James Lane Allen

Flute and Violin

And other Kentucky Tales and Romances

James Lane Allen

Flute and Violin
And other Kentucky Tales and Romances

ISBN/EAN: 9783744673730

Printed in Europe, USA, Canada, Australia, Japan

Cover: Foto ©Thomas Meinert / pixelio.de

More available books at **www.hansebooks.com**

FLUTE AND VIOLIN
AND OTHER KENTUCKY TALES AND ROMANCES

By James Lane Allen

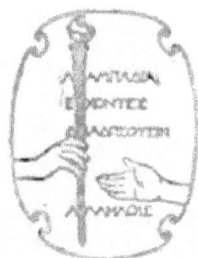

Biographical Edition

NEW YORK AND LONDON
HARPER & BROTHERS, PUBLISHERS
1899

To her

FROM WHOSE FRAIL BODY HE DREW LIFE IN THE
BEGINNING, FROM WHOSE STRONG SPIRIT HE
WILL DRAW LIFE UNTIL THE CLOSE, THESE
TALES, WITH ALL OTHERS HAPLY HERE-
AFTER TO BE WRITTEN, ARE DEDI-
CATED AS A PERISHABLE MONU-
MENT OF INEFFABLE
REMEMBRANCE

INTRODUCTORY SKETCH.

THESE tales were published a few years ago. Since then, although not left like unturned stones, but kept constantly rolling, they have nevertheless gathered their moss: those stories that take root on earlier stories, those small fictions that rapidly spread over other small fictions—and conceal them. Thus, in certain quarters, it has been told and believed that the actual experience of a young Kentucky monk is laid bare in "The White Cowl"; that a well-known original furnished the portrait of the nun in "Sister Dolorosa"; that a tragic incident, saddening the career of a famous American sculptor, formed the basis of the romance entitled "Posthumous Fame." Once, on a railway train, an indignant lady demonstrated to the author how unmistakable her own husband had been used to make up the character of *Gordon Helm*, and protested that she was ill pleased at the thought—the author not caring to assure her that still less was he pleased at the thought, and that her indignation was catching.

This is a good place in which to cleanse away these and other patches of moss, which serve to make his plain, underlying inventions appear too highly variegated with adventitious greenness. For instance, the author wishes to avow to the indignant lady of the railway that he never had the slightest need of her husband either in his fiction or out of it. So, many a monk has borne the name of *Father Palemon;* but touching the monastic life, or the pre-monastic, or the post-monastic life, of any one of these he possesses, as a fact, not the filmiest tradition. Nuns have veiled themselves as *Sister Dolorosa* through centuries that all but go back to the *Mater Dolorosa* herself; but to him they are as so many halos, so much pious, impersonal dust. There is nothing whatsoever of reality behind " Posthumous Fame "— and nothing real in it. As respects this story, those who run may read; and, better still, those who read may run.

The truth is different, however, in the matter of the other tales completing the collection. Here some real personages have been evoked and convoked, and possibly provoked, at will—not their will. In *Flute and Violin* there is a man and there is a boy. As to the man, the opening paragraph of the story may be taken to contain literal truth. Also the second and the third and the fourth. But beyond this point, the *Reverend James Moore* of the tale has nothing to do with the Reverend James Moore of history. The former imaginary gentleman, having assumed the name, the pulpit, the professorship, and the virtues of the latter real one, thereafter claimed the right to be original. True, one of the living female descendants of the historic parson (another indignant woman) once wrote to the author, protesting that, inasmuch as she was herself actually descended from this very man, he could not possibly have died a bachelor. The author in turn could not possibly remind this lady that her reasoning along here was a little treacherous; that, come to the worst, he was talking about his *James Moore* and not her James Moore. Instead, he hastened to render to her—and her ancestor—

the justice she demanded; and in "The Choir Invisible" he compelled his own *James Moore* to marry, and endowed him with as many daughters as seemed desirable; the entire family emerging in a body from a drop of ink.

The boy in *Flute and Violin*—he is not a portrait from an original: the author hopes he is an original from a portrait. There used to be a boarding-house in Lexington where the author fared and wayfared at intervals, and on the wall of the dining-room of this house, opposite his seat, hung a life-size portrait of a poor little outcast lad. They grew to be great friends, these two—the man regularly at his meals (irregularly if possible), and the lad forever hungry, forever ragged, forever friendless, standing there by the table from day to day, and perceived only by the man. A torn cap sat above his frowzy hair; an old buttonless shirt opened down his bosom; the cast-off waistcoat of a man hung around his little shoulders; the very heart and soul of him, looking out of those shy, appealing eyes, seemed ready to be laid like a free gift in the palm of any one for a few kind words. These were the first materials out of which the author tried to create the little violinist of a century ago. As to the violin, he, when a lad, experienced the ecstasy —and the agony—of awaiting the day when he should become the possessor of a new one, in place of the old cornstalk. The first piece of music that *he* ever learned was "O, Thou Fount of Every Blessing"; and to this day his flesh winces as he recalls the fact that a certain note which was always right when he whistled the hymn was always wrong when he flourished the bow.

The story, "King Solomon of Kentucky," is founded upon facts—upon many facts. The existence of an old vagabond and hero, who once went by that name, the selling of him for vagrancy, the cholera, the grave-digging and all that. Scarce the name of a character or a line of description in this tale but was taken from the local history of the time. The old French confectioner figured in it, the old French dancing-master, the old music-dealer. The description of M. Xaupi's ball, what there is of it, is actual enough. One of the costumes—"a white satin with ethereal silk overdress embroidered in an oak-leaf of green"—was the wedding-dress of the author's own mother, she having been married in the spring of that awful year of 1833. It is a pleasure to be able to recall in this place an act of gratitude, nearly half a century due: a year or two ago the grave of King Solomon was hunted out in the Lexington cemetery, and for the first time marked with fitness.

The story, "Two Gentlemen of Kentucky," has a good deal of actuality behind it—biographical actuality. There once lived on a blue-grass farm, in slave times, an old negro preacher named Peter Cotton, though possibly he might better have been called Peter Wool; comforting him was a consort named Phyllis. As a matter of record he besought his mistress to embroider texts of Scripture on the tails of his Sunday coat, and his mistress obliged him—so romantic often is reality. The books mentioned in the story as those he cared for were in truth Peter's books. He was a good gospel preacher as well as a good marrying preacher—a double qualification much insisted on, one hears, among the people of his race, and perhaps not duly regarded by the occupants of "white pulpits": that is, he divided his time fairly between wedding his sinners to Heaven and marrying them to each other. So much for the Peter Cotton of local history whom the author never laid eyes on. As

for the *Peter Cotton* of the story, another old negro
enters into his make. When the author was a lad he
was much used to frequent, by permission, the private
grounds of a wealthy gentleman living alone on the edge
of Lexington. Those grounds — were there ever any
others like them?—lawns, hedges, forest trees and evergreens, vines, fruits, flowers, birds, sun and shade, songs
and quiet! They are all mirage now, lifted away from
the earth. Often not a soul would be at home, for the
great man was down - town, busy with his banks and
courts of law. So that the solitary keeper of this Eden
was an old negro gardener, the faithful servitor and
friend of his master. To the lad's astonishment he was
named "Fish." "Fish," as to his piscatorial countenance, might have traced his ancestors through some
haphazard union of a black bass and a speckled trout,
save only the eyes which squinted at the flounder. The
teeth were clearly derived from a man-eating shark. But
he had the soul if not the features of a gentleman; and
he abounded in humanity to the boy. The *Peter Cotton* of the story, therefore, is in part his tribute of gratitude and affection (the best of literature is gratitude) to
this old gardener, who many a time loaded him down
with flowers, but never, alas! with fruit. The boy had a
two-sided conception of desire, but "Fish" had a one-
sided conception of duty, and gave him everything that
could be smelled, nothing that could be eaten. A cup
of cold water was the limit of his generosity; and if the
water had happened to have a fruity flavor, he would no
doubt have saved it for his master.

That master was not the original of the other of
"The Two Gentlemen." No original existed. The
author attempted to exhibit, in a way, a type of Ken-

tucky gentleman farmer, who at the close of the Civil
War abandoned the country for the towns, and led rather
idle, useless lives.   In England objection was made to
this character on the ground that the trail of Colonel
Newcome is over the colonels of American fiction.   It
is a point curiously mismade, curiously misconceived.
The truth is, about the same time that Thackeray found
the lineaments and elements of his good and mighty
anglo-Saxon gentleman in that branch of the race, had
he been living in certain parts of the United States he
would have found essentially the same lineaments and
elements diffused through this.   Among the Kentucky
gentlemen of the old school there were characters that
forced you to think of Colonel Newcome.   Not because
they were imitations of Colonel Newcome, for they may
never have heard of him, but because they themselves
were made of the same stuff.   And if to write of this
local type, however inadequately, is to suggest some poor
resemblance, as a pool might resemble an ocean, the
point to be enforced is not the influence of Thackeray's
work upon literature, but the influence of life upon
Thackeray's work.   So that he gathered together out
of the deeps of the race, and put together in the image
of his own genius, a type of man that was the widely
diffused creation of the race itself.

In looking over these tales, written several years ago,
the author feels like one who goes back to walk across a
land that he inhabits no longer.   They have for him the
silence of overgrown pathways, along which feet pass
never again.

NEW YORK CITY,
August 15, 1899.

CONTENTS.

FLUTE AND VIOLIN.

ffiute and Violin.

THE PARSON'S MAGIC FLUTE.

ON one of the dim walls of Christ Church, in Lexington, Kentucky, there hangs, framed in thin black wood, an old rectangular slab of marble. A legend sets forth that the tablet is in memory of the Reverend James Moore, first minister of Christ Church and President of Transylvania University, who departed this life in the year 1814, at the age of forty-nine. Just beneath runs the record that he was learned, liberal, amiable, and pious.

Save this concise but not unsatisfactory summary, little is now known touching the reverend gentleman. A search through other sources of information does, indeed, result in reclaiming certain facts. Thus, it appears that he was a Virginian, and that he came to Lexington in the year 1792—when Kentucky ceased to be a county of Virginia, and became a State. At first he was a candidate for the ministry of the Presbyterian

Church; but the Transylvania Presbytery having reproved him for the liberality of his sermons, James kicked against such rigor in his brethren, and turned for refuge to the bosom of the Episcopal Communion. But this body did not offer much of a bosom to take refuge in.

Virginia Episcopalians there were in and around the little wooden town; but so rampant was the spirit of the French Revolution and the influence of French infidelity that a celebrated local historian, who knew thoroughly the society of the place, though writing of it long afterwards, declared that about the last thing it would have been thought possible to establish there was an Episcopal church.

Not so thought James. He beat the canebrakes and scoured the buffalo trails for his Virginia Episcopalians, huddled them into a dilapidated little frame house on the site of the present building, and there fired so deadly a volley of sermons at the sinners free of charge that they all became living Christians. Indeed, he fired so long and so well that, several years later—under favor of Heaven and through the success of a lottery with a one-thousand-dollar prize and nine hundred and seventy-four blanks—there was built and furnished a small brick church, over which he was regularly called to officiate twice a month, at a salary of two hundred dollars a year.

Here authentic history ends, except for the additional fact that in the university he sat in the chair of logic, metaphysics, moral philosophy, and belles-lettres — a large chair to sit in with ill-matched legs and most uncertain bottom. Another authority is careful to state that he had a singularly sweet breath and beautiful

"HE HAD BEAUTIFUL MANNERS."

manners. Thus it has been well with the parson as respects his posthumous fame; for how many of our fellow - creatures are learned without being amiable, amiable without being pious, and pious without having beautiful manners!

And yet the best that may be related of him is not told in the books; and it is only when we have allowed the dust to settle once more upon the histories, and have peered deep into the mists of oral tradition, that the parson is discovered standing there in spirit and the flesh, but muffled and ghost-like, as a figure seen through a dense fog.

A tall, thinnish man, with silky pale-brown hair, worn long and put back behind his ears, the high tops of which bent forward a little under the weight, and thus took on the most remarkable air of paying incessant attention to everybody and everything; set far out in front of these ears, as though it did not wish to be disturbed by what was heard, a white, wind-splitting face, calm, beardless, and seeming never to have been cold, or to have dropped the kindly dew of perspiration; under the serene peak of this forehead a pair of large gray eyes, patient and dreamy, being habitually turned inward upon a mind toiling with hard abstractions; having within him a conscience burning always like a planet; a bachelor—being a logician; therefore sweet-tempered. never having sipped the sour cup of experience; gazing covertly at womankind from behind the delicate veil of unfamiliarity that lends enchantment; being a bachelor and a bookworm, therefore already old at forty, and a little run down in his toilets, a little frayed out at the elbows and the knees, a little seamy along the back, a little deficient at the heels; in pocket

poor always, and always the poorer because of a spend-
thrift habit in the matter of secret charities ; kneeling
down by his small hard bed every morning and praying
that during the day his logical faculty might discharge
its function morally, and that his moral faculty might
discharge its function logically, and that over all the
operations of all his other faculties he might find heavenly grace to exercise both a logical and a moral control; at night kneeling down again to ask forgiveness
that, despite his prayer of the morning, one or more of
these same faculties — he knew and called them all
familiarly by name, being a metaphysician — had gone
wrong in a manner the most abnormal, shameless, and
unforeseen ; thus, on the whole, a man shy and dry ;
gentle, lovable ; timid, resolute ; forgetful, remorseful ;
eccentric, impulsive, thinking too well of every human
creature but himself ; an illogical logician, an erring
moralist, a wool - gathered philosopher, but, humanly
speaking, almost a perfect man.

Well, the parson had a flute — a little one — and the
older he grew, and the more patient and dreamy his
gray eyes, always the more and more devotedly he blew
this little friend. How the fond soul must have loved
it ! They say that during his last days as he lay
propped high on white pillows, once, in a moment of
wandering consciousness, he stretched forth his hand
and in fancy lifting it from the white counterpane, carried it gently to his lips. Then, as his long, delicate
fingers traced out the spirit ditties of no tone and his
mouth pursed itself in the fashion of one who is softly
blowing, his whole face was overspread with a halo of
ecstatic peace.

And yet, for all the love he bore it, the parson was

never known to blow his flute between the hours of sun-
rise and sunset — that is, never but once. Alas, that
memorable day! But when the night fell and he came
home—home to the two-story log-house of the widow
Spurlock; when the widow had given him his supper
of coffee sweetened with brown sugar, hot johnny-cake,
with perhaps a cold joint of venison and cabbage pickle;
when he had taken from the supper table, by her permission, the solitary tallow dip in its little brass candle-
stick, and climbed the rude steep stairs to his room above;
when he had pulled the leathern string that lifted the
latch, entered, shut the door behind him on the world,
placed the candle on a little deal table covered with
text-books and sermons, and seated himself beside it in
a rush-bottomed chair—then— He began to play?
No; then there was dead silence.

For about half an hour this silence continued. The
widow Spurlock used to say that the parson was giving
his supper time to settle; but, alas! it must have settled almost immediately, so heavy was the johnny-cake.
Howbeit, at the close of such an interval, any one standing at the foot of the steps below, or listening beneath
the window on the street outside, would have heard the
silence broken.

At first the parson blew low, peculiar notes, such as a
kind and faithful shepherd might blow at nightfall as
an invitation for his scattered wandering sheep to gather
home about him. Perhaps it was a way he had of calling in the disordered flock of his faculties—some weary,
some wounded, some torn by thorns, some with their
fleeces, which had been washed white in the morning
prayer, now bearing many a stain. But when they had
all answered, as it were, to this musical roll-call, and had

taken their due places within the fold of his brain, obedient, attentive, however weary, however suffering, then
the flute was laid aside, and once more there fell upon
the room intense stillness ; the poor student had entered
upon his long nightly labors.

Hours passed. Not a sound was to be heard but the
rustle of book leaves, now rapidly, now slowly turned, or
the stewing of sap in the end of a log on the hearth, or
the faint drumming of fingers on the table—those long
fingers, the tips of which seemed not so full of particles
of blood as of notes of music, circulating impatiently
back and forth from his heart. At length, as midnight
drew near, and the candle began to sputter in the sock-
et, the parson closed the last book with a decisive snap,
drew a deep breath, buried his face in his hands for a
moment, as if asking a silent blessing on the day's work,
and then, reaching for his flute, squared himself before
the dying embers, and began in truth to play. This
was the one brief, pure pleasure he allowed himself.

It was not a musical roll-call that he now blew, but a
dismissal for the night. One might say that he was
playing the cradle song of his mind. And what a cradle song it was ! A succession of undertone, silver-
clear, simple melodies; apparently one for each faculty,
as though he was having something kind to say to them
all ; thanking some for the manner in which they had
served him during the day, the music here being brave
and spirited ; sympathizing with others that had been
unjustly or too rudely put upon, the music here being
plaintive and soothing ; and finally granting his pardon
to any such as had not used him quite fairly, the music
here having a searching, troubled quality, though end-
ing in the faintest breath of love and peace.

It was not known whence the parson had these melodies; but come whence they might, they were airs of heavenly sweetness, and as he played them, one by one his faculties seemed to fall asleep like quieted children. His long, out-stretched legs relaxed their tension, his feet fell over sidewise on the hearth-stone, his eyes closed, his head sank towards his shoulder. Still, he managed to hold on to his flute, faintly puffing a few notes at greater intervals, until at last, by the dropping of the flute from his hands or the sudden rolling of his big head backward, he would awaken with a violent jerk. The next minute he would be asleep in bed, with one ear out on guard, listening for the first sound that should awake him in the morning.

Such having been the parson's fixed habit as long as any one had known him, it is hard to believe that five years before his death he abruptly ceased to play his flute and never touched it again. But from this point the narrative becomes so mysterious that it were better to have the testimony of witnesses.

II.

Every bachelor in this world is secretly watched by some woman. The parson was watched by several, but most closely by two. One of these was the widow Spurlock, a personage of savory countenance and wholesome figure—who was accused by the widow Babcock, living at the other end of the town, of having robust intentions towards her lodger. This piece of slander had no connection with the fact that she had used the point of her carving knife to enlarge in the door of his room

the hole through which the latch-
string passed, in order that she might
increase the ventilation. The aperture for ventilation thus formed was
exactly the size of one of her innocent black eyes.

The other woman was an infirm,
ill-favored beldam by the name of
Arsena Furnace, who lived alone just
across the street, and whose bedroom
was on the second floor, on a level
with the parson's. Being on terms
of great intimacy with the widow Spurlock, she persuad-
ed the latter that the parson's room was poorly lighted
for one who used his eyes so much, and that the win-
dow-curtain of red calico should be taken down. On
the same principle of requiring less sun because having
less use for her eyes, she hung before her own window
a faded curtain, transparent only from within. Thus
these two devoted, conscientious souls conspired to
provide the parson unawares with a sufficiency of air
and light.

On Friday night, then, of August 31, 1809—for this
was the exact date—the parson played his flute as
usual, because the two women were sitting together below and distinctly heard him. It was unusual for them
to be up at such an hour, but on that day the drawing of the lottery had come off, and they had held tickets, and were discussing their disappointment in having
drawn blanks. Towards midnight the exquisite notes
of the flute floated down to them from the parson's
room.

"I suppose he'll keep on playing those same old

tunes as long as there is a thimbleful of wind in him.
I wish he'd learn some new ones," said the hag, taking
her cold pipe from her cold lips, and turning her eyes
towards her companion with a look of some impatience.

"He might be better employed at such an hour than
playing on the flute," replied the widow, sighing audibly
and smoothing a crease out of her apron.

As by-and-by the notes of the flute became intermit-
tent, showing that the parson was beginning to fall
asleep, Arsena said good-night, and crossing the street
to her house, mounted to the front window. Yes, there
he was; the long legs stretched out towards the hearth,
head sunk sidewise on his shoulder, flute still at his
lips, the sputtering candle throwing its shadowy light
over his white weary face, now wearing a smile. Without doubt he played his flute that night as usual; and
Arsena, tired of the sight, turned away and went to bed.

A few minutes later the widow Spurlock placed an
eye at the aperture of ventilation, wishing to see whether the logs on the fire were in danger of rolling out and
setting fire to the parson's bed; but suddenly remembering that it was August, and that there was no fire,
she glanced around to see whether his candle needed
snuffing. Happening, however, to discover the parson
in the act of shedding his coat, she withdrew her eye,
and hastened precipitately down-stairs, but sighing so
loud that he surely must have heard her had not his
faculty of external perception been already fast asleep.

At about three o'clock on the afternoon of the next
day, as Arsena was sweeping the floor of her kitchen,
there reached her ears a sound which caused her to listen for a moment, broom in air. It was the parson
playing—playing at three o'clock in the afternoon!—

and playing—she strained her ears again and again to
make sure—playing a Virginia reel. Still, not believing her ears, she hastened aloft to the front window and
looked across the street. At the same instant the widow Spurlock, in a state of equal excitement, hurried to
the front door of her house, and threw a quick glance
up at Arsena's window. The hag thrust a skinny hand
through a slit in the curtain and beckoned energetically,
and a moment later the two women stood with their
heads close together watching the strange performance.

Some mysterious change had come over the parson
and over the spirit of his musical faculty. He sat upright in his chair, looking ten years younger, his whole
figure animated, his foot beating time so audibly that it
could be heard across the street, a vivid bloom on his
lifeless cheeks, his head rocking to and fro like a ship
in a storm, and his usually dreamy, patient gray eyes now
rolled up towards the ceiling in sentimental perturbation.
And how he played that Virginia reel! Not once, but
over and over, and faster and faster, until the notes
seemed to get into the particles of his blood and set
them to dancing. And when he had finished that, he
snatched his handkerchief from his pocket, dashed it
across his lips, blew his nose with a resounding snort,
and settling his figure into a more determined attitude,
began another. And the way he went at that! And
when he finished that, the way he went at another! Two
negro boys, passing along the street with a spinning-
wheel, put it down and paused to listen ; then, catching
the infection of the music, they began to dance. And
then the widow Spurlock, catching the infection also,
began to dance, and bouncing into the middle of the
room, there actually did dance until her tucking-comb

rolled out, and—ahem!—one of her stockings slipped
down. Then the parson struck up the "Fisher's Horn-
pipe," and the widow, still in sympathy, against her will,
sang the words:

> " Did you ever see the Devil
> With his wood and iron shovel,
> A-hoeing up coal
> For to burn your soul?"

" He's bewitched," said old Arsena, trembling and
sick with terror.

" By *whom?*" cried the widow Spurlock, indignantly,
laying a heavy hand on Arsena's shoulder.

" By his flute," replied Arsena, more fearfully.

At length the parson, as if in for it, and possessed to
go all lengths, jumped from his chair, laid the flute on
the table, and disappeared in a hidden corner of the
room. Here he kept closely locked a large brass-nailed
hair trunk, over which hung a looking-glass. For ten
minutes the two women waited for him to reappear, and
then he did reappear, not in the same clothes, but wearing the ball dress of a Virginia gentleman of an older
time, perhaps his grandfather's—knee-breeches, silk
stockings, silver buckles, low shoes, laces at his wrists,
laces at his throat and down his bosom. And to make
the dress complete he had actually tied a blue ribbon
around his long silky hair. Stepping airily and gal-
lantly to the table, he seized the flute, and with a little
wave of it through the air he began to play, and to tread
the mazes of the minuet, about the room, this way and
that, winding and bowing, turning and gliding, but all
the time fingering and blowing for dear life.

" Who would have thought it was in him?" said Arsena, her fear changed to admiration.

"*I* would!" said the widow.

While he was in the midst of this performance the two women had their attention withdrawn from him in a rather singular way. A poor lad hobbling on a crutch made his appearance in the street below, and rapidly but timidly swung himself along to the widow Spurlock's door. There he paused a moment, as if overcome by mortification, but finally knocked. His summons not being answered, he presently knocked more loudly.

"Hist!" said the widow to him, in a half-tone, opening a narrow slit in the curtain. "What do you want, David?"

The boy wheeled and looked up, his face at once crimson with shame. "I want to see the parson," he said, in a voice scarcely audible.

"The parson's not at home," replied the widow, sharply. "He's out; studying up a sermon." And she closed the curtain.

An expression of despair came into the boy's face, and for a moment in physical weakness he sat down on the door-step. He heard the notes of the flute in the room above; he knew that the parson *was* at home; but presently he got up and moved away.

The women did not glance after his retreating figure, being reabsorbed by the movements of the parson. Whence had he that air of grace and high-born courtesy? that vivacity of youth?

"He must be in love," said Arsena. "He must be in love with the widow Babcock."

"He's no more in love with her than *I* am," replied her companion, with a toss of her head.

A few moments later the parson, whose motions had been gradually growing less animated, ceased dancing,

"HE BEGAN TO PLAY."

and disappeared once more in the corner of the room,
soon emerging therefrom dressed in his own clothes,
but still wearing on his hair the blue ribbon, which he
had forgotten to untie. Seating himself in his chair by
the table, he thrust his hands into his pockets, and with
his eyes on the floor seemed to pass into a trance of
rather demure and dissatisfying reflections.

When he came down to supper that night he still
wore his hair in the forgotten queue, and it may have
been this that gave him such an air of lamb-like meekness. The widow durst ask him no questions, for
there was that in him which held familiarity at a distance; but although he ate with unusual heartiness,
perhaps on account of such unusual exercise, he did
not lift his eyes from his plate, and thanked her for all
her civilities with a gratitude that was singularly plaintive.

That night he did not play his flute. The next day
being Sunday, and the new church not yet being opened,
he kept his room. Early in the afternoon a messenger
handed to the widow a note for him, which, being sealed,
she promptly delivered. On reading it he uttered a
quick, smothered cry of grief and alarm, seized his hat,
and hurried from the house. The afternoon passed and
he did not return. Darkness fell, supper hour came
and went, the widow put a candle in his room, and then
went across to commune with Arsena on these unusual
proceedings.

Not long afterwards they saw him enter his room carrying under his arm a violin case. This he deposited
on the table, and sitting down beside it, lifted out a boy's
violin.

"A *boy's* violin!" muttered Arsena.

"A *boy's* violin !" muttered the widow ; and the two
women looked significantly into each other's eyes.

" Humph !"

" Humph !"

By-and-by the parson replaced the violin in the box
and sat motionless beside it, one of his arms hanging
listlessly at his side, the other lying on the table.   The
candle shone full in his face, and a storm of emotions
passed over it.   At length they saw him take up the
violin again, go to the opposite wall of the room, mount
a chair, knot the loose strings together, and hang the
violin on a nail above his meagre shelf of books.   Upon
it he hung the bow.   Then they saw him drive a nail in
the wall close to the other, take his flute from the table,
tie around it a piece of blue ribbon he had picked up
off the floor, and hang it also on the wall.   After this he
went back to the table, threw himself in his chair, buried
his head in his arms, and remained motionless until the
candle burned out.

"What's the meaning of all this ?" said one of the
two women, as they separated below.

" I'll find out if it's the last act of my life," said the
other.

But find out she never did.   For question the parson
directly she dared not ; and neither to her nor any one
else did he ever vouchsafe an explanation.   Whenever,
in the thousand ways a woman can, she would hint her
desire to fathom the mystery, he would baffle her by as-
suming an air of complete unconsciousness, or repel her
by a look of warning so cold that she hurriedly changed
the subject.

As time passed on it became evident that some grave
occurrence indeed had befallen him.   Thenceforth, and

during the five re-
maining years of his
life, he was never quite
the same. For months
his faculties, long used
to being soothed at
midnight by the music
of the flute, were like
children put to bed
hungry and refused to
be quieted, so that
sleep came to him
only after hours of
waiting and tossing,
and his health suffer-
ed in consequence.
And then in all things
he lived like one who
was watching himself
closely as a person not
to be trusted.

Certainly he was a
sadder man. Often
the two women would
see him lift his eyes
from his books at
night, and turn them
long and wistfully
towards the wall of the room where, gathering cobwebs
and dust, hung the flute and the violin.

If any one should feel interested in having this whole
mystery cleared up, he may read the following tale of a
boy's violin.

III.

A BOY'S VIOLIN.

ON Friday, the 31st of August, 1809—that being the day of the drawing of the lottery for finishing and furnishing the new Episcopal church—at about ten o'clock in the morning, there might have been seen hobbling slowly along the streets, in the direction of the public square, a little lad by the name of David. He was idle and lonesome, not wholly through his fault. If there had been white bootblacks in those days, he might now have been busy around a tavern door polishing the noble toes of some old Revolutionary soldier; or if there had been newsboys, he might have been selling the *Gazette* or the *Reporter*—the two papers which the town afforded at that time. But there were enough negro slaves to polish all the boots in the town for nothing when the boots got polished at all, as was often not the case; and if people wanted to buy a newspaper, they went to the office of the editor and publisher, laid the silver down on the counter, and received a copy from the hands of that great man himself.

The lad was not even out on a joyous summer vacation, for as yet there was not a public school in the town, and his mother was too poor to send him to a private one, teaching him as best she could at home. This home was one of the rudest of the log-cabins of the town, built by his father, who had been killed a few years before in a tavern brawl. His mother earned a scant livelihood, sometimes by taking in coarse sewing for the hands of the hemp factory, sometimes by her loom, on which with rare skill she wove the finest fabrics of the time.

As he hobbled on towards the public square, he came to an elm-tree which cast a thick cooling shade on the sidewalk, and sitting down, he laid his rickety crutch beside him, and drew out of the pocket of his home-made tow breeches a tangled mass of articles—pieces of violin strings, all of which had plainly seen service under the bow at many a dance; three old screws, belonging in their times to different violin heads; two lumps of resin, one a rather large lump of dark color and common quality, the other a small lump of transparent amber wrapped sacredly to itself in a little brown paper bag labelled "Cucumber Seed;" a pair of epaulets, the brass fringes of which were tarnished and torn; and further miscellany.

These treasures he laid out one by one, first brushing the dirt off the sidewalk with the palm of one dirty hand, and then putting his mouth close down to blow away any loose particles that might remain to soil them; and when they were all displayed, he propped himself on one elbow, and stretched his figure caressingly beside them.

A pretty picture the lad made as he lay there dreaming over his earthly possessions—a pretty picture in the shade of the great elm, that sultry morning of August, three-quarters of a century ago! The presence of the crutch showed there was something sad about it; and so there was; for if you had glanced at the little bare brown foot, set toes upward on the curb-stone, you would have discovered that the fellow to it was missing —cut off about two inches above the ankle. And if this

had caused you to throw a look of sympathy at his face,
something yet sadder must long have held your attention. Set jauntily on the back of his head was a weath-
er-beaten dark blue cloth cap, the patent-leather frontlet
of which was gone; and beneath the ragged edge of
this there fell down over his forehead and temples and
ears a tangled mass of soft yellow hair, slightly curling.
His eyes were large, and of a blue to match the depths
of the calm sky above the tree-tops; the long lashes
which curtained them were brown; his lips were red,
his nose delicate and fine, and his cheeks tanned to the
color of ripe peaches. It was a singularly winning face,
intelligent, frank, not describable. On it now rested a
smile, half joyous, half sad, as though his mind was full
of bright hopes, the realization of which was far away.
From his neck fell the wide collar of a white cotton
shirt, clean but frayed at the elbows, and open and buttonless down his bosom. Over this he wore an old-
fashioned satin waistcoat of a man, also frayed and buttonless. His dress was completed by a pair of baggy
tow breeches, held up by a single tow suspender fastened to big brown horn buttons.

After a while he sat up, letting his foot hang down
over the curb-stone, and uncoiling the longest of the
treble strings, he put one end between his shining teeth,
and stretched it tight by holding the other end off between his thumb and forefinger. Then, waving in the
air in his other hand an imaginary bow, with his head
resting a little on one side, his eyelids drooping, his
mind in a state of dreamy delight, the little musician began to play—began to play the violin that he had long
been working for, and hoped would some day become
his own.

It was nothing to him now that his whole performance consisted of one broken string. It was nothing
to him, as his body rocked gently to and fro, that he
could not hear the music which ravished his soul. So
real was that music to him that at intervals, with a little frown cf vexation as though things were not going
perfectly, he would stop, take up the small lump of cost-
ly resin, and pretend to rub it vigorously on the hair of
the fancied bow. Then he would awake that delicious
music again, playing more ecstatically, more passionately than before.

At that moment there appeared in the street, about a
hundred yards off, the Reverend James Moore, who was
also moving in the direction of the public square, his
face more cool and white than usual, although the morning was never more sultry.

He had arisen with an all but overwhelming sense of
the importance of that day. Fifteen years are an immense period in a brief human life, especially fifteen
years of spiritual toil, hardships, and discouragements,
rebuffs, weaknesses, and burdens, and for fifteen such
years he had spent himself for his Episcopalians, some
of whom read too freely Tom Paine and Rousseau,
some loved too well the taverns of the town, some
wrangled too fiercely over their land suits. What wonder if this day, which, despite all drawbacks, was to witness the raising of money for equipping the first brick
church, was a proud and happy one to his meek but
victorious spirit! What wonder if, as he had gotten
out of bed that morning, he had prayed with unusual
fervor that for this day in especial his faculties, from
the least to the greatest, and from the weakest to
the strongest, might discharge their functions perfectly,

and that the drawing of the lottery might come off de-
cently and in good order; and that—yes, this too was
in the parson's prayer—that if it were the will of Heav-
en and just to the other holders of tickets, the right
one of the vestry-men might draw the thousand-dollar
prize; for he felt very sure that otherwise there would
be little peace in the church for many a day to come,
and that for him personally the path-way of life would
be more slippery and thorny.

So that now as he hurried down the street he was
happy; but he was anxious; and being excited for both
reasons, the way was already prepared for him to lose
that many-handed self-control which he had prayed so
hard to retain.

He passed within the shade of the great elm, and
then suddenly came to a full stop. A few yards in
front of him the boy was performing his imaginary violin solo on a broken string, and the sight went straight
to the heart of that musical faculty whose shy divinity
was the flute. For a few moments he stood looking on
in silence, with all the sympathy of a musician for a
comrade in poverty and distress.

Other ties also bound him to the boy. If the divine
voice had said to the Reverend James Moore: "Among
all the people of this town, it will be allowed you to
save but one soul. Choose you which that shall be," he
would have replied: "Lord, this is a hard saying, for I
wish to save them all. But if I must choose, let it be
the soul of this lad."

The boy's father and he had been boyhood friends in
Virginia, room-mates and classmates in college, and together they had come to Kentucky. Summoned to the
tavern on the night of the fatal brawl, he had reached

the scene only in time to lay his old playfellow's head
on his bosom, and hear his last words :

"Be kind to my boy!... Be a better father to him
than I have been!... Watch over him and help him!...
Guard him from tempta-
tion!... Be kind to him
in his little weaknesses!
... Win his heart, and
you can do everything
with him!... Promise me
this!"

"So help me Heaven,
all that I can do for him
I will do!"

From that moment he had taken upon his conscience,
already toiling beneath its load of cares, the burden of
this sacred responsibility. During the three years of
his guardianship that had elapsed, this burden had not
grown lighter; for apparently he had failed to acquire

any influence over the lad, or to establish the least friend-
ship with him. It was a difficult nature that had been
bequeathed him to master — sensitive, emotional, delicate, wayward, gay, rebellious of restraint, loving freedom like the poet and the artist. The Reverend James
Moore, sitting in the chair of logic, moral philosophy,
metaphysics, and belles-lettres ; lecturing daily to young
men on all the powers and operations of the human
mind, taking it to pieces and putting it together and
understanding it so perfectly, knowing by name every
possible form of fallacy and root of evil—the Reverend
James Moore, when he came to study the living mind
of this boy, confessed to himself that he was as great a
dunce as the greatest in his classes. But he loved the
boy, nevertheless, with the lonely resources of his nature, and he never lost hope that he would turn to him
in the end.

How long he might have stood now looking on and
absorbed with the scene, it is impossible to say ; for the
lad, happening to look up and see him, instantly, with a
sidelong scoop of his hand, the treasures on the sidewalk disappeared in a cavernous pocket, and the next
moment he had seized his crutch, and was busy fumbling at a loosened nail.

" Why, good-morning, David," cried the parson, cheerily, but with some embarrassment, stepping briskly forward, and looking down upon the little figure now hanging its head with guilt. " You've got the coolest seat
in town," he continued, "and I wish I had time to sit
down and enjoy it with you ; but the drawing comes
off at the lottery this morning, and I must hurry down
to see who gets the capital prize." A shade of anxiety
settled on his face as he said this. " But here's the

morning paper," he added, drawing out of his coat-pock-
et the coveted sheet of the weekly *Reporter*, which he
was in the habit of sending to the lad's mother, knowing
that her silver was picked up with the point of her needle. " Take it to your mother, and tell her she must be
sure to go to see the wax figures." What a persuasive
smile overspread his face as he said this! " And *you*
must be certain to go too! They'll be fine. Good-bye."

He let one hand rest gently on the lad's blue cloth
cap, and looked down into the upturned face with an
expression that could scarcely have been more tender.

" He looks feverish," he said to himself as he walked
away, and then his thoughts turned to the lottery.

"Good-bye," replied the boy, in a low voice, lifting his
dark blue eyes slowly to the patient gray ones. " I'm
glad he's gone!" he added to himself; but he nevertheless gazed after the disappearing figure with shy
fondness. Then he also began to think of the lottery.

If Mr. Leuba should draw the prize, he might give
Tom Leuba a new violin ; and if he gave Tom a new
violin, then he had promised to give him Tom's old one.
It had been nearly a year since Mr. Leuba had said to
him, laughing, in his dry, hard little fashion :

"Now, David, you must be smart and run my errands
while Tom's at school of mornings ; and some of these
days, when I get rich enough, I'll give Tom a new violin
and I'll give you his old one." ı

"Oh, Mr. Leuba !" David had cried, his voice quiver-
ing with excitement, and his whole countenance beam-
ing with delight, " I'll wait on you forever, if you'll give
me Tom's old violin."

Yes, nearly a whole year had passed since then—
a lifetime of waiting and disappointment. Many an

errand he had run for Mr. Leuba. Many a bit of a thing
Mr. Leuba had given him : pieces of violin strings, odd
worn-out screws, bits of resin, old epaulets, and a few
fourpences ; but the day had never come when he had
given him Tom's violin.

Now if Mr. Leuba would only draw the prize ! As
he lay on his back on the sidewalk, with the footless
stump of a leg crossed over the other, he held the newspaper between his eyes and the green limbs of the elm
overhead, and eagerly read for the last time the adver-.
tisement of the lottery. Then, as he finished reading it,
his eyes were suddenly riveted upon a remarkable notice printed just beneath.

This notice stated that Messrs. Ollendorf and Mason
respectfully acquainted the ladies and gentlemen of Lex-
ington·that they had opened at the Kentucky Hotel a
new and elegant collection of wax figures, judged by
connoisseurs to be equal, if not superior, to any exhib-
ited in America. Among which are the following characters : An excellent representation of General George
Washington giving orders to the Marquis de la Fayette,
his aid. In another scene the General is represented
as a fallen victim to death, and the tears of America,
represented by a beautiful female weeping over him—
which makes it a most interesting scene. His Excel-
lency Thomas Jefferson. General Buonaparte in mar-
shal action. General Hamilton and Colonel Burr. In
this interesting scene the Colonel is represented in
the attitude of firing, while the General stands at his
distance waiting the result of the first fire : both accu-
rate likenesses. The death of General Braddock, who
fell in Braddock's Defeat. An Indian is represented
as scalping the General, while one of his men, in an

attempt to rescue him out of the hands of the Indians,
was overtaken by another Indian, who is ready to split
him with his tomahawk. Mrs. Jerome Buonaparte, for-
merly Miss Patterson. The Sleeping Beauty. Eliza
Wharton, or the American coquette, with her favorite
gallant and her intimate friend Miss Julia Granby. The
Museum will be open from ten o'clock in the morning
'til nine in the evening. Admittance fifty cents for
grown persons; children half price. Profiles taken
with accuracy at the Museum.

The greatest attraction of the whole Museum will be
a large magnificent painting of Christ in the Garden of
Gethsemane.

All this for a quarter! The newspaper suddenly
dropped from his hands into the dirt of the street—he
had no quarter! For a moment he sat as immovable
as if the thought had turned him into stone; but the
next moment he had sprung from the sidewalk and was
speeding home to his mother. Never before had the
stub of the little crutch been plied so nimbly among the
stones of the rough sidewalk. Never before had he
made a prettier picture, with the blue cap pushed far
back from his forehead, his yellow hair blowing about
his face, the old black satin waistcoat flopping like a
pair of disjointed wings against his sides, the open newspaper streaming backward from his hand, and his face
alive with hope.

IV.

Two hours later he issued from the house, and set his
face in the direction of the museum—a face full of excitement still, but full also of pain, because he had no

money, and saw no chance of getting any. It was a
dull time of the year for his mother's work. Only the
day before she had been paid a month's earnings, and
already the money had been laid out for the frugal ex-
penses of the household. It would be a long time before any more would come in, and in the mean time the
exhibition of wax figures would have been moved to
some other town. When he had told her that the parson had said that she must go to see them, she had
smiled fondly at him from beside her loom, and quietly
shaken her head with inward resignation; but when he
told her the parson had said *he* must be sure to go too,
the smile had faded into an expression of fixed sadness.

On his way down town he passed the little music
store of Mr. Leuba, which was one block this side of the
Kentucky Hotel. He was all eagerness to reach the
museum, but his ear caught the sounds of the violin,
and he forgot everything else in his desire to go in and
speak with Tom, for Tom was his lord and master.

"Tom, are you going to see the wax figures?" he cried,
with trembling haste, curling himself on top of the keg
of nails in his accustomed corner of the little lumber-
room. But Tom paid no attention to the question or
the questioner, being absorbed in executing an intricate
passage of "O Thou Fount of every Blessing!" For
the moment David forgot his question himself, absorbed
likewise in witnessing this envied performance.

When Tom had finished, he laid the violin across his
knees and wiped his brow with his shirt-sleeves. "Don't
you know that you oughtn't to talk to me when I'm performing?" he said, loftily, still not deigning to look at
his offending auditor. "Don't you know that it dis-
turbs a fiddler to be spoken to when he's performing?"

"EXECUTING AN INTRICATE PASSAGE."

Tom was an overgrown, rawboned lad of some fifteen years, with stubby red hair, no eyebrows, large watery blue eyes, and a long neck with a big Adam's apple.

"I didn't mean to interrupt you, Tom," said David, in a tone of the deepest penitence. "You know that I'd rather hear you play than anything."

"Father got the thousand-dollar prize," said Tom coldly, accepting the apology for the sake of the compliment.

"Oh, *Tom!* I'm so glad! *Hurrah!*" shouted David, waving his old blue cap around his head, his face transfigured with joy, his heart leaping with a sudden hope, and now at last he would get the violin.

"What are *you* glad for?" said Tom, with dreadful severity. "He's *my* father; he's not *your* father;" and for the first time he bestowed a glance upon the little figure curled up on the nail keg, and bending eagerly towards him with clasped hands.

"I *know* he's *your* father, Tom, but—"

"Well, then, what are you *glad* for?" insisted Tom. "You're not going to get any of the money."

"I know *that*, Tom," said David, coloring deeply, "but—"

"Well, then, what *are* you glad for?"

"I don't think I'm so *very* glad, Tom," replied David, sorrowfully.

But Tom had taken up the bow and was rubbing the resin on it. He used a great deal of resin in his playing, and would often proudly call David's attention to how much of it would settle as a white dust under the bridge. David was too well used to Tom's rebuffs to mind them long, and as he now looked on at this resining process, the sunlight came back into his face.

"Please let me try it once, Tom—just *once*." Experience had long ago taught him that this was asking too much of Tom; but with the new hope that the violin might now soon become his, his desire to handle it was ungovernable.

"Now look here, David," replied Tom, with a great show of kindness in his manner, "I'd let you try it once, but you'd spoil the tone. It's taken me a long time to get a good tone into this fiddle, and you'd take it all out the very first whack. As soon as you learn to get a good tone out of it, I'll let you play on it. Don't you *know* you'd spoil it, if I was to let you try it *now ?*" he added, suddenly wheeling with tremendous energy upon his timid petitioner.

"I'm afraid I would, Tom," replied David, with a voice full of anguish.

"But just listen to me," said Tom; and taking up the violin, he rendered the opening passage of "O Thou Fount of every Blessing!" Scarcely had he finished when a customer entered the shop, and he hurried to the front, leaving the violin and the bow on the chair that he had quitted.

No sooner was he gone than the little figure slipped noiselessly from its perch, and hobbling quickly to the chair on which the violin lay, stood beside it in silent love. Touch it he durst not; but his sensitive, delicate hands passed tremblingly over it, and his eyes dwelt upon it with unspeakable longing. Then, with a sigh, he turned away, and hastened to the front of the shop. Tom had already dismissed his customer, and was standing in the door, looking down the street in the direction of the Kentucky Hotel, where a small crowd had collected around the entrance of the museum.

As David stepped out upon the sidewalk, it was the sight of this crowd that recalled him to a new sorrow.

"Tom," he cried, with longing, "are you going to see the wax figures?"

"Of course I'm going," he replied, carelessly. "We're all going."

"When, Tom?" asked David, with breathless interest.

"Whenever we want to, of course," replied Tom. "I'm not going just once; I'm going as often as I like."

"Why don't you go now, Tom? It's so hot—they might melt."

This startling view of the case was not without its effect on Tom, although a suggestion from such a source was not to be respected. He merely threw his eyes up towards the heavens and said, sturdily: "You ninny! they'll not melt. Don't you see it's going to rain and turn cooler?"

"I'll bet you *I'd* not wait for it to turn cooler. I'll bet you *I'd* be in there before you could say Jack Roberson, if *I* had a quarter," said David, with resolution.

V.

All that long afternoon he hung in feverish excitement around the door of the museum. There was scarce a travelling show in Kentucky in those days. It was not strange if to this idler of the streets, in whom imagination was all-powerful, and in whose heart quivered ungovernable yearnings for the heroic, the poetic, and the beautiful, this day of the first exhibition of wax figures was the most memorable of his life.

It was so easy for everybody to go in who wished; so

impossible for him. Groups of gay ladies slipped their
silver half-dollars through the variegated meshes of their
silken purses. The men came in jolly twos and threes,
and would sometimes draw out great rolls of bills. Now
a kind-faced farmer passed in, dropping into the hands
of the door-keeper a half-dollar for himself, and three
quarters for three sleek negroes that followed at his
heels; and now a manufacturer with a couple of ap-
prentices — lads of David's age and friends of his.
Poor little fellow! at many a shop of the town he had
begged to be taken as an apprentice himself, but no one
would have him because he was lame.

And now the people were beginning to pour out, and
he hovered about them, hoping in this way to get some
idea of what was going on inside. Once, with the courage of despair, he seized the arm of a lad as he came
out.

"Oh, Bobby, *tell* me all about it!"

But Bobby shook him off, and skipped away to tell
somebody else who didn't want to hear.

After a while two sweet-faced ladies dressed in
mourning appeared. As they passed down the street
he was standing on the sidewalk, and there must have
been something in his face to attract the attention of
one of them, for she paused, and in the gentlest manner
said :

"My little man, how did you like the wax figures and
the picture?"

"Oh, madam," he replied, his eyes filling, "I have
not seen them !"

"But you will see them, I hope," she said, moving
away, but bestowing on him the lingering smile of bereft motherhood.

The twilight fell, and still he lingered, until, with a sudden remorseful thought of his mother, he turned away and passed up the dark street. His tongue was parched, there was a lump in his throat, and a numb pain about his heart. Far up the street he paused and looked back. A lantern had been swung out over the entrance of the museum, and the people were still passing in.

VI.

A happy man was the Reverend James Moore the next morning. The lottery had been a complete success, and he would henceforth have a comfortable church, in which the better to save the souls of his fellow-creatures. The leading vestry-man had drawn the capital prize, and while the other members who had drawn blanks were not exactly satisfied, on the whole the result seemed as good as providential. As he walked down town at an early hour, he was conscious of suffering from a dangerous elation of spirit; and more than once his silent prayer had been : " Lord, let me not be puffed up this day ! Let me not be blinded with happiness ! Keep the eyes of my soul clear, that I overlook no duty ! What have I, unworthy servant, done that I should be so fortunate ?"

Now and then, as he passed along, a church member would wring his hand and offer congratulations. After about fifteen years of a more or less stranded condition a magnificent incoming tide of prosperity now seemed to lift him off his very feet.

From wandering rather blindly about the streets for a while, he started for the new church, remembering

that he had an engagement with a committee of ladies.
who had taken in charge the furnishing of it. But when
he reached there, no one had arrived but the widow
Babcock. She was very beautiful ; and looking at womankind from behind his veil of unfamiliarity, the parson, despite his logic, had always felt a desire to lift that
veil when standing in her presence. The intoxication
of his mood was not now lessened by coming upon her
so unexpectedly alone.

"My dear Mrs. Babcock," he said, offering her his
hand in his beautiful manner, "it seems peculiarly fitting that you should be the first of the ladies to reach
the spot ; for it would have pained me to think you less
zealous than the others. The vestry needs not only
your taste in furniture, but the influence of your presence."

The widow dropped her eyes, the gallantry of the
speech being so unusual. "I came early on purpose,"
she replied, in a voice singularly low and tremulous. "I
wanted to see you alone. Oh, Mr. Moore, the ladies of
this town owe you such a debt of gratitude ! You have
been such a comfort to those who are sad, such a support to those who needed strengthening ! And who has
needed these things as much as I ?"

As she spoke, the parson, with a slight look of apprehension, had put his back against the wall, as was apt
to be his way when talking with ladies.

"Who has needed these things as I have ?" continued the widow, taking a step forward, and with increasing agitation. "Oh, Mr. Moore, I should be an ungrate-
ful woman if I did not mingle my congratulations with
the others. And I want to do this now with my whole
soul. May God bless you, and crown the labors of

"THE WIDOW DROPPED HER EYES."

your life with every desire of your heart!" And saying this, the widow laid the soft tips of one hand on
one of the parson's shoulders, and raising herself slightly on tiptoe, kissed him.

"Oh, Mrs. Babcock!" cried the dismayed logician,
"what have you done?" But the next moment, the logician giving place to the man, he grasped one of her
hands, and murmuring, "May God bless *you* for *that!*"
seized his hat, and hurried out into the street.

The most careless observer might have been interested in watching his movements as he walked
away.

He carried his hat in his hand, forgetting to put it
on. Several persons spoke to him on the street, but he
did not hear them. He strode a block or two in one
direction, and then a block or two in another.

"If she does it again," he muttered to himself—"if
she does it again, I'll marry her!... Old?... I could
run a mile in a minute!"

As he was passing the music-store, the dealer called
out to him:

"Come in, parson. I've got a present for you."

"A—present—for—*me?*" repeated the parson, blank
with amazement. In his life the little music-dealer had
never made him a present.

"Yes, a present," repeated the fortunate vestry-man,
whose dry heart, like a small seed-pod, the wind of good-
fortune had opened, so that a few rattling germs of generosity dropped out. Opening a drawer behind his
counter, he now took out a roll of music. "Here's some
new music for your flute," he said. "Accept it with my
compliments."

New music for his flute! The parson turned it over

dreamily, and it seemed that the last element of disorder had come to derange his faculties.

"And Mrs. Leuba sends her compliments, and would
like to have you to dinner," added the shopkeeper,
looking across the counter with some amusement at the
expression of the parson, who now appeared as much
shocked as though his whole nervous system had been
suddenly put in connection with a galvanic battery of
politeness.

It was a very gay dinner, having been gotten up to
celebrate the drawing of the prize. The entire company
were to go in the afternoon to see the waxworks, and
some of the ladies wore especial toilets, with a view to
having their profiles taken.

" Have you been to see the waxworks, Mr. Moore ?"
inquired a spinster roguishly, wiping a drop of soup
from her underlip.

The unusual dinner, the merriment, the sense of many
ladies present. mellowed the parson like old wine.

" No, madam." he replied, giddily ; " but I shall go
this very afternoon.   I find it impossible any longer to
deny myself the pleasure of beholding the great American Coquette and the Sleeping Beauty.   I must take
my black sheep," he continued, with expanding warmth.
" I must drive my entire flock of soiled lambs into the
favored and refining presence of Miss Julia Granby."

Keeping to this resolution, as soon as dinner was
over he made his excuses to the company, and set off
to collect a certain class of boys which he had scraped
together by hook and crook from the by-ways of the
town, and about an hour later he might have been seen
driving them before him towards the entrance of the
museum.   There he shouldered his way cheerfully up

to the door, and shoved each of the lads good-naturedly
in, finally passing in himself, with a general glance at
the by-standers, as if to say, " Was there ever another
man as happy in this world ?"

But he soon came out, leaving his wild lambs to
browse at will in those fresh pastures, and took his way
up street homeward. He seemed to be under some necessity of shaking them off in order to enjoy the solitude of his thoughts.

" If she does it again ! . . . If she does it again ! . . .
Whee! whee! whee!—whee! whee! whee!" and he began to whistle for his flute with a nameless longing.

It was soon after this that the two women heard him
playing the reel, and watched him perform certain later
incredible evolutions.   For whether one event, or all
events combined, had betrayed him into this outbreak,
henceforth he was quite beside himself.

Is it possible that on this day the Reverend James
Moore had driven the ancient, rusty, creaky chariot of
his faculties too near the sun of love?

VII.

A sad day it had been meantime for the poor lad.

He had gotten up in the morning listless and dull
and sick at the sight of his breakfast. But he had
feigned to be quite well that he might have permission
to set off down-town. There was no chance of his being able to get into the museum, but he was drawn
irresistibly thither for the mere pleasure of standing
around and watching the people, and hoping that something — *something* would turn up. He was still there

when his dinner - hour came, but he never thought of
this. Once, when the door-keeper was at leisure, he had
hobbled up and said to him, with a desperate effort to
smile, " Sir, if I were rich, I'd live in your museum for
about five years."

But the door - keeper had pushed him rudely back,
telling him to be off and not obstruct the sidewalk.

He was still standing near the entrance
when the parson came down the street driving his flock of boys. Ah,
if he had only joined that

class, as time
after time he
had been asked to do !
All at once his face lit
up with a fortunate in-
spiration, and pushing
his way to the very
side of the door-keeper, he placed himself there that
the parson might see him and take him with the oth-

ers; for had he not said that *he* must be sure to go?
But when the parson came up, this purpose had failed
him, and he had apparently shrunk to half his size behind the bulk of the door-keeper, fearing most of all
things that the parson would discover him and know
why he was there.

He was still lingering outside when the parson reappeared and started homeward; and he sat down and
watched him out of sight. He seemed cruelly hurt, and
his eyes filled with tears.

"*I'd* have taken *him* in the very first one," he said,
choking down a sob; and then, as if he felt this to
be unjust, he murmured over and over: "Maybe he
forgot me; maybe he didn't mean it; maybe he forgot me."

Perhaps an hour later, slowly and with many pauses,
he drew near the door of the parson's home. There he
lifted his hand three times before he could knock.

"The parson's not at home," the widow Spurlock had
called sharply down to him.

With this the last hope had died out of his bosom;
for having dwelt long on the parson's kindness to him
—upon all the parson's tireless efforts to befriend him—
he had summoned the courage at last to go and ask
him to lend him a quarter.

With little thought of whither he went, he now turned
back down-town, but some time later he was still standing at the entrance of the museum.

He looked up the street again. All the Leubas were
coming, Tom walking, with a very haughty air, a few
feet ahead.

"Why don't you go in?" he said, loudly, walking up
to David and jingling the silver in his pockets. "What

are you standing out here for? If you *want* to go in,
why don't you *go* in?"

"Oh, Tom!" cried David, in a whisper of eager confidence, his utterance choked with a sob, "I haven't got
any money."

"I'd hate to be as poor as *you* are," said Tom, contemptuously. "I'm going this evening, and to-night,
and as often as I want," and he turned gayly away to
join the others.

He was left alone again, and his cup of bitterness,
which had been filling drop by drop, now ran over.

Several groups came up just at that moment. There
was a pressure and a jostling of the throng. As Mr.
Leuba, who had made his way up to the door-keeper,
drew a handful of silver from his pocket, some one accidentally struck his elbow, and several pieces fell to
the pavement. Then there was laughter and a scram-
bling as these were picked up and returned. But out
through the legs of the crowd one bright silver quarter
rolled unseen down the sloping sidewalk towards the
spot where David was standing.

It was all done in an instant. He saw it coming;
the little crutch was set forward a pace, the little body
was swung silently forward, and as the quarter fell over
on its shining side, the dirty sole of a brown foot covered it.

The next minute, with a sense of triumph and bounding joy, the poverty-tortured, friendless little thief had
crossed the threshold of the museum, and stood face to
face with the Redeemer of the world; for the picture
was so hung as to catch the eye upon entering, and it
arrested his quick, roving glance and held it in awe-
stricken fascination. Unconscious of his own move-

BEFORE THE PICTURE.

ments, he drew nearer and nearer, until he stood a few feet in front of the arc of spectators, with his breathing all but suspended, and one hand crushing the old blue cloth cap against his naked bosom.

It was a strange meeting. The large rude painting possessed no claim to art. But to him it was an overwhelming revelation, for he had never seen any pictures, and he was gifted with an untutored love of painting. Over him, therefore, it exercised an inthralling influence, and it was as though he stood in the visible presence of One whom he knew that the parson preached of and his mother worshipped.

Forgetful of his surroundings, long he stood and gazed. Whether it may have been the thought of the stolen quarter that brought him to himself, at length he drew a deep breath, and looked quickly around with a frightened air. From across the room he saw Mr. Leuba watching him gravely, as it seemed to his guilty conscience, with fearful sternness. A burning flush dyed his face, and he shrank back, concealing himself among the crowd. The next moment, without ever having seen or so much as thought of anything else in the museum, he slipped out into the street.

There the eyes of everybody seemed turned upon him. Where should he go? Not home. Not to Mr. Leuba's music-store. No; he could never look into Mr. Leuba's face again. And Tom? He could hear Tom crying out, wherever he should meet him, "You stole a quarter from father."

In utter terror and shame, he hurried away out to the southern end of the town, where there was an abandoned rope-walk.

It was a neglected place, damp and unhealthy. In

the farthest corner of it he lay down and hid himself in
a clump of iron-weeds. Slowly the moments dragged
themselves along. Of what was he thinking? Of his
mother? Of the parson? Of the violin that would
now never be his? Of that wonderful sorrowful face
which he had seen in the painting? The few noises of
the little town grew very faint, the droning of the bum-
blebee on the purple tufts of the weed overhead very
loud, and louder still the beating of his heart against
the green grass as he lay on his side, with his head on
his blue cap and his cheek in his hand. And then he
fell asleep.

When he awoke he started up bewildered. The sun
had set, and the heavy dews of twilight were falling. A
chill ran through him; and then the recollection of
what had happened came over him with a feeling of
desolation. When it was quite dark he left his hiding-
place and started back up-town.

He could reach home in several ways, but a certain
fear drew him into the street which led past the music-
store. If he could only see Mr. Leuba, he felt sure
that he could tell by the expression of his face whether
he had missed the quarter. At some distance off he
saw by the light of the windows Mr. Leuba standing in
front of his shop talking to a group of men. Noiselessly he drew near, noiselessly he was passing without
the courage to look up.

"Stop, David. Come in here a moment. I want to
talk to you."

As Mr. Leuba spoke, he apologized to the gentlemen
for leaving, and turned back into the rear of the shop.
Faint, and trembling so that he could scarcely stand,
his face of a deadly whiteness, the boy followed.

"David," said Mr. Leuba—in his whole life he had never spoken so kindly; perhaps his heart had been touched by some belated feeling, as he had studied the boy's face before the picture in the museum, and certainly it had been singularly opened by his good-fortune—"David," he said, "I promised when I got rich enough I'd give Tom a new violin, and give you his old one. Well, I gave him a new one to-day; so here's yours," and going to a corner of the room, he took up the box, brought it back, and would have laid it on the boy's arm, only there was no arm extended to receive it.

"Take it! It's yours!"

"Oh, Mr. Leuba!"

It was all he could say. He had expected to be charged with stealing the quarter, and instead there was held out to him the one treasure in the world—the violin of which he had dreamed so long, for which he had served so faithfully.

"Oh, Mr. Leuba!"

There was a pitiful note in the cry, but the dealer was not the man to hear it, or to notice the look of angelic contrition on the upturned face. He merely took the lad's arm, bent it around the violin, patted the ragged cap, and said, a little impatiently:

"Come, come! they're waiting for me at the door. To-morrow you can come down and run some more errands for me," and he led the way to the front of the shop and resumed his conversation.

Slowly along the dark street the lad toiled homeward with his treasure. At any other time he would have sat down on the first curb-stone, opened the box, and in ecstatic joy have lifted out that peerless instrument;

or he would have sped home with it to his mother,
flying along on his one crutch as if on the winds of
heaven. But now he could not look at it, and something clogged his gait so that he loitered and faltered
and sometimes stood still irresolute.

But at last he approached the log-cabin which was
his home. A rude fence enclosed the yard, and inside this fence there grew a hedge of lilacs. When
he was within a few feet of the gate he paused, and
did what he had never done before—he put his face
close to the panels of the fence, and with a look of
guilt and sorrow peeped through the lilacs at the face
of his mother, who was sitting in the light of the open
door-way.

She was thinking of him. He knew that by the
patient sweetness of her smile. All the heart went out
of him at the sight, and hurrying forward, he put the
violin down at her feet, and threw his arms around her
neck, and buried his head on her bosom.

VIII.

After he had made his confession, a restless and
feverish night he had of it, often springing up from his
troubled dreams and calling to her in the darkness.
But the next morning he insisted upon getting up for a
while.

Towards the afternoon he grew worse again, and
took to his bed, the yellow head tossing to and fro,
the eyes bright and restless, and his face burning. At
length he looked up and said to his mother, in the
manner of one who forms a difficult resolution: " Send

for the parson. Tell him I am sick and want to see
him."

It was this summons that the widow Spurlock had
delivered on the Sunday afternoon when the parson

had quitted the house with such a cry of distress. He
had not so much as thought of the boy since the Friday
morning previous.

"How is it possible," he exclaimed, as he hurried

on—"how is it *possible* that I *could* have forgotten
him?"

The boy's mother met him outside the house and
drew him into an adjoining room, silently, for her tears
were falling. He sank into the first chair.

"Is he so ill?" he asked, under his trembling breath.

"I'm afraid he's going to be very ill. And to see
him in so much trouble—"

"What is the matter? In God's name, has anything happened to him?"

She turned her face away to hide her grief. "He
said he would tell you himself. Oh, if I've been too
hard with him! But I did it for the best. I didn't
know until the doctor came that he was going to be ill,
or I would have waited. Do anything you can to quiet
him—anything he should ask you to do," she implored,
and pointed towards the door of the room in which the
boy lay.

Conscience-stricken and speechless, the parson opened it and entered.

The small white bed stood against the wall beneath
an open window, and one bright-headed sunflower,
growing against the house outside, leaned in and fixed
its kind face anxiously upon the sufferer's.

The figure of the boy was stretched along the edge
of the bed, his cheek on one hand and his eyes turned
steadfastly towards the middle of the room, where, on a
table, the violin lay exposed to view

He looked quickly towards the door as the parson
entered, and an expression of relief passed over his
face.

"Why, David," said the parson, chidingly, and crossing to the bed with a bright smile. "Sick? This will

never do;" and he sat down, imprisoning one of the burning palms in his own.

The boy said nothing, but looked at him searchingly, as though needing to lay aside masks and disguises and penetrate at once to the bottom truth. Then he asked, " Are you mad at me ?"

" My poor boy !" said the parson, his lips trembling a little as he tightened his pressure—" my poor boy! why should *I* be mad at *you* ?"

" You never could do anything with me."

" Never mind that now," said the parson, soothingly, but adding, with bitterness, " it was all my fault—all my fault."

" It wasn't your fault," said the boy. " It was mine."

A change had come over him in his treatment of the parson. Shyness had disappeared, as is apt to be the case with the sick.

" I want to ask you something," he added, confidentially.

" Anything—anything ! Ask me anything !"

" Do you remember the wax figures ?"

" Oh yes, I remember them very well," said the parson, quickly, uneasily.

" I wanted to see 'em, and I didn't have any money, and I stole a quarter from Mr. Leuba."

Despite himself a cry escaped the parson's lips, and dropping the boy's hand, he started from his chair and walked rapidly to and fro across the room, with the fangs of remorse fixed deep in his conscience.

" Why didn't you come to me ?" he asked at length, in a tone of helpless entreaty. " Why didn't you come to me ? Oh, if you had only come to me !"

" I did come to you," replied the boy.

"When?" asked the parson, coming back to the bedside.

"About three o'clock yesterday."

About three o'clock yesterday!   And what was he
doing at that time?   He bent his head over to his very
knees, hiding his face in his hands.

"But why didn't you let me know it?   Why didn't
you come in?"

"Mrs. Spurlock told me you were at work on a sermon."

"God forgive me!" murmured the parson. with a
groan.

"I thought you'd lend me a quarter," said the boy, simply. "You took the other boys, and you told me *I* must be certain to go. I thought you'd lend me a quarter till I could pay you back."

"Oh, David!" cried the parson, getting down on his knees by the bedside, and putting his arms around the boy's neck, "I would have lent you—I would have given you—anything I have in this poor world!"

The boy threw his arms around the parson's neck and clasped him close. "Forgive me!"

"Oh, boy! boy! can you forgive *me?*" Sobs stifled the parson's utterance, and he went to a window on the opposite side of the room.

When he turned his face inward again, he saw the boy's gaze fixed once more intently upon the violin.

"There's something I want you to do for me," he said. "Mr. Leuba gave me a violin last night, and mamma says I ought to sell it and pay him back. Mamma says it will be a good lesson for me." The words seemed wrung from his heart's core. "I thought I'd ask *you* to sell it for me. The doctor says I may be sick a long time, and it worries me." He began to grow excited, and tossed from side to side.

"Don't worry," said the parson, "I'll sell it for you."

The boy looked at the violin again. To him it was priceless, and his eyes grew heavy with love for it. Then he said, cautiously: "I thought *you'd* get a good price for it. I don't think I could take less than a hundred dollars. It's worth more than that, but if I have to sell it, I don't think I *could* take less than a hundred dollars," and he fixed his burning eyes on the parson's.

"Don't worry! I'll sell it for you. Oh yes, you can

easily get a hundred dollars for it. I'll bring you a hundred dollars for it by to-morrow morning."

As the parson was on the point of leaving the room, with the violin under his arm, he paused with his hand on the latch, an anxious look gathering in his face. Then he came back, laid the violin on the table, and going to the bedside, took the boy's hands in both of his own.

"David," said the moral philosopher, wrestling in his consciousness with the problem of evil—" David, was it the face of the Saviour that you wished to see? Was it *this* that tempted you to—" and he bent over the boy breathless.

"I wanted to see the Sleeping Beauty."

The parson turned away with a sigh of acute disappointment.

It was on this night that he was seen to enter his room with a boy's violin under his arm, and later to hang it, and hang his beloved flute, tied with a blue ribbon, above the meagre top shelf of books—Fuller's *Gospel*, Petrarch, Volney's *Ruins*, Zollicoffer's *Sermons*, and the *Horrors of San Domingo*. After that he remained motionless at his table, with his head bowed on his folded arms, until the candle went out, leaving him in inner and outer darkness. Moralist, logician, philosopher, he studied the transgression, laying it at last solely to his own charge.

At daybreak he stood outside the house with the physician who had been with the boy during the night. "Will he die?" he asked.

The physician tapped his forehead with his forefinger. "The chances are against him. The case has peculiar complications. All night it has been nothing but the wax figures and the stolen quarter and the violin. His mother has tried to persuade him not to sell it. But he won't bear the sight of it now, although he is wild at the thought of selling it."

"David," said the parson, kneeling by the bedside, and speaking in a tone pitiful enough to have recalled a soul from the other world—" David, here's the money for the violin; here's the hundred dollars," and he pressed it into one of the boy's palms. The hand closed upon it, but there was no recognition. It was half a year's salary.

The first sermon that the parson preached in the new church was on the Sunday after the boy's death. It was expected that he would rise to the occasion and surpass himself, which, indeed, he did, drawing tears even from the eyes of those who knew not that they could shed them, and all through making the greatest effort to keep back his own. The subject of the sermon was "The Temptations of the Poor." The sermon of the following fortnight was on the " Besetting Sin," the drift of it going to show that the besetting sin may be the one pure and exquisite pleasure of life, involving only the exercise of the loftiest faculty. And this was followed by a third sermon on "The Kiss that Betrayeth," in which the parson ransacked history for illustrations to show that every species of man—ancient, mediæval, and modern—had been betrayed in this way. During the delivery of this sermon the parson looked so cold and even severe that it was not understood why the emotions of any one should have been touched, or why the widow Babcock should have lowered her veil and wept bitterly.

And thus being ever the more loved and revered as

he grew ever the more lovable and saint-like, he passed
onward to the close.   But not until the end came did
he once stretch forth a hand to touch his flute ; and
it was only in imagination then that he grasped it. to
sound the final roll-call of his wandering faculties, and
to blow a last good-night to his tired spirit.

King Solomon of Kentucky.

I.

It had been a year of strange disturbances—a deso-
lating drought, a hurly-burly of destructive tempests, killing frosts in the tender valleys, mortal fevers in the tender homes. Now came tidings that all day the wail of
myriads of locusts was heard in the green woods of Virginia and Tennessee ; now that Lake Erie was blocked
with ice on the very verge of summer, so that in the
Niagara new rocks and islands showed their startling
faces. In the Blue-glass Region of Kentucky countless
caterpillars were crawling over the ripening apple orchards and leaving the trees as stark as when tossed in
the thin air of bitter February days.

Then, flying low and heavily through drought and
tempest and frost and plague, like the royal presence
of disaster, that had been but heralded by its mournful train, came nearer and nearer the dark angel of the
pestilence.

M. Xaupi had given a great ball only the night before
in the dancing-rooms over the confectionery of M. Giron—that M. Giron who made the tall pyramids of mé-
ringues and macaroons for wedding-suppers, and spun
around them a cloud of candied webbing as white and
misty as the veil of the bride. It was the opening co-
tillon party of the summer. The men came in blue

5

cloth coats with brass buttons, buff waistcoats, and
laced and ruffled shirts; the ladies came in white satins with ethereal silk overdresses, embroidered in the
figure of a gold beetle or an oak leaf of green. The
walls of the ball-room were painted to represent landscapes of blooming orange-trees, set here and there in
clustering tubs; and the chandeliers and sconces were
lighted with innumerable wax-candles, yellow and green
and rose.

Only the day before, also, Clatterbuck had opened
for the summer a new villa-house, six miles out in the
country, with a dancing-pavilion in a grove of maples
and oaks, a pleasure-boat on a sheet of crystal water,
and a cellar stocked with old sherry, Sauterne, and
Château Margaux wines, with anisette, " Perfect Love,"
and Guigholet cordials.

Down on Water Street, near where now stands a railway station, Hugh Lonney, urging that the fear of cholera was not the only incentive to cleanliness, had just
fitted up a sumptuous bath-house, where cold and shower
baths might be had at twelve and a half cents each, or
hot ones at three for half a dollar

Yes, the summer of 1833 was at hand, and there must
be new pleasures, new luxuries; for Lexington was the
Athens of the West and the Kentucky Birmingham.

Old Peter Leuba felt the truth of this, as he stepped
smiling out of his little music-store on Main Street, and,
rubbing his hands briskly together, surveyed once more
his newly-arranged windows, in which were displayed
gold and silver epaulets, bottles of Jamaica rum, garden
seeds from Philadelphia, drums and guitars and harps.
Dewees & Grant felt it in their drug-store on Cheapside, as they sent off a large order for calomel and su-

perior Maccoboy, rappee, and Lancaster snuff. Bluff little Daukins Tegway felt it, as he hurried on the morning of that day to the office of the *Observer and Reporter,* and advertised that he would willingly exchange his beautiful assortment of painted muslins and Dunstable bonnets for flax and feathers. On the threshold he met a florid farmer, who had just offered ten dollars' reward for a likely runaway boy with a long fresh scar across his face ; and to-morrow the paper would contain one more of those tragical little cuts, representing an African slave scampering away at the top of his speed, with a stick swung across his shoulder and a bundle dangling down his back. In front of Postlethwaite's Tavern, where now stands the Phœnix Hotel, a company of idlers, leaning back in Windsor chairs and planting their feet against the opposite wall on a level with their heads, smoked and chewed and yawned, as they discussed the administration of Jackson and arranged for the coming of Daniel Webster in June, when they would give him a great barbecue, and roast in his honor a buffalo bull taken from the herd emparked near Ashland. They hailed a passing merchant, who, however, would hear nothing of the bull, but fell to praising his Rocky Mountain beaver and Goose Creek salt; and another, who turned a deaf ear to Daniel Webster, and invited them to drop in and examine his choice essences of peppermint, bergamot, and lavender.

But of all the scenes that might have been observed in Lexington on that day, the most remarkable occurred in front of the old court-house at the hour of high noon. On the mellow stroke of the clock in the steeple above the sheriff stepped briskly forth, closely followed by a man of powerful frame, whom he commanded to station

himself on the pavement several feet off. A crowd of
men and boys had already collected in anticipation, and
others came quickly up as the clear voice of the sheriff
was heard across the open public square and old market-place.

He stood on the topmost of the court-house steps,
and for a moment looked down on the crowd with the
usual air of official severity.

"Gentlemen," he then cried out sharply, "by an or-
dah of the cou't I now offah this man at public sale to
the highes' biddah. He is able-bodied but lazy, without visible property or means of suppoht, an' of dissolute habits. He is therefoh adjudged guilty of high
misdemeanahs, an' is to be sole into labah foh a twelvemonth. How much, then, am I offahed foh the vagrant?
How much am I offahed foh ole King Sol'mon?"

Nothing was offered for old King Solomon. The
spectators formed themselves into a ring around the
big vagrant and settled down to enjoy the performance.

"Staht 'im, somebody."

Somebody started a laugh, which rippled around the
circle.

The sheriff looked on with an expression of unre-
laxed severity, but catching the eye of an acquaintance
on the outskirts, he exchanged a lightning wink of secret appreciation. Then he lifted off his tight beaver
hat, wiped out of his eyes a little shower of perspiration
which rolled suddenly down from above, and warmed
a degree to his theme.

"Come, gentlemen," he said, more suasively, "it's too
hot to stan' heah all day. Make me an offah! You all
know ole King Sol'mon; don't wait to be interduced.
How much, then, to staht 'im? Say fifty dollahs!

Twenty-five! Fifteen! Ten! Why, gentlemen! Not *ten* dollahs? Remembah this is the Blue-grass Region of Kentucky—the land of Boone an' Kenton, the home of Henry Clay!" he added, in an oratorical *crescendo*.

"He ain't wuth his victuals," said an oily little tavern-keeper, folding his arms restfully over his own stomach and cocking up one piggish eye into his neighbor's face. "He ain't wuth his 'taters."

"Buy 'im foh 'is rags!" cried a young law-student, with a Blackstone under his arm, to the town rag-picker opposite, who was unconsciously ogling the vagrant's apparel.

"I *might* buy 'im foh 'is *scalp*," drawled a farmer, who had taken part in all kinds of scalp contests and was now known to be busily engaged in collecting crow scalps for a match soon to come off between two rival counties.

"I think I'll buy 'im foh a hat-sign," said a manufacturer of ten-dollar Castor and Rhorum hats. This sally drew merry attention to the vagrant's hat, and the merchant felt rewarded.

"You'd bettah say the town ought to buy 'im an' put 'im up on top of the cou't-house as a scarecrow foh the cholera," said some one else.

"What news of the cholera did the stage-coach bring this mohning?" quickly inquired his neighbor in his ear; and the two immediately fell into low, grave talk, forgot the auction, and turned away.

"Stop, gentlemen, stop!" cried the sheriff, who had watched the rising tide of good-humor, and now saw his chance to float in on it with spreading sails. "You're runnin' the price in the wrong direction—down, not up. The law requires that he be sole to the highes' biddah, not the lowes'. As loyal citizens, uphole the

constitution of the commonwealth of Kentucky an'
make me an offah; the man is really a great bargain.
In the first place, he would cos' his ownah little or
nothin', because, as you see, he keeps himself in cigahs
an' clo'es; then, his main article of diet is whiskey—a
supply of which he always has on han'. He don't even
need a bed, foh you know he sleeps jus' as well on any
doohstep; noh a chair, foh he prefers to sit roun' on the
curb-stones. Remembah, too, gentlemen, that ole King
Sol'mon is a Virginian—from the same neighbohhood as
Mr. Clay. Remembah that he is well educated, that he is
an *awful* Whig, an' that he has smoked mo' of the stumps
of Mr. Clay's cigahs than any other man in existence.
If you don't b'lieve *me*, gentlemen, yondah goes Mr.
Clay now; call *him* ovah an' ask 'im foh yo'se'ves."

He paused, and pointed with his right forefinger towards Main street, along which the spectators, with a
sudden craning of necks, beheld the familiar figure of
the passing statesman.

"But you don't need *any*body to tell you these fac's,
gentlemen," he continued. "You merely need to be reminded that ole King Sol'mon is no ohdinary man. Mo'-
ovah he has a kine heaht, he nevah spoke a rough wohd
to anybody in this worl',' an' he is as proud as Tecumseh
of his good name an' charactah. An', gentlemen," he
added, bridling with an air of mock gallantry and laying
a hand on his heart, "if anythin' fu'thah is required in
the way of a puffect encomium, we all know that there
isn't anothah man among us who cuts as wide a swath
among the ladies. The'foh, if you have any appreciation of virtue, any magnanimity of heaht; if you set a
propah valuation upon the descendants of Virginia, that
mothah of Presidents; if you believe in the pure laws

of Kentucky as the pioneer bride of the Union; if you love America an' love the worl'—make me a gen'rous, high-toned offah foh ole King Sol'mon!"

He ended his peroration amid a shout of laughter and applause, and, feeling satisfied that it was a good time for returning to a more practical treatment of his subject, proceeded in a sincere tone:

" He can easily earn from one to two dollahs a day, an' from three to six hundred a yeah. There's not anothah white man in town capable of doin' as much work. There's not a niggah han' in the hemp factories with such muscles an' such a chest. *Look* at 'em! An', if you don't b'lieve me, step fo'wahd and *feel* 'em. How much, then, is bid foh 'im?"

"One dollah!" said the owner of a hemp factory, who had walked forward and felt the vagrant's arm, laughing, but coloring up also as the eyes of all were quickly turned upon him. In those days it was not an unheard-of thing for the muscles of a human being to be thus examined when being sold into servitude to a new master.

"Thank you!" cried the sheriff, cheerily. "One precinc' heard from! One dollah! I am offahed one dollah foh ole King Sol'mon. One dollah foh the king! Make it a half. One dollah an' a half. Make it a half. One dol-dol-dol-dollah!"

Two medical students, returning from lectures at the old Medical Hall, now joined the group, and the sheriff explained:

" One dollah is bid foh the vagrant ole King Sol'mon, who is to be sole into labah foh a twelvemonth. Is there any othah bid? Are you all done? One dollah, once—"

"Dollah and a half," said one of the students, and remarked half jestingly under his breath to his companion, "I'll buy him on the chance of his dying. We'll dissect him."

"Would you own his body if he *should* die?"

"If he dies while bound to me, I'll arrange *that.*"

"One dollah an' a half," resumed the sheriff; and falling into the tone of a facile auctioneer he rattled on:

"One dollah an' a half foh ole Sol'mon—sol, sol, sol, —do, re, mi, fa, sol—do, re, mi, fa, sol! Why, gentlemen, you can set the king to music!"

All this time the vagrant had stood in the centre of that close ring of jeering and humorous by-standers— —a baffling text from which to have preached a sermon on the infirmities of our imperfect humanity. Some years before, perhaps as a master-stroke of derision, there had been given to him that title which could but heighten the contrast of his personality and estate with every suggestion of the ancient sacred magnificence; and never had the mockery seemed so fine as at this moment, when he was led forth into the streets to receive the lowest sentence of the law upon his poverty and dissolute idleness. He was apparently in the very prime of life—a striking figure, for nature at least had truly done some royal work on him. Over six feet in height, erect, with limbs well shaped and sinewy, with chest and neck full of the lines of great power, a large head thickly covered with long reddish hair, eyes blue, face beardless, complexion fair but discolored by low passions and excesses—such was old King Solomon. He wore a stiff, high, black Castor hat of the period, with the crown smashed in and the torn rim hanging down over one ear; a black cloth coat in the old style,

ragged and buttonless; a white cotton shirt, with the
broad collar crumpled, wide open at the neck and down
his sunburnt bosom; blue jeans pantaloons, patched at
the seat and the knees; and ragged cotton socks that
fell down over the tops of his dusty shoes, which were
open at the heels.

In one corner of his sensual mouth rested the stump
of a cigar. Once during the proceedings he had produced another, lighted it, and continued quietly smoking. If he took to himself any shame as the central
figure of this ignoble performance, no one knew it.
There was something almost royal in his unconcern.
The humor, the badinage, the open contempt, of which
he was the public target, fell thick and fast upon him,
but as harmlessly as would balls of pith upon a coat of
mail. In truth, there was that in his great, lazy, gentle,
good-humored bulk and bearing which made the gibes
seem all but despicable. He shuffled from one foot to
the other as though he found it a trial to stand up so
long, but all the while looking the spectators full in the
eyes without the least impatience. He suffered the
man of the factory to walk round him and push and
pinch his muscles as calmly as though he had been the
show bull at a country fair. Once only, when the sheriff
had pointed across the street at the figure of Mr. Clay,
he had looked quickly in that direction with a kindling
light in his eye and a passing flush on his face. For
the rest, he seemed like a man who has drained his cup
of human life and has nothing left him but to fill again
and drink without the least surprise or eagerness.

The bidding between the man of the factory and the
·student had gone slowly on. The price had reached
ten dollars. The heat was intense, the sheriff tired.

Then something occurred to revivify the scene. Across
the market-place and towards the steps of the court-
house there suddenly came trundling along in breathless haste a huge old negress, carrying on one arm a
large shallow basket containing apple crab-lanterns and
fresh gingerbread. With a series of half-articulate
grunts and snorts she approached the edge of the
crowd and tried to force her way through. She coaxed,
she begged, she elbowed and pushed and scolded, now
laughing, and now with the passion of tears in her thick,
excited voice. All at once, catching sight of the sheriff,
she lifted one ponderous brown arm, naked to the elbow, and waved her hand to him above the heads of
those in front.

"Hole on, marseter! Hole on!" she cried, in a tone
of humorous entreaty. "Don' knock 'im off till I
come! Gim *me* a bid at 'im!"

The sheriff paused and smiled. The crowd made
way tumultuously, with broad laughter and comment.

"Stan' aside theah an' let Aun' Charlotte in!"

"*Now* you'll see biddin'!"

"Get out of the way foh Aun' Charlotte!"

"Up, my free niggah! Hurrah foh Kentucky!"

A moment more and she stood inside the ring of
spectators, her basket on the pavement at her feet, her
hands plumped akimbo into her fathomless sides, her
head up, and her soft, motherly eyes turned eagerly
upon the sheriff. Of the crowd she seemed unconscious, and on the vagrant before her she had not cast
a single glance.

She was dressed with perfect neatness. A red and
yellow Madras kerchief was bound about her head in a
high coil, and another was crossed over the bosom of

her stiffly starched and smoothly ironed blue cottonade dress. Rivulets of perspiration ran down over her nose, her temples, and around her ears, and disappeared mysteriously in the creases of her brown neck. A single drop accidentally hung glistening like a diamond on the circlet of one of her large brass ear-rings.

The sheriff looked at her a moment, smiling, but a little disconcerted. The spectacle was unprecedented.

" What do you want heah, Aun' Charlotte ?" he asked, kindly. " You can't sell yo' pies an' gingerbread heah."

" I don' *wan'* sell no pies en gingerbread," she replied, contemptuously. "I wan' bid on *him,*" and she nodded sidewise at the vagrant.

" White folks allers sellin' niggahs to wuk fuh *dem ;* I gwine buy a white man to wuk fuh *me.* En he gwine t' git a mighty hard mistiss, you heah *me !*"

The eyes of the sheriff twinkled with delight.

" Ten dollahs is offahed foh ole King Sol'mon. Is theah any othah bid ? Are you all done?"

" 'Leben," she said.

Two young ragamuffins crawled among the legs of the crowd up to her basket and filched pies and cake beneath her very nose.

" Twelve !" cried the student, laughing.

" Thirteen !" she laughed too, but her eyes flashed.

" *You are bidding against a niggah,*" whispered the student's companion in his ear.

" So I am ; let's be off," answered the other, with a hot flush on his proud face.

Thus the sale was ended, and the crowd variously dispersed. In a distant corner of the court-yard the ragged urchins were devouring their unexpected booty. The old negress drew a red handkerchief out of her bosom,

untied a knot in a corner of it, and counted out the
money to the sheriff.   Only she and the vagrant were
now left on the spot.

"You have bought me.   What do you want me to
do?" he asked quietly.

"Lohd, honey!" she answered, in a low tone of affec-
tionate chiding, "I don' wan' you to do *nothin'!* I wuzn'
gwine t' 'low dem white folks to buy you.   Dey'd wuk
you till you dropped dead.   You go 'long en do ez you
please."

She gave a cunning chuckle of triumph in thus setting at naught the ends of justice, and, in a voice rich
and musical with affection, she said, as she gave him a
little push :

"You bettah be gittin' out o' dis blazin' sun.   G' on
home!   I be 'long by-en-by."

He turned and moved slowly away in the direction of
Water Street, where she lived ; and she, taking up her
basket, shuffled across the market-place towards Cheapside, muttering to herself the while :

"I come mighty nigh gittin' dah too late, foolin' 'long
wid dese pies.   Sellin' *him* 'ca'se he don' wuk!   Umph!
If all de men in dis town dat don' wuk wuz to be tuk
up en sole, d' wouldn' be 'nough money in de town to
buy 'em!   Don' I see 'em settin' 'roun' dese taverns
f'om mohnin' till night?"

She snorted out her indignation and disgust, and
sitting down on the sidewalk, under a Lombardy poplar, uncovered her wares and kept the flies away with a
locust bough, not discovering, in her alternating good
and ill humor, that half of them had been filched by her
old tormentors.

This was the memorable scene enacted in Lexington

on that memorable day of the year 1833—a day that
passed so briskly. For whoever met and spoke together asked the one question : Will the cholera come
to Lexington? And the answer always gave a nervous
haste to business—a keener thrill to pleasure. It was
of the cholera that the negro woman heard two sweet
passing ladies speak as she spread her wares on the
sidewalk. They were on their way to a little picture-
gallery just opened opposite M. Giron's ball-room, and
in one breath she heard them discussing their toilets for
the evening and in the next several portraits by Jouett.

So the day passed, the night came on, and M. Xaupi
gave his brilliant ball. Poor old Xaupi — poor little
Frenchman! whirled as a gamin of Paris through the
mazes of the Revolution, and lately come all the way
to Lexington to teach the people how to dance. Hop
about blithely on thy dry legs, basking this night in
the waxen radiance of manners and melodies and
graces! Where will be thy tunes and airs to-morrow?
Ay, smile and prompt away! On and on! Swing corners, ladies and gentlemen! Form the basket! Hands
all around!

While the bows were still darting across the strings,
out of the low, red east there shot a long, tremulous
bow of light up towards the zenith. And then, could
human sight have beheld the invisible, it might have
seen hovering over the town, over the ball-room, over
M. Xaupi, the awful presence of the plague.

But knowing nothing of this, the heated revellers went
merrily home in the chill air of the red and saffron
dawn. And knowing nothing of it also, a man awakened on the door-step of a house opposite the ball-room,
where he had long since fallen asleep. His limbs were

cramped and a shiver ran through his frame. Staggering to his feet, he made his way down to the house of
Free Charlotte, mounted to his room by means of a
stair-way opening on the street, threw off his outer gar-
ments, kicked off his shoes, and taking a bottle from a
closet pressed it several times to his lips with long outward breaths of satisfaction. Then, casting his great
white bulk upon the bed, in a minute more he had sunk
into a heavy sleep,—the usual drunken sleep of old
King Solomon.

He, too, had attended M. Xaupi's ball, in his own way
and in his proper character, being drawn to the place
for the pleasure of seeing the fine ladies arrive and float
in, like large white moths of the summer night ; of looking in through the open windows at the many-colored
waxen lights and the snowy arms and shoulders, of
having blown out to him the perfume and the music ;
not worthy to go in, being the lowest of the low, but attending from a door-step of the street opposite—with
a certain rich passion in his nature for splendor and
revelry and sensuous beauty.

II.

About 10 o'clock the sunlight entered through the
shutters and awoke him. He threw one arm up over
his eyes to intercept the burning rays. As he lay out-
stretched and stripped of grotesque rags, it could be
better seen in what a mould nature had cast his figure.
His breast, bare and tanned, was barred by full, arch-
ing ribs and knotted by crossing muscles ; and his
shirt-sleeve, falling away to the shoulder from his bent

arm, revealed its crowded muscles in the high relief of heroic bronze. For, although he had been sold as a vagrant, old King Solomon had in earlier years followed the trade of a digger of cellars, and the strenuous use of mattock and spade had developed every sinew to the utmost. His whole person, now half naked and in repose, was full of the suggestions of unspent power. Only his face, swollen and red, only his eyes, bloodshot and dull, bore the impress of wasted vitality. There, all too plainly stamped, were the passions long since raging and still on fire.

The sunlight had stirred him to but a low degree of consciousness, and some minutes passed before he realized that a stifling, resinous fume impregnated the air. He sniffed it quickly; through the window seemed to come the smell of burning tar. He sat up on the edge of the bed and vainly tried to clear his thoughts.

The room was a clean but poor habitation—uncarpeted, whitewashed, with a piece or two of the cheapest furniture, and a row of pegs on one wall, where usually hung those tattered coats and pantaloons, miscellaneously collected, that were his purple and fine linen. He turned his eyes in this direction now and noticed that his clothes were missing. The old shoes had disappeared from their corner; the cigar stumps, picked up here and there in the streets according to his wont, were gone from the mantel-piece. Near the door was a large bundle tied up in a sheet. In a state of bewilderment, he asked himself what it all meant. Then a sense of the silence in the street below possessed him. At this hour he was used to hear noises enough—from Hugh Lonney's new bath-house on one side, from Harry Sikes's barber-shop on the other.

A mysterious feeling of terror crept over and helped to sober him. How long had he lain asleep? By degrees he seemed to remember that two or three times he had awakened far enough to drink from the bottle under his pillow, only to sink again into heavier stupefaction. By degrees, too, he seemed to remember that other things had happened—a driving of vehicles this way and that, a hurrying of people along the street. He had thought it the breaking-up of M. Xaupi's ball. More than once had not some one shaken and tried to arouse him? Through the wall of Harry Sikes's barbershop had he not heard cries of pain—sobs of distress?

He staggered to the window, threw open the shutters, and, kneeling at the sill, looked out. The street was deserted. The houses opposite were closed. Cats were sleeping in the silent door-ways. But as he looked up and down he caught sight of people hurrying along cross-streets. From a distant lumber-yard came the muffled sound of rapid hammerings. On the air was the faint roll of vehicles—the hush and the vague noises of a general terrifying commotion.

In the middle of the street below him a keg was burning, and, as he looked, the hoops gave way, the tar spread out like a stream of black lava, and a cloud of inky smoke and deep-red furious flame burst upward through the sagging air. Just beneath the window a common cart had been backed close up to the door of the house. In it had been thrown a few small articles of furniture, and on the bottom bedclothes had been spread out as if for a pallet. While he looked old Charlotte hurried out with a pillow.

He called down to her in a strange, unsteady voice:

"What is the matter? What are you doing, Aunt Charlotte?"

She uttered a cry, dropped the pillow, and stared up at him. Her face looked dry and wrinkled.

"My God! De chol'ra's in town! I'm waitin' on you! Dress, en come down en fetch de bun'le by de dooh." And she hurried back into the house.

But he continued leaning on his folded arms, his brain stunned by the shock of the intelligence. Suddenly he leaned far out and looked down at the closed shutters of the barber-shop. Old Charlotte reappeared.

"Where is Harry Sikes?" he asked.

"Dead en buried."

"When did he die?"

"Yestidd'y evenin'."

"What day is this?"

"Sadd'y."

M. Xaupi's ball had been on Thursday evening. That night the cholera had broken out. He had lain in his drunken stupor ever since. Their talk had lasted but a minute, but she looked up anxiously and urged him.

"D' ain' no time to was'e, honey! D' ain' no time to was'e. I done got dis cyart to tek you 'way in, en I be ready to start in a minute. Put yo' clo'es on en bring de bun'le wid all yo' yudder things in it."

With incredible activity she climbed into the cart and began to roll up the bedclothes. In reality she had made up her mind to put him into the cart, and the pallet had been made for him to lie and finish his drunken sleep on, while she drove him away to a place of safety.

Still he did not move from the window-sill. He was

6

thinking of Harry Sikes, who had shaved him many a
time for nothing. Then he suddenly called down to
her:

"Have many died of the cholera? Are there many
cases in town?"

She went on with her preparations and took no notice of him. He repeated the question. She got down
quickly from the cart and began to mount the staircase.
He went back to bed, pulled the sheet up over him,
and propped himself up among the pillows. Her soft,
heavy footsteps slurred on the stair-way as though her
strength were failing, and as soon as she entered the
room she sank into a chair, overcome with terror. He
looked at her with a sudden sense of pity.

"Don't be frightened," he said, kindly. "It might
only make it the worse for you."

"I can' he'p it, honey," she answered, wringing her
hands and rocking herself to and fro; "de ole niggah
can' he'p it. If de Lohd jes spah me to git out'n dis
town wid you! Honey, ain' you able to put on yo'
clo'es?"

"You've tied them all up in the sheet."

"De Lohd he'p de crazy ole niggah!"

She started up and tugged at the bundle, and laid
out a suit of his clothes, if things so incongruous could
be called a suit.

"Have many people died of the cholera?"

"Dey been dyin' like sheep ev' since yestidd'y
mohnin'—all day, en all las' night, en dis mohnin'!
De man he done lock up de huss, en dey been buryin'
'em in cyarts. En de grave-diggah he done run away,
en hit look like d' ain' nobody to dig de graves."

She bent over the bundle, tying again the four corners of the sheet. Through the window came the sound of the quick hammers driving nails. She threw up her arms into the air, and then seizing the bundle dragged it rapidly to the door.

"You heah dat? Dey nailin' up cawfins in de lum-bah-yahd! Put on yo' clo'es, honey, en come on."

A resolution had suddenly taken shape in his mind.

"Go on away and save your life. Don't wait for me ; I'm not going. And good-bye, Aunt Charlotte, in case I don't see you any more. You've been very kind to me—kinder than I deserved. Where have you put my mattock and spade?"

He said this very quietly, and sat up on the edge of the bed, his feet hanging down, and his hand stretched out towards her.

"Honey," she explained, coaxingly, from where she stood, "can't you sobah up a little en put on yo' clo'es? I gwine to tek you 'way to de country. You don' wan' no tools. You can' dig no cellahs now. De chol'ra's in town en de people's dyin' like sheep."

"I expect they will need me," he answered.

She perceived now that he was sober. For an instant her own fear was forgotten in an outburst of resentment and indignation.

"Dig graves fuh 'em, when dey put you up on de block en sell you same ez you wuz a niggah! Dig graves fuh 'em, when dey allers callin' you names on de street en makin' fun o' you!"

"They are not to blame. I have brought it on my-self."

"But we can' stay heah en die o' de chol'ra!"

"You mustn't stay. You must go away at once."

"But if I go, who gwine tek cyah o' *you*?"

"Nobody."

She came quickly across the room to the bed, fell on her knees, clasped his feet to her breast, and looked up into his face with an expression of imploring tenderness. Then, with incoherent cries and with sobs and tears, she pleaded with him—pleaded for dear life; his and her own.

It was a strange scene. What historian of the heart will ever be able to do justice to those peculiar ties which bound the heart of the negro in years gone by to a race of not always worthy masters? This old Virginia nurse had known King Solomon when he was a boy playing with her young master, till that young master died on the way to Kentucky.

At the death of her mistress she had become free with a little property. By thrift and industry she had greatly enlarged this. Years passed and she became the only surviving member of the Virginian household, which had emigrated early in the century to the Bluegrass Region. The same wave of emigration had brought in old King Solomon from the same neighborhood. As she had risen in life, he had sunk. She sat on the sidewalks selling her fruits and cakes; he sat on the sidewalks more idle, more ragged and dissolute. On no other basis than these facts she began to assume a sort of maternal pitying care of him, patching his rags, letting him have money for his vices, and when, a year or two before, he had ceased working almost entirely, giving him a room in her house and taking in payment what he chose to pay.

He brushed his hand quickly across his eyes as she knelt before him now, clasping his feet to her bosom. From coaxing him as an intractable child she had, in the old servile fashion, fallen to imploring him, with touching forgetfulness of their real relations:

"O my marseter! O my marseter Solomon! Go 'way en save yo' life, en tek yo' po' ole niggah wid you!"

But his resolution was formed, and he refused to go. A hurried footstep paused beneath the window and a loud voice called up. The old nurse got up and went to the window. A man was standing by the cart at her door.

"For God's sake let me have this cart to take my wife and little children away to the country! There is not a vehicle to be had in town. I will pay you—" He stopped, seeing the distress on her face.

"Is he dead?" he asked, for he knew of her care of old King Solomon.

"He *will* die!" she sobbed. "Tilt de t'ings out on de pavement. I gwine t' stay wid 'im en tek cyah o' 'im."

III.

A little later, dressed once more in grotesque rags and carrying on his shoulder a rusty mattock and a rusty spade, old King Solomon appeared in the street below and stood looking up and down it with an air of anxious indecision. Then shuffling along rapidly to the corner of Mill Street, he turned up towards Main.

Here a full sense of the terror came to him. A man, hurrying along with his head down, ran full against him and cursed him for the delay:

"Get out of my way, you old beast!" he cried. "If the cholera would carry you off it would be a blessing to the town."

Two or three little children, already orphaned and hungry, wandered past, crying and wringing their hands. A crowd of negro men with the muscles of athletes, some with naked arms, some naked to the waist, their eyes dilated, their mouths hanging open, sped along in tumultuous disorder. The plague had broken out in the hemp factory and scattered them beyond control.

He grew suddenly faint and sick. His senses swam, his heart seemed to cease beating, his tongue burned, his throat was dry, his spine like ice. For a moment the contagion of deadly fear overcame him, and, unable to stand, he reeled to the edge of the sidewalk and sat down.

Before him along the street passed the flying people —men on horseback with their wives behind and children in front, families in carts and wagons, merchants in two-wheeled gigs and sulkies. A huge red and yellow stage-coach rolled ponderously by, filled within, on top, in front, and behind with a company of riotous students of law and of medicine. A rapid chorus of voices shouted to him as they passed :

" Good-bye, Solomon !"

" The cholera'll have you befoah sunset !"

" Better be diggin' yoah grave, Solomon ! That 'll be yoah last cellah."

" Dig us a big wine cellah undah the Medical Hall while we are away."

" And leave yo' body there ! We want yo' skeleton."

" Good-bye, old Solomon !"

A wretched carry-all passed with a household of more wretched women ; their tawdry and gay attire, their haggard and painted and ghastly faces, looking horrible in the blaze of the pitiless sunlight. They, too, simpered and hailed him and spent upon him their hardened and degraded badinage. Then there rolled by a high-swung carriage, with the most luxurious of cushions, upholstered with morocco, with a coat-of-arms, a driver and a footman in livery, and drawn by sparkling, prancing horses. Lying back on the satin cushions a fine gentleman ; at the window of the carriage two rosy children, who pointed their fingers at the vagrant and turned and looked into their father's face, so that he leaned forward, smiled, leaned back again, and was whirled away to a place of safety.

Thus they passed him, as he sat down on the sidewalk—even physicians from their patients, pastors from their stricken flocks. Why should not he flee? He had no ties, except the faithful affection of an old negress. Should he not at least save her life by going away, seeing that she would not leave him?

The orphaned children wandered past again, sobbing more wearily. He called them to him.

"Why do you not go home? Where is your mother?" he asked.

"She is dead in the house," they answered; "and no one has come to bury her."

Slowly down the street was coming a short funeral train. It passed—a rude cortege : a common cart, in the bottom of which rested a box of plain boards containing the body of the old French dancing-master; walking behind it, with a cambric handkerchief to his eyes, the old French confectioner ; at his side, wearing the robes of his office and carrying an umbrella to ward off the burning sun, the beloved Bishop Smith ; and behind them, two by two and with linked arms, perhaps a dozen men, most of whom had been at the ball.

No head was lifted or eye turned to notice the vagrant seated on the sidewalk. But when the train had passed he rose, laid his mattock and spade across his shoulder, and, stepping out into the street, fell into line at the end of the procession.

They moved down Short Street to the old burying-ground, where the Baptist church-yard is to-day. As they entered it, two grave-diggers passed out and hurried away. Those before them had fled. They had been at work but a few hours. Overcome with horror at the sight of the dead arriving more and more rapidly, they, too, deserted that post of peril. No one was left. Here and there in the church-yard could be seen bodies awaiting interment. Old King Solomon stepped quietly forward and, getting down into one of the half-finished graves, began to dig.

The vagrant had happened upon an avocation.

IV.

All summer long, Clatterbuck's dancing-pavilion was as silent in its grove of oaks as a temple of the Druids, and his pleasure-boat nestled in its moorings, with no hand to feather an oar in the little lake. All summer long, no athletic young Kentuckians came to bathe their white bodies in Hugh Lonney's new bath-house for twelve and a half cents, and no one read Daukins Tegway's advertisement that he was willing to exchange his Dunstable bonnets for flax and feathers. The likely runaway boy, with a long, fresh scar across his face, was never found, nor the buffalo bull roasted for Daniel Webster, and Peter Leuba's guitars were never thrummed on any moonlit verandas. Only Dewees and Grant were busy, dispensing, not snuff, but calomel.

Grass grew in the deserted streets. Gardens became little wildernesses of rank weeds and riotous creepers. Around shut window-lattices roses clambered and shed their perfume into the poisoned air, or dropped their faded petals to strew the echoless thresholds. In darkened rooms family portraits gazed on sad vacancy or looked helplessly dowrr on rigid sheeted forms.

In the trees of poplar and locust along the streets the unmolested birds built and brooded. The oriole swung its hempen nest from a bough over the door of the spider-tenanted factory, and in front of the old Medical Hall the blue-jay shot up his angry crest and screamed harshly down at the passing bier. In a cage hung against the wall of a house in a retired street a mocking-bird sung, beat its breast against the bars, sung more passionately, grew silent and dropped dead from its perch, never knowing that its mistress had long since become a clod to its full-throated requiem.

Famine lurked in the wake of the pestilence. Markets were closed. A few shops were kept open to furnish necessary supplies. Now and then some old negro might have been seen, driving a meat-wagon in from the country, his nostrils stuffed with white cotton saturated with camphor. Oftener the only visible figure in the streets was that of a faithful priest going about among his perishing fold, or that of the bishop moving hither and thither on his ceaseless ministrations.

But over all the ravages of that terrible time there towered highest the solitary figure of that powerful grave-digger, who, nerved by the spectacle of the common misfortune, by one heroic effort rose for the time

above the wrecks of his own nature. In the thick of
the plague, in the very garden spot of the pestilence, he
ruled like an unterrified king. Through days unnaturally chill with gray cloud and drizzling rain, or unnaturally hot with the fierce sun and suffocating damps
that appeared to steam forth from subterranean cal-
drons, he worked unfaltering, sometimes with a helper,
sometimes with none. There were times when, ex-
hausted, he would lie down in the half-dug graves and
there sleep until able to go on ; and many a midnight
found him under the spectral moon, all but hidden by
the rank nightshade as he bent over to mark out the
lines of one of those narrow mortal cellars.

V.

Nature soon smiles upon her own ravages and strews
our graves with flowers, not as memories, but for other
flowers when the spring returns.

It was one cool, brilliant morning late in that autumn. The air blew fresh and invigorating, as though
on the earth there were no corruption, no death. Far
southward had flown the plague. A spectator in the
open court-square might have seen many signs of life
returning to the town. Students hurried along, talking
eagerly. Merchants met for the first time and spoke of
the winter trade. An old negress, gayly and neatly
dressed, came into the market-place, and sitting down
on a sidewalk displayed her yellow and red apples and
fragrant gingerbread. She hummed to herself an old
cradle-song, and in her soft, motherly black eyes shone
a mild, happy radiance. A group of young ragamuffins

eyed her longingly from a distance. Court was to open
for the first time since the spring. The hour was early,
and one by one the lawyers passed slowly in. On the
steps of the court-house three men were standing:
Thomas Brown, the sheriff; old Peter Leuba, who had
just walked over from his music-store on Main Street;
and little M. Giron, the French confectioner. Each wore
mourning on his hat, and their voices were low and grave.

"Gentlemen," the sheriff was saying, "it was on this
very spot the day befoah the cholera broke out that I
sole 'im as a vagrant. An' I did the meanes' thing a
man can evah do. I hel' 'im up to public ridicule foh
his weaknesses an' made spoht of 'is infirmities. I
laughed at 'is povahty an' 'is ole clo'es. I delivahed
on 'im as complete an oration of sarcastic detraction as
I could prepare on the spot, out of my own meanness
an' with the vulgah sympathies of the crowd. Gentlemen, if I only had that crowd heah now, an' ole King
Sol'mon standin' in the midst of it, that I might ask 'im
to accept a humble public apology, offahed from the
heaht of one who feels himself unworthy to shake 'is
han'! But, gentlemen, that crowd will nevah reassem-
ble. Neahly ev'ry man of them is dead, an' ole King
Sol'mon buried them."

"He buried my friend Adolphe Xaupi," said François
Giron, touching his eyes with his handkerchief.

"There is a case of my best Jamaica rum for him
whenever he comes for it," said old Leuba, clearing his
throat.

"But, gentlemen, while we are speakin' of ole King
Sol'mon we ought not to fohget who it is that has sup-
pohted 'im. Yondah she sits on the sidewalk, sellin'
'er apples an' gingerbread."

The three men looked in the direction indicated.

"Heah comes ole King Sol'mon now," exclaimed the sheriff.

Across the open square the vagrant was seen walking slowly along with his habitual air of quiet, unobtrusive preoccupation. A minute more and he had come over and passed into the court-house by a side door.

"Is Mr. Clay to be in court to-day?"

"He is expected, I think."

"Then let's go in; there will be a crowd."

"I don't know; so many are dead."

They turned and entered and found seats as quietly as possible; for a strange and sorrowful hush brooded over the court-room. Until the bar assembled, it had not been realized how many were gone. The silence was that of a common overwhelming disaster. No one spoke with his neighbor, no one observed the vagrant as he entered and made his way to a seat on one of the meanest benches, a little apart from the others. He had not sat there since the day of his indictment for vagrancy. The judge took his seat and, making a great effort to control himself, passed his eyes slowly over the court-room. All at once he caught sight of old King Solomon sitting against the wall in an obscure corner; and before any one could know what he was doing, he hurried down and walked up to the vagrant and grasped his hand. He tried to speak, but could not. Old King Solomon had buried his wife and daughter—buried them one clouded midnight, with no one present but himself.

Then the oldest member of the bar started up and followed the example; and then the other members, rising by a common impulse, filed slowly back and one by one wrung that hard and powerful hand. After them came the other persons in the court-room. The vagrant, the grave-digger, had risen and stood against the wall, at first with a white face and a dazed expression, not knowing what it meant; afterwards, when he understood it, his head dropped suddenly forward and his tears fell thick and hot upon the hands that he could not see. And his were not the only tears. Not a man in the long file but paid his tribute of emotion as he stepped forward to honor that image of sadly eclipsed but still effulgent humanity. It was not grief, it was not gratitude, nor any sense of making reparation for the past. It was the softening influence of an act of heroism, which makes every man feel himself a brother hand in hand with every other—such power has a single act of moral greatness to reverse the relations of men, lifting up one, and bringing all others to do him homage.

It was the coronation scene in the life of old King Solomon of Kentucky.

TWO GENTLEMEN OF KENTUCKY.

Two Gentlemen of Kentucky.

"The woods are hushed, their music is no more:
  The leaf is dead, the yearning passed away:
New leaf, new life—the days of frost are o'er:
  New life, new love, to suit the newer day."

THE WOODS ARE HUSHED.

It was near the middle of the afternoon of an autumnal day, on the wide, grassy plateau of Central Kentucky.

The Eternal Power seemed to have quitted the universe and left all nature folded in the calm of the Eternal Peace. Around the pale-blue dome of the heavens a few pearl-colored clouds hung motionless, as though the wind had been withdrawn to other skies. Not a crimson leaf floated downward through the soft, silvery light that filled the atmosphere and created the sense of lonely, unimaginable spaces. This light overhung the far-rolling landscape of field and meadow and wood, crowning with faint radiance the remoter low-swelling hill-tops and deepening into dreamy half-shadows on their eastern slopes. Nearer, it fell in a white flake on an unstirred sheet of water which lay along the edge of a mass of sombre-hued woodland, and nearer still it touched to spring-like brilliancy a level, green meadow on the hither edge of the water, where a group of Durham cattle stood with reversed flanks near the gleam-

7

ing trunks of some leafless sycamores. Still nearer, it
caught the top of the brown foliage of a little bent oak-
tree and burned it into a silvery flame. It lit on the back
and the wings of a crow flying heavily in the path of its
rays, and made his blackness as white as the breast of
a swan. In the immediate foreground, it sparkled in
minute gleams along the stalks of the coarse, dead
weeds that fell away from the legs and the flanks of a
white horse, and slanted across the face of the rider
and through the ends of his gray hair, which straggled
trom beneath his soft black hat.

The horse, old and patient and gentle, stood with
low-stretched neck and closed eyes half asleep in the
faint glow of the waning heat; and the rider, the sole
human presence in all the field, sat looking across the
silent autumnal landscape, sunk in reverie. Both horse
and rider seemed but harmonious elements in the panorama of still-life, and completed the picture of a closing scene.

To the man it was a closing scene. From the rank,
fallow field through which he had been riding he was
now surveying, for the last time, the many features of a
landscape that had been familiar to him from the beginning of memory. In the afternoon and the autumn
of his age he was about to rend the last ties that bound
him to his former life, and, like one who had survived
his own destiny, turn his face towards a future that was
void of everything he held significant or dear.

The Civil War had only the year before reached its
ever-memorable close. From where he sat there was
not a home in sight, as there was not one beyond the
reach of his vision, but had felt its influence. Some of
his neighbors had come home from its camps and pris-

ons, aged or altered as though by half a lifetime of
years. The bones of some lay whitening on its battle-
fields. Families, reassembled around their hearth-stones,
spoke in low tones unceasingly of defeat and victory,
heroism and death. Suspicion and distrust and es-
trangement prevailed. Former friends met each other
on the turnpikes without speaking; brothers avoided
each other in the streets of the neighboring town. The
rich had grown poor; the poor had become rich. Many
of the latter were preparing to move West. The negroes were drifting blindly hither and thither, deserting
the country and flocking to the towns. Even the once
united church of his neighborhood was jarred by the
unstrung and discordant spirit of the times. At affect-
ing passages in the sermons men grew pale and set
their teeth fiercely; women suddenly lowered their black
veils and rocked to and fro in their pews; for it is always at the bar of Conscience and before the very altar
of God that the human heart is most wrung by a sense
of its losses and the memory of its wrongs. The war
had divided the people of Kentucky as the false mother
would have severed the child.

It had not left the old man unscathed. His younger
brother had fallen early in the conflict, borne to the end
of his brief warfare by his impetuous valor; his aged
mother had sunk under the tidings of the death of her
latest-born; his sister was estranged from him by his
political differences with her husband; his old family
servants, men and women, had left him, and grass and
weeds had already grown over the door-steps of the
shut, noiseless cabins. Nay, the whole vast social system of the old régime had fallen, and he was henceforth but a useless fragment of the ruins.

All at once his mind turned from the cracked and smoky mirror of the times and dwelt fondly upon the scenes of the past. The silent fields around him seemed again alive with the negroes, singing as they followed the ploughs down the corn-rows or swung the cradles through the bearded wheat. Again, in a frenzy of merriment, the strains of the old fiddles issued from crevices of cabin-doors to the rhythmic beat of hands and feet that shook the rafters and the roof. Now he was sitting on his porch, and one little negro was blacking his shoes, another leading his saddle-horse to the stiles, a third bringing his hat, and a fourth handing him a glass of ice-cold sangaree; or now he lay under the locust-trees in his yard, falling asleep in the drowsy heat of the summer afternoon, while one waved over him a bough of pungent walnut leaves, until he lost consciousness and by-and-by awoke to find that they both had fallen asleep side by side on the grass and that the abandoned fly-brush lay full across his face.

From where he sat also were seen slopes on which picnics were danced under the broad shade of maples and elms in June by those whom death and war had scattered like the transitory leaves that once had sheltered them. In this direction lay the district school-house where on Friday evenings there were wont to be speeches and debates; in that, lay the blacksmith's shop where of old he and his neighbors had met on horseback of Saturday afternoons to hear the news, get the mails, discuss elections, and pitch quoits. In the valley beyond stood the church at which all had assembled on calm Sunday mornings like the members of one united family. Along with these scenes went many a chastened reminiscence of bridal and funeral and simpler events that had made up the annals of his country life.

The reader will have a clearer insight into the character and past career of Colonel Romulus Fields by remembering that he represented a fair type of that social order which had existed in rank perfection over the blue-grass plains of Kentucky during the final decades of the old régime. Perhaps of all agriculturists in the United States the inhabitants of that region had spent the most nearly idyllic life, on account of the beauty of the climate, the richness of the land, the spacious comfort of their homes, the efficiency of their negroes, and the characteristic contentedness of their dispositions. Thus nature and history combined to make them a peculiar class, a cross between the aristocratic and the bucolic, being as simple as shepherds and as proud as kings, and not seldom exhibiting among both men and women types of character which were as remarkable for pure, tender, noble states of feeling as they were commonplace in powers and cultivation of mind.

It was upon this luxurious social growth that the war naturally fell as a killing frost, and upon no single specimen with more blighting power than upon Colonel Fields. For destiny had quarried and chiselled him, to serve as an ornament in the barbaric temple of human bondage. There *were* ornaments in that temple, and he was one. A slave-holder with Southern sympathies, a man educated not beyond the ideas of his generation, convinced that slavery was an evil, yet seeing no present way of removing it, he had of all things been a model master. As such he had gone on record in Kentucky, and no doubt in a Higher Court; and as such his

efforts had been put forth to secure the passage of many
of those milder laws for which his State was distin-
guished.   Often, in those dark days, his face, anxious
and sad, was to be seen amid the throng that surrounded the blocks on which slaves were sold at auction ; and more than one poor wretch he had bought to
save him from separation from his family or from being
sold into the Southern plantations—afterwards riding
far and near to find him a home on one of the neighboring farms.

But all those days were over.   He had but to place
the whole picture of the present beside the whole picture of the past to realize what the contrast meant for
him.

At length he gathered the bridle reins from the neck
of his old horse and turned his head homeward.   As
he rode slowly on, every spot gave up its memories.
He dismounted when he came to the cattle and walked
among them, stroking their soft flanks and feeling in
the palm of his hand the rasp of their salt-loving
tongues ; on his sideboard at home was many a silver
cup which told of premiums on cattle at the great fairs.
It was in this very pond that as a boy he had learned
to swim on a cherry rail.   When he entered the woods,
the sight of the walnut-trees and the hickory-nut trees,
loaded on the topmost branches, gave him a sudden
pang.

Beyond the woods he came upon the garden, which
he had kept as his mother had left it—an old-fashioned
garden with an arbor in the centre, covered with Isa-
bella grape-vines on one side and Catawba on the
other ; with walks branching thence in four directions,
and along them beds of jump-up-johnnies, sweet-will-

iams, daffodils, sweet-peas, larkspur, and thyme, flags
and the sensitive-plant, celestial and maiden's-blush
roses. He stopped and looked over the fence at the
very spot where he had found his mother on the day
when the news of the battle came.

She had been kneeling, trowel in hand, driving away
vigorously at the loamy earth, and, as she saw him
coming, had risen and turned towards him her face
with the ancient pink bloom on her clear cheeks and
the light of a pure, strong soul in her gentle eyes.
Overcome by his emotions, he had blindly faltered out
the words, " Mother, John was among the killed !"   For
a moment she had looked at him as though stunned by
a blow.   Then a violent flush had overspread her features, and then an ashen pallor; after which, with a
sudden proud dilating of her form as though with joy,
she had sunk down like the tenderest of her lily-stalks,
cut from its root.

Beyond the garden he came to the empty cabin and
the great wood-pile.   At this hour it used to be a scene
of hilarious activity—the little negroes sitting perched
in chattering groups on the topmost logs or playing
leap-frog in the dust, while some picked up baskets of
chips or dragged a back-log into the cabins.

At last he drew near the wooden stiles and saw the
large house of which he was the solitary occupant.
What darkened rooms and noiseless halls !   What beds,
all ready, that nobody now came to sleep in, and cush-
ioned old chairs that nobody rocked !   The house and
the contents of its attic, presses, and drawers could
have told much of the history of Kentucky from almost
its beginning ; for its foundations had been laid by his
father near the beginning of the century, and through

its doors had passed a long train of forms, from the veterans of the Revolution to the soldiers of the Civil War. Old coats hung up in closets; old dresses folded away in drawers; saddle-bags and buckskin-leggins; hunting-jackets, powder-horns, and militiamen hats; looms and knitting-needles; snuffboxes and reticules —what a treasure-house of the past it was! And now the only thing that had the springs of life within its bosom was the great, sweet-voiced clock, whose faithful face had kept unchanged amid all the swift pageantry of changes.

He dismounted at the stiles and handed the reins to a gray-haired negro, who had hobbled up to receive them with a smile and a gesture of the deepest respect.

"Peter," he said, very simply, "I am going to sell the place and move to town. I can't live here any longer."

With these words he passed through the yard-gate, walked slowly up the broad pavement, and entered the house.

MUSIC NO MORE.

On the disappearing form of the colonel was fixed an ancient pair of eyes that looked out at him from behind a still more ancient pair of silver-rimmed spectacles with an expression of indescribable solicitude and love.

These eyes were set in the head of an old gentleman —for such he was—named Peter Cotton, who was the only one of the colonel's former slaves that had remained inseparable from his person and his altered fortunes. In early manhood Peter had been a wood-chopper; but he had one day had his leg broken by the limb of a falling tree, and afterwards, out of consideration for his limp, had been made supervisor of the wood-pile, gardener, and a sort of nondescript servitor of his master's luxurious needs.

Nay, in larger and deeper characters must his history be writ, he having been, in days gone by, one of those ministers of the gospel whom conscientious Kentucky masters often urged to the exercise of spiritual functions in behalf of their benighted people. In course of preparation for this august work, Peter had learned to read and had come to possess a well-chosen library of three several volumes — *Webster's Spelling-Book*, *The Pilgrim's Progress*, and the Bible. But even these unusual acquisitions he deemed not enough; for being touched with a spark of poetic fire from heaven, and fired by the African's fondness for all that is conspicuous in dress, he had conceived for himself the creation of a unique garment which should symbolize in perfection the claims and consolations of his apostolic office. This was nothing less than a sacred blue-jeans coat that he had had his old mistress make him, with very long and spacious tails, whereon, at his further direction, she embroidered sundry texts of Scripture which it pleased him to regard as the fit visible annunciations of his holy calling. And inasmuch as his mistress, who had had the coat woven on her own looms from the wool of her finest sheep, was, like other gentlewomen of her time, rarely skilled in the accomplishments of the needle, and was moreover in full sympathy with the piety of his intent, she wrought of these passages a border enriched with such intricate curves, marvellous flourishes, and harmonious letterings, that Solomon never reflected the glory in which Peter was arrayed whenever he put it on. For after much prayer that the Almighty wisdom would aid his reason in the difficult task of selecting the most appropriate texts, Peter had chosen seven—one for each day in the week —with such tact, and no doubt heavenly guidance, that when braided together they did truly constitute an eloquent epitome of Christian duty, hope, and pleading.

From first to last they were as follows: "Woe is unto me if I preach not the gospel;" "Servants, be obedient to them that are your masters according to the flesh;" "Come unto me, all ye that labour and are heavy laden;" "Consider the lilies of the field, how they grow; they toil not, neither do they spin;" "Now abideth faith, hope, and charity, these three; but the greatest of these is charity;" "I would not have you to be ignorant, brethren, concerning them which are asleep;" "For as in Adam all die, even so in Christ shall all be made alive." This concatenation of texts Peter wished to have duly solemnized, and therefore, when the work was finished, he further requested his mistress to close the entire chain with the word "Amen," introduced in some suitable place.

But the only spot now left vacant was one of a few square inches, located just where the coat-tails hung over the end of Peter's spine; so that when any one stood full in Peter's rear, he could but marvel at the sight of so solemn a word emblazoned in so unusual a locality.

Panoplied in this robe of righteousness, and with a worn leathern Bible in his hand, Peter used to go around of Sundays, and during the week, by night, preaching from cabin to cabin the gospel of his heavenly Master.

The angriest lightnings of the sultriest skies often played amid the darkness upon those sacred coat-tails

and around that girdle of everlasting texts, as though
the evil spirits of the air would fain have burned them
and scattered their ashes on the roaring winds. The
slow-sifting snows of winter whitened them as though
to chill their spiritual fires; but winter and summer,
year after year, in weariness of body, often in sore
distress of mind, for miles along this lonely road and
for miles across that rugged way, Peter trudged on
and on, withal perhaps as meek a spirit as ever grew
foot-sore in the paths of its Master. Many a poor over-
burdened slave took fresh heart and strength from the
sight of that celestial raiment; many a stubborn, rebellious spirit, whose flesh but lately quivered under the
lash, was brought low by its humble teaching; many a
worn-out old frame, racked with pain in its last illness,
pressed a fevered lip to its hopeful hem; and many a
dying eye closed in death peacefully fixed on its immortal pledges.

When Peter started abroad, if a storm threatened, he
carried an old cotton umbrella of immense size; and as
the storm burst, he gathered the tails of his coat carefully up under his armpits that they might be kept
dry. Or if caught by a tempest without his umbrella, he
would take his coat off and roll it up inside out, leaving
his body exposed to the fury of the elements. No care,
however, could keep it from growing old and worn and
faded; and when the slaves were set free and he was
called upon by the interposition of Providence to lay it
finally aside, it was covered by many a patch and stain
as proofs of its devoted usage.

One after another the colonel's old servants, gathering their children about them, had left him, to begin
their new life. He bade them all a kind good-bye, and

into the palm of each silently pressed some gift that he
knew would soon be needed.　But no inducement could
make Peter or Phillis, his wife, budge from their cabin.
"Go, Peter!　Go, Phillis!" the colonel had said time
and again.　"No one is happier that you are free than
I am; and you can call on me for what you need to set
you up in business."　But Peter and Phillis asked to
stay with him.　Then suddenly, several months before
the time at which this sketch opens, Phillis had died,
leaving the colonel and Peter as the only relics of that
populous life which had once filled the house and the cabins.　The colonel had succeeded in hiring a woman to
do Phillis's work; but her presence was a strange note of
discord in the old domestic harmony, and only saddened
the recollections of its vanished peace.

Peter had a short, stout figure, dark-brown skin,
smooth-shaven face, eyes round, deep-set and wide
apart, and a short, stub nose which dipped suddenly
into his head, making it easy for him to wear the silver-
rimmed spectacles left him by his old mistress.　A peculiar conformation of the muscles between the eyes
and the nose gave him the quizzical expression of one
who is about to sneeze, and this was heightened by a
twinkle in the eyes which seemed caught from the
shining of an inner sun upon his tranquil heart.

Sometimes, however, his face grew sad enough.　It
was sad on this afternoon while he watched the colonel
walk slowly up the pavement, well overgrown with
weeds, and enter the house, which the setting sun
touched with the last radiance of the finished day.

NEW LIFE.

About two years after the close of the war, therefore, the colonel and Peter were to be found in Lexington, ready to turn over a new leaf in the volumes of their lives, which already had an old - fashioned binding, a somewhat musty odor, and but few unwritten leaves remaining.

After a long, dry summer you may have seen two gnarled old apple - trees, that stood with interlocked arms on the western slope of some quiet hill-side, make a melancholy show of blooming out again in the autumn of the year and dallying with the idle buds that mock their sapless branches. Much the same was the belated, fruitless efflorescence of the colonel and Peter.

The colonel had no business habits, no political ambition, no wish to grow richer. He was too old for society, and without near family ties. For some time he wandered through the streets like one lost—sick with yearning for the fields and woods, for his cattle, for familiar faces. He haunted Cheapside and the court-house square, where the farmers always assembled when they came to town ; and if his eye lighted on one, he would button-hole him on the street-corner and lead him into a grocery and sit down for a quiet chat. Sometimes he would meet an aimless, melancholy wanderer like himself, and the two would go off and discuss over and over again their departed days ; and several times he came unexpectedly upon some of his old servants who had fallen into bitter want, and who more than repaid him for the help he gave by contrasting the hard-

ships of a life of freedom with the ease of their shackled
years.

In the course of time, he could but observe that human life in the town was reshaping itself slowly and
painfully, but with resolute energy. The colossal structure of slavery had fallen, scattering its ruins far and
wide over the State ; but out of the very débris was being taken the material to lay the deeper foundations of
the new social edifice. Men and women as old as he
were beginning life over and trying to fit themselves for
it by changing the whole attitude and habit of their
minds—by taking on a new heart and spirit. But when
a great building falls, there is always some rubbish,
and the colonel and others like him were part of this.
Henceforth they possessed only an antiquarian sort of
interest, like the stamped bricks of Nebuchadnezzar.

Nevertheless he made a show of doing something,
and in a year or two opened on Cheapside a store for
the sale of hardware and agricultural implements. He
knew more about the latter than anything else ; and,
furthermore, he secretly felt that a business of this kind
would enable him to establish in town a kind of head-
quarters for the farmers. His account-books were to
be kept on a system of twelve months' credit; and he
resolved that if one of his customers couldn't pay then,
it would make no difference.

Business began slowly. The farmers dropped in and
found a good lounging-place. On county-court days,
which were great market-days for the sale of sheep,
horses, mules, and cattle in front of the colonel's door,
they swarmed in from the hot sun and sat around on
the counter and the ploughs and machines till the entrance was blocked to other customers.

When a customer did come in, the colonel, who was probably talking with some old acquaintance, would tell him just to look around and pick out what he wanted and the price would be all right. If one of those acquaintances asked for a pound of nails, the colonel would scoop up some ten pounds and say, "I reckon that's about a pound, Tom." He had never seen a pound of nails in his life; and if one had been weighed on his scales, he would have said the scales were wrong.

He had no great idea of commercial despatch. One morning a lady came in for some carpet-tacks, an article that he had forgotten to lay in. But he at once sent off an order for enough to have tacked a carpet pretty well all over Kentucky; and when they came, two weeks later, he told Peter to take her up a dozen papers with his compliments. He had laid in, however, an ample and especially fine assortment of pocket-knives, for that instrument had always been to him one of gracious and very winning qualities. Then when a friend dropped in he would say, "General, don't you need a new pocket-knife?" and, taking out one, would open all the blades and commend the metal and the handle. The "general" would inquire the price, and the colonel, having shut the blades, would hand it to him, saying in a careless, fond way, "I reckon I won't charge you anything for that." His mind could not come down to the low level of such ignoble barter, and he gave away the whole case of knives.

These were the pleasanter aspects of his business life, which did not lack as well its tedium and crosses. Thus there were many dark stormy days when no one he cared to see came in; and he then became rather a pathetic figure, wandering absently around amid the symbols of his past activity, and stroking the ploughs, like dumb companions. Or he would stand at the door and look across at the old court-house, where he had seen many a slave sold and had listened to the great Kentucky orators.

But what hurt him most was the talk of the new farming and the abuse of the old which he was forced to hear; and he generally refused to handle the improved implements and mechanical devices by which labor and waste were to be saved.

Altogether he grew tired of " the thing," and sold out at the end of the year with a loss of over a thousand dollars, though he insisted he had done a good business.

As he was then seen much on the streets again and several times heard to make remarks in regard to the sidewalks, gutters, and crossings, when they happened to be in bad condition, the *Daily Press* one morning published a card stating that if Colonel Romulus Fields would consent to make the race for mayor he would receive the support of many Democrats, adding a tribute to his virtues and his influential past. It touched the colonel, and he walked down-town with a rather commanding figure the next morning. But it pained him to see how many of his acquaintances returned his salutations very coldly; and just as he was passing the Northern Bank he met the young opposition candidate—a little red-haired fellow, walking between two ladies, with a rose-bud in his button-hole—who refused to speak at all, but made the ladies laugh by some remark he uttered as the colonel passed. The card had been inserted humorously, but he took it seriously; and when his friends found this out, they rallied round him.

The day of election drew near. They told him he must buy votes. He said he wouldn't buy a vote to be mayor of the New Jerusalem. They told him he must "mix" and "treat." He refused. Foreseeing he had no chance, they besought him to withdraw. He said he would not. They told him he wouldn't poll twenty votes. He replied that *one* would satisfy him, provided it was neither begged nor bought. When his defeat was announced, he accepted it as another evidence that he had no part in the present—no chance of redeeming his idleness.

A sense of this weighed heavily on him at times; but it is not likely that he realized how pitifully he was undergoing a moral shrinkage in consequence of mere disuse. Actually, extinction had set in with him long prior to dissolution, and he was dead years before his heart ceased beating. The very basic virtues on which had rested his once spacious and stately character were now but the mouldy corner-stones of a crumbling ruin.

It was a subtle evidence of deterioration in manliness that he had taken to dress. When he had lived in the country, he had never dressed up unless he came to town. When he had moved to town, he thought he must remain dressed up all the time; and this fact first fixed his attention on a matter which afterwards began to be loved for its own sake. Usually he wore a Derby hat, a black diagonal coat, gray trousers, and a white necktie. But the article of attire in which he took chief pleasure was hose; and the better to show the gay colors of these, he wore low-cut shoes of the finest calfskin, turned up at the toes. Thus his feet kept pace with the present, however far his head may have lagged in the past; and it may be that this stream of fresh fashions, flowing perennially over his lower extremities

8

like water about the roots of a tree, kept him from dry-
ing up altogether.

Peter always polished his shoes with too much blacking, perhaps thinking that the more the blacking the
greater the proof of love.   He wore his clothes about a
season and a half—having several suits—and then
passed them on to Peter, who, foreseeing the joy of
such an inheritance, bought no new ones.   In the act
of transferring them the colonel made no comment until he came to the hose, from which he seemed unable
to part without a final tribute of esteem, as: "These
are fine, Peter;" or, "Peter, these are nearly as good
as new."   Thus Peter, too, was dragged through the
whims of fashion.   To have seen the colonel walking
about his grounds and garden followed by Peter, just a
year and a half behind in dress and a yard and a half
behind in space, one might well have taken the rear figure for the colonel's double, slightly the worse for wear,
somewhat shrunken, and cast into a heavy shadow.

Time hung so heavily on his hands at night that with
a happy inspiration he added a dress suit to his ward-
robe, and accepted the first invitation to an evening
party.

He grew excited as the hour approached, and dressed
in a great fidget for fear he should be too late.

"How do I look, Peter?" he inquired at length, surprised at his own appearance.

"Splendid, Marse Rom," replied Peter, bringing in
the shoes with more blacking on them than ever before.

"I think," said the colonel, apologetically—"I think
I'd look better if I'd put a little powder on.   I don't
know what makes me so red in the face."

But his heart began to sink before he reached his

hostess's, and he had a fearful sense of being the observed of all observers as he slipped through the hall
and passed rapidly up to the gentlemen's room. He
stayed there after the others had gone down, bewildered and lonely, dreading to go down himself. By-
and-by the musicians struck up a waltz, and with a
little cracked laugh at his own performance he cut a
few shines of an unremembered pattern; but his ankles
snapped audibly, and he suddenly stopped with the
thought of what Peter would say if he should catch him
at these antics. Then he boldly went down-stairs.

He had touched the new human life around him at
various points: as he now stretched out his arms
towards its society, for the first time he completely realized how far removed it was from him. Here he saw
'a younger generation — the flowers of the new social
order — sprung from the very soil of fraternal battle-
fields, but blooming together as the emblems of oblivious peace. He saw fathers, who had fought madly on
opposite sides, talking quietly in corners as they watched
their children dancing, or heard them toasting their old
generals and their campaigns over their champagne in
the supper-room. He was glad of it; but it made him
feel, at the same time, that, instead of treading the
velvety floors, he ought to step up and take his place
among the canvases of old-time portraits that looked
down from the walls.

The dancing he had done had been not under the
blinding glare of gaslight, but by the glimmer of tallow-
dips and star-candles and the ruddy glow of cavernous
firesides—not to the accompaniment of an orchestra of
wind-instruments and strings, but to a chorus of girls'
sweet voices, as they trod simpler measures, or to the

maddening sway of a gray-haired negro fiddler standing
on a chair in the chimney-corner. Still, it is significant to note that his saddest thought, long after leaving,
was that his shirt bosom had not lain down smooth, but
stuck out like a huge cracked egg-shell ; and that when,
in imitation of the others, he had laid his white silk
handkerchief across his bosom inside his vest, it had
slipped out during the evening, and had been found by
him, on confronting a mirror, flapping over his stomach
like a little white masonic apron.

"Did you have a nice time, Marse Rom?" inquired
Peter, as they drove home through the darkness.

"Splendid time, Peter, splendid time," replied the
colonel, nervously.

"Did you dance any, Marse Rom?"

"I didn't *dance*. Oh, I *could* have danced if I'd *wanted* to ; but I didn't."

Peter helped the colonel out of the carriage with pitying gentleness when they reached home. It was the first
and only party.

Peter also had been finding out that his occupation
was gone.

Soon after moving to town, he had tendered his pas-
toral services to one of the fashionable churches of the
city—not because it was fashionable, but because it
was made up of his brethren. In reply he was invited
to preach a trial sermon, which he did with gracious
unction.

It was a strange scene, as one calm Sunday morning
he stood on the edge of the pulpit, dressed in a suit of
the colonel's old clothes, with one hand in his trousers-
pocket, and his lame leg set a little forward at an angle
familiar to those who know the statues of Henry Clay.

How self-possessed he seemed, yet with what a rush of memories did he pass his eyes slowly over that vast assemblage of his emancipated people! With what feelings must he have contrasted those silk hats, and walking-canes, and broadcloths; those gloves and satins, laces and feathers, jewelry and fans—that whole many-colored panorama of life — with the weary, sad, and sullen audiences that had often heard him of old under the forest trees or by the banks of some turbulent stream!

In a voice husky, but heard beyond the flirtation of the uttermost pew, he took his text: "Consider the lilies of the field, how they grow; they toil not, neither do they spin." From this he tried to preach a new sermon, suited to the newer day. But several times the thoughts of the past were too much for him, and he broke down with emotion.

The next day a grave committee waited on him and reported that the sense of the congregation was to call a colored gentleman from Louisville. Private objections to Peter were that he had a broken leg, wore Colonel Fields's second-hand clothes, which were too big for him, preached in the old-fashioned way, and lacked self-control and repose of manner.

Peter accepted his rebuff as sweetly as Socrates might have done. Humming the burden of an old hymn, he took his righteous coat from a nail in the wall and folded it away in a little brass-nailed deer-skin trunk, laying over it the spelling-book and the *Pilgrim's Progress*, which he had ceased to read. Thenceforth his relations to his people were never intimate, and even from the other servants of the colonel's household he stood apart. But the colonel took Peter's rejection

greatly to heart, and the next morning gave him the
new silk socks he had worn at the party.   In paying his
servants the colonel would sometimes say, "Peter, I
reckon I'd better begin to pay you a salary; that's the
style now."   But Peter would turn off, saying he didn't
"have no use fur no salary."

Thus both of them dropped more and more out of
life, but as they did so drew more and more closely to
each other.   The colonel had bought a home on the
edge of the town, with some ten acres of beautiful ground
surrounding.   A high osage-orange hedge shut it in,
and forest trees, chiefly maples and elms, gave to the
lawn and house abundant shade.   Wild-grape vines, the
Virginia-creeper, and the climbing-oak swung their long
festoons from summit to summit, while honeysuckles,
clematis, and the Mexican-vine clambered over arbors
and trellises, or along the chipped stone of the low,
old-fashioned house.   Just outside the door of the colonel's bedroom slept an ancient, broken sundial.

The place seemed always in half-shadow, with hedge-
rows of box, clumps of dark holly, darker firs half a century old, and aged, crape-like cedars.

It was in the seclusion of this retreat, which looked
almost like a wild bit of country set down on the edge
of the town, that the colonel and Peter spent more of
their time as they fell farther in the rear of onward
events.   There were no such flower-gardens in the city,
and pretty much the whole town went thither for its
flowers, preferring them to those that were to be had
for a price at the nurseries.

There was, perhaps, a suggestion of pathetic humor in
the fact that it should have called on the colonel and
Peter, themselves so nearly defunct, to furnish the flow-

ers for so many funerals ; but, it is certain, almost weekly the two old gentlemen received this chastening admonition of their all-but-spent mortality.   The colonel
cultivated the rarest fruits also, and had under glass
varieties that were not friendly to the climate; so that
by means of the fruits and flowers there was established
a pleasant social bond with many who otherwise would
never have sought them out.

But others came for better reasons.   To a few deep-
seeing eyes the colonel and Peter were ruined landmarks
on a fading historic landscape, and their devoted friend-
ship was the last steady burning-down of that pure
flame of love which can never again shine out in the
future of the two races.   Hence a softened charm invested the drowsy quietude of that shadowy paradise
in which the old master without a slave and the old
slave without a master still kept up a brave pantomime
of their obsolete relations.   No one ever saw in their
intercourse ought but the finest courtesy, the most delicate consideration.   The very tones of their voices in
addressing each other were as good as sermons on gentleness, their antiquated playfulness as melodious as
the babble of distant water.   To be near them was to
be exorcised of evil passions.

The sun of their day had indeed long since set ; but
like twin clouds lifted high and motionless into some
far quarter of the gray twilight skies, they were still radiant with the glow of the invisible orb.

Henceforth the colonel's appearances in public were
few and regular.   He went to church on Sundays,
where he sat on the edge of the choir in the centre of
the building, and sang an ancient bass of his own im-
provisation to the older hymns, and glanced furtively

around to see whether any one noticed that he could not sing the new ones. At the Sunday-school picnics the committee of arrangements allowed him to carve the mutton, and after dinner to swing the smallest children gently beneath the trees. He was seen on Commencement Day at Morrison Chapel, where he always gave his bouquet to the valedictorian. It was the speech of that young gentleman that always touched him, consisting as it did of farewells.

In the autumn he might sometimes be noticed sitting high up in the amphitheatre at the fair, a little blue around the nose, and looking absently over into the ring where the judges were grouped around the music-stand. Once he had strutted around as a judge himself, with a blue ribbon in his button-hole, while the band played "Sweet Alice, Ben Bolt," and "Gentle Annie." The ring seemed full of young men now, and no one even thought of offering him the privileges of the grounds. In his day the great feature of the exhibition had been cattle ; now everything was turned into a horse-show. He was always glad to get home again to Peter, his true yoke-fellow. For just as two old oxen—one white and one black—that have long toiled under the same yoke will, when turned out to graze at last in the widest pasture, come and put themselves horn to horn and flank to flank, so the colonel and Peter were never so happy as when ruminating side by side.

NEW LOVE.

In their eventless life the slightest incident acquired the importance of a history. Thus, one day in June, Peter discovered a young couple love-making in the shrubbery, and with the deepest agitation reported the fact to the colonel.

Never before, probably, had the fluttering of the dear god's wings brought more dismay than to these ancient involuntary guardsmen of his hiding-place. The colonel was at first for breaking up what he considered a piece of underhand proceedings, but Peter reasoned stoutly that if the pair were driven out they would simply go to some other retreat; and without getting the approval of his conscience to this view, the colonel contented himself with merely repeating that they ought to go straight and tell the girl's parents. Those parents lived just across the street outside his grounds. The young lady he knew very well himself, having a few years before given her the privilege of making herself at home among his flowers. It certainly looked hard to drive her out now, just when she was making the best possible use of his kindness and her opportunity. Moreover, Peter walked down street and ascertained that the young fellow was an energetic farmer living a few miles from town, and son of one of the colonel's former friends; on both of which accounts the latter's heart went out to him. So when, a few days later, the colonel, followed by Peter, crept up breathlessly and peeped through the bushes at the pair strolling along the shady perfumed walks, and so plainly happy in that happiness which comes but once in a lifetime, they not only abandoned the idea of betraying the secret, but afterwards kept away from that part of the grounds, lest they should be an interruption.

" Peter," stammered the colonel, who had been trying to get the words out for three days, "do you suppose he has already—*asked* her?"

"Some's pow'ful quick on de trigger, en some's
mighty slow," replied Peter, neutrally.   " En some," he
added, exhaustively, "don't use de trigger 't all !"

" I always thought there had to be asking done by
somebody," remarked the colonel, a little vaguely.

" I nuver axed Phillis !" exclaimed Peter, with a certain air of triumph.

" Did Phillis ask *you*, Peter?" inquired the colonel,
blushing and confidential.

"No, no, Marse Rom !   I couldn't er stood dat from
no 'oman !" replied Peter, laughing and shaking his
head.

The colonel was sitting on the stone steps in front of
the house, and Peter stood below, leaning against a
Corinthian column, hat in hand, as he went on to tell
his love-story.

" Hit all happ'n dis way, Marse Rom. We wuz gwine
have pra'r-meetin', en I 'lowed to walk home wid Phillis
en ax 'er on de road.   I been 'lowin' to ax 'er heap o'
times befo', but I ain' jes nuver done so.   So I says to
myse'f, says I, ' I jes mek my sermon to-night kiner lead
up to whut I gwine tell Phillis on de road home.'   So I
tuk my tex' from de *lef'* tail o' my coat : ' De greates' o'
dese is charity;' caze I knowed charity wuz same ez
love.   En all de time I wuz preachin' an' glorifyin'
charity en identifyin' charity wid love, I couldn' he'p
thinkin' 'bout what I gwine say to Phillis on de road
home.   Dat mek me feel better ; en de better I *feel*, de
better I *preach*, so hit boun' to mek my *heahchs* feel better likewise—Phillis 'mong um.   So Phillis she jes sot
dah listenin' en listenin' en lookin' like we wuz a'ready
on de road home, till I got so wuked up in my feelin's I
jes knowed de time wuz come.   By-en-by, I had n' mo'

'n done preachin' en wuz lookin' roun' to git my Bible
en my hat, 'fo' up popped dat big Charity Green, who
been settin' 'longside o' Phillis en tekin' ev'y las' thing I
said to *her*se'f. En she tuk hole o' my han' en squeeze
it, en say she felt mos' like shoutin'. En 'fo' I knowed
it, I jes see Phillis wrap 'er shawl roun' 'er head en tu'n
'er nose up at me right quick en flip out de dooh. De
dogs howl mighty mou'nful when I walk home by myse'f *dat* night," added Peter, laughing to himself, " en I
ain' preach dat sermon no mo' tell atter me en Phillis
wuz married.

"Hit wuz long time," he continued, " 'fo' Phillis come
to heah me preach any mo'. But 'long 'bout de nex'
fall we had big meetin', en heap mo' um j'ined. But
Phillis, she ain't nuver j'ined yit. I preached mighty
nigh all roun' my coat-tails till I say to myse'f, D' ain't
but one tex' lef', en I jes got to fetch 'er wid dat! De
tex' wuz on de *right* tail o' my coat : 'Come unto me,
all ye dat labor en is heavy laden.' Hit wuz a ve'y mo-
mentous sermon, en all 'long I jes see Phillis wras'lin'
wid 'erse'f, en I say, ' She *got* to come *dis* night, de
Lohd he'pin' me.' En I had n' mo' 'n said de word, 'fo'
she jes walked down en guv me 'er han'.

"Den we had de baptizin' in Elkhorn Creek, en de
watter wuz deep en de curren' tol'ble swif'. Hit look to
me like dere wuz five hundred uv um on de creek side.
By-en-by I stood on de edge o' de watter, en Phillis she
come down to let me baptize 'er. En me en 'er j'ined
han's en waded out in the creek, mighty slow, caze
Phillis didn' have no shot roun' de bottom uv 'er dress,
en it kep' bobbin' on top de watter till I pushed it down.
But by-en-by we got 'way out in de creek, en bof uv us
wuz tremblin'. En I says to 'er ve'y kin'ly, ' When I

put you un'er de watter, Phillis, you mus' try en hole
yo'se'f stiff, so I can lif' you up easy.' But I hadn't
mo' 'n jes got 'er laid back over de watter ready to
souze 'er un'er when 'er feet flew up off de bottom uv
de creek, en when I retched out to fetch 'er up, I stepped
in a hole ; en 'fo' I knowed it, we wuz flounderin' roun'
in de watter, en de hymn dey was singin' on de
bank sounded mighty confused-like. En Phillis she
swallowed some watter, en all 't oncet she jes grap
me right tight roun' de neck, en say mighty quick,
says she, ' I gwine marry whoever gits me out'n dis yere
watter !'

"En by-en-by, when me en 'er wuz walkin' up de
bank o' de creek, drippin' all over, I says to 'er, says I :

"'Does you 'member what you said back yon'er in
de watter, Phillis ?'

"'I ain' out'n no watter yit,' says she, ve'y con-
temptuous.

"'When does you consider yo'se'f out'n de watter?'
says I, ve'y humble.

"'When I git dese soakin' clo'es off'n my back,'
says she.

"Hit wuz good dark when we got home, en atter a
while I crope up to de dooh o' Phillis's cabin en put
my eye down to de key-hole, en see Phillis jes settin'
'fo' dem blazin' walnut logs dressed up in 'er new red
linsey dress, en 'er eyes shinin'. En I shuk so I 'mos'
faint. Den I tap easy on de dooh, en say in a mighty
tremblin' tone, says I :

"'Is you out'n de watter yit, Phillis ?'

"'I got on dry dress,' says she.

"'Does you 'member what you said back yon'er in
de watter, Phillis ?' says I.

"'De latch-string on de outside de dooh,' says she, mighty sof'.

"En I walked in."

As Peter drew near the end of this reminiscence, his voice sank to a key of inimitable tenderness; and when it was ended he stood a few minutes, scraping the gravel with the toe of his boot, his head dropped forward. Then he added, huskily:

"Phillis been dead heap o' years now;" and turned away.

This recalling of the scenes of a time long gone by may have awakened in the breast of the colonel some gentle memory; for after Peter was gone he continued to sit a while in silent musing. Then getting up, he walked in the falling twilight across the yard and through the gardens until he came to a secluded spot in the most distant corner. There he stooped or rather knelt down and passed his hands, as though with mute benediction, over a little bed of old-fashioned China pinks. When he had moved in from the country he had brought nothing away from his mother's garden but these, and in all the years since no one had ever pulled them, as Peter well knew; for one day the colonel had said, with his face turned away:

"Let them have all the flowers they want; but leave the pinks."

He continued kneeling over them now, touching them softly with his fingers, as though they were the fragrant, never-changing symbols of voiceless communion with his past. Still it may have been only the early dew of the evening that glistened on them when he rose and slowly walked away, leaving the pale moonbeams to haunt the spot.

Certainly after this day he showed increasing concern in the young lovers who were holding clandestine
meetings in his grounds.

"Peter," he would say, "why, if they love each other,
don't they get married ?   Something may happen."

"I been spectin' some'n' to happ'n fur some time, ez
dey been quar'lin' right smart lately," replied Peter,
laughing.

Whether or not he was justified in this prediction,
before the end of another week the colonel read a notice of their elopement and marriage ; and several days
later he came up from down-town and told Peter that
everything had been forgiven the young pair, who had
gone to house-keeping in the country.   It gave him
pleasure to think he had helped to perpetuate the race
of blue-grass farmers.

THE YEARNING PASSED AWAY.

It was in the twilight of a late autumn day in the
same year that nature gave the colonel the first direct
intimation to prepare for the last summons.   They had
been passing along the garden walks, where a few pale
flowers were trying to flourish up to the very winter's
edge, and where the dry leaves had gathered unswept
and rustled beneath their feet.   All at once the colonel
turned to Peter, who was a yard and a half behind, as
usual, and said :

"Give me your arm, Peter, I feel tired ;" and thus the
two, for the first time in all their lifetime walking
abreast, passed slowly on.

"Peter," said the colonel, gravely, a minute or two

later, "we are like two dried-up stalks of fodder. I wonder the Lord lets us live any longer."

"I reck'n He's managin' to use us *some* way, or we wouldn' be heah," said Peter.

"Well, all I have to say is, that if He's using me, He can't be in much of a hurry for his work," replied the colonel.

"He uses snails, en I *know* we ain' ez slow ez *dem*," argued Peter, composedly.

"I don't know. I think a snail must have made more progress since the war than I have."

The idea of his uselessness seemed to weigh on him, for a little later he remarked, with a sort of mortified smile:

"Do you think, Peter, that we would pass for what they call representative men of the New South?"

"We done *had* ou' day, Marse Rom," replied Peter. "We got to pass fur what we *wuz*. Mebbe de *Lohd's* got mo' use fur us yit 'n *people* has," he added, after a pause.

From this time on the colonel's strength gradually failed him; but it was not until the following spring that the end came.

A night or two before his death his mind wandered backward, after the familiar manner of the dying, and his delirious dreams showed the shifting, faded pictures that renewed themselves for the last time on his wasting memory. It must have been that he was once more amid the scenes of his active farm life, for his broken snatches of talk ran thus:

"Come, boys, get your cradles! Look where the sun is! You are late getting to work this morning. That is the finest field of wheat in the county. Be careful about the bundles! Make them the same size and tie them tight. That swath is too wide, and you don't hold your cradle right, Tom. . . .

"Sell *Peter! Sell Peter Cotton!* No, sir! You might buy *me* some day and work *me* in your cotton-field; but as long as he's mine, you can't buy Peter, and you can't buy any of *my* negroes. . . .

"Boys! boys! If you don't work faster, you won't finish this field to-day. . . . You'd better go in the shade and rest now. The sun's very hot. Don't drink too much ice-water. There's a jug of whisky in the fence-corner. Give them a good dram around, and tell them to work slow till the sun gets lower.". . .

Once during the night a sweet smile played over his features as he repeated a few words that were part of an old rustic song and dance. Arranged, not as they came broken and incoherent from his lips, but as he once had sung them, they were as follows:

> "O Sister Phœbe! How merry were we
> When we sat under the juniper-tree,
>   The juniper-tree, heigho!
> Put this hat on your head! Keep your head warm:
> Take a sweet kiss! It will do you no harm,
>   Do you no harm, I know!"

After this he sank into a quieter sleep, but soon stirred with a look of intense pain.

"Helen! Helen!" he murmured. "Will you break your promise? Have you changed in your feelings towards me? I have brought you the pinks. Won't you take the pinks, Helen?"

Then he sighed as he added, "It wasn't her fault. If she had only known—"

Who was the Helen of that far-away time? Was this the colonel's love-story?

But during all the night, whithersoever his mind wandered, at intervals it returned to the burden of a single strain—the harvesting. Towards daybreak he took it up again for the last time:

"O boys, boys, *boys!* If you don't work faster you won't finish the field to-day. Look how low the sun is!... I am going to the house. They can't finish the field to-day. Let them do what they can, but don't let them work late. I want Peter to go to the house with me. Tell him to come on."...

In the faint gray of the morning, Peter, who had been watching by the bedside all night, stole out of the room, and going into the garden pulled a handful of pinks— a thing he had never done before—and, re-entering the colonel's bedroom, put them in a vase near his sleeping face. Soon afterwards the colonel opened his eyes and looked around him. At the foot of the bed stood Peter, and on one side sat the physician and a friend. The night-lamp burned low, and through the folds of the curtains came the white light of early day.

"Put out the lamp and open the curtains," he said, feebly. "It's day." When they had drawn the curtains aside, his eyes fell on the pinks, sweet and fresh with the dew on them. He stretched out his hand and touched them caressingly, and his eyes sought Peter's with a look of grateful understanding.

"I want to be alone with Peter for a while," he said, turning his face towards the others.

When they were left alone, it was some minutes before anything was said. Peter, not knowing what he did, but knowing what was coming, had gone to the win-

9

dow and hid himself behind the curtains, drawing them tightly around his form as though to shroud himself from sorrow.

At length the colonel said, "Come here!"

Peter, almost staggering forward, fell at the foot of the bed, and, clasping the colonel's feet with one arm, pressed his cheek against them.

"Come closer!"

Peter crept on his knees and buried his head on the colonel's thigh.

" Come up here—*closer;*" and putting one arm around Peter's neck he laid the other hand softly on his head, and looked long and tenderly into his eyes. " I've got to leave you, Peter. Don't you feel sorry for me?"

"Oh, Marse Rom!" cried Peter, hiding his face, his whole form shaken by sobs.

" Peter," added, the colonel with ineffable gentleness, "if I had served my Master as faithfully as you have served yours, I should not feel ashamed to stand in his presence."

" If my Marseter is ez mussiful to me ez you have been—"

" I have fixed things so that you will be comfortable after I am gone. When your time comes, I should like you to be laid close to me. We can take the long sleep together. Are you willing?"

"That's whar I want to be laid."

The colonel stretched out his hand to the vase, and taking the bunch of pinks, said very calmly :

" Leave these in my hand; I'll carry them with me." A moment more, and he added :

" If I shouldn't wake up any more, good-bye, Peter!"

" Good-bye, Marse Rom!"

And they shook hands a long time. After this the
colonel lay back on the pillows. His soft, silvery hair
contrasted strongly with his child-like, unspoiled, open
face. To the day of his death, as is apt to be true of
those who have lived pure lives but never married, he
had a boyish strain in him—a softness of nature, showing itself even now in the gentle expression of his
mouth. His brown eyes had in them the same boyish
look when, just as he was falling asleep, he scarcely
opened them to say:

"Pray, Peter."

Peter, on his knees, and looking across the colonel's
face towards the open door, through which the rays of
the rising sun streamed in upon his hoary head, prayed,
while the colonel fell asleep, adding a few words for
himself now left alone.

Several hours later, memory led the colonel back
again through the dim gate-way of the past, and out of
that gate-way his spirit finally took flight into the future.

Peter lingered a year. The place went to the colonel's
sister, but he was allowed to remain in his quarters.
With much thinking of the past, his mind fell into a
lightness and a weakness. Sometimes he would be
heard crooning the burden of old hymns, or sometimes
seen sitting beside the old brass-nailed trunk, fumbling
with the spelling-book and *The Pilgrim's Progress*. Oft-
en, too, he walked out to the cemetery on the edge of
the town, and each time could hardly find the colonel's
grave amid the multitude of the dead.

One gusty day in spring, the Scotch sexton, busy with
the blades of blue-grass springing from the animated
mould, saw his familiar figure standing motionless beside
the colonel's resting-place. He had taken off his hat

—one of the colonel's last bequests—and laid it on the colonel's head-stone. On his body he wore a strange coat of faded blue, patched and weather-stained, and so moth-eaten that parts of the curious tails had dropped entirely away. In one hand he held an open Bible, and on a much-soiled page he was pointing with his finger to the following words :

"I would not have you ignorant, brethren, concerning them which are asleep."

It would seem that, impelled by love and faith, and guided by his wandering reason, he had come forth to preach his last sermon on the immortality of the soul over the dust of his dead master.

The sexton led him home, and soon afterwards a friend, who had loved them both, laid him beside the colonel. ·

It was perhaps fitting that his winding-sheet should be the vestment in which, years agone, he had preached to his fellow-slaves in bondage; for if it so be that the dead of this planet shall come forth from their graves clad in the trappings of mortality, then Peter should arise on the Resurrection Day wearing his old jeans coat.

THE WHITE COWL.

The White Cowl.

In a shadowy solitary valley of Southern Kentucky and beside a noiseless stream there stands to-day a great French abbey of white-cowled Trappist monks. It is the loneliest of human habitations. Though not a ruin, an atmosphere of gray antiquity hangs about and forever haunts it. The pale-gleaming cross on the spire looks as though it would fall to the earth, weary of its aged unchangeableness. The long Gothic windows; the rudely carven wooden crucifixes, suggesting the very infancy of holy art; the partly encompassing wall, seemingly built to resist a siege; the iron gate of the porter's lodge, locked against profane intrusion—all are the voiceless but eloquent emblems of a past that still enchains the memory by its associations as it once enthralled the reason by its power.

Over the placid stream and across the fields to the woody crests around float only the sounds of the same sweet monastery bells that in the quiet evening air ages ago summoned a ruder world to nightly rest and pious thoughts of heaven. Within the abbey at midnight are heard the voices of monks chanting the self-same masses that ages ago were sung by others, who all night long from icy chapel floors lifted up piteous hands with intercession for poor souls suffering in purgatory. One almost expects to see coming along the dusty Kentucky road which winds through the valley meek brown palmers returning from the Holy Sepulchre, or through an upper window of the abbey to descry lance and visor and battle-axe flashing in the sunlight as they wind up a distant hill-side to the storming of some perilous citadel.

Ineffable influences, too, seem to bless the spot. Here, forsooth, some saint, retiring to the wilderness to subdue the devil in his flesh, lived and struggled and suffered and died, leaving his life as an heroic pattern for others who in the same hard way should wish to win the fullest grace of Christlike character. Perhaps even one of the old monks, long since halting towards the close of his pilgrimage, will reverently lead you down the aisle to the dim sepulchre of some martyr, whose relics repose under the altar while his virtues perpetually exhale heavenward like gracious incense.

The beauty of the region, and especially of the grounds surrounding the abbey, thus seems but a touching mockery. What have these inward-gazing, heavenward-gazing souls to do with the loveliness of Nature, with change of season, or flight of years, with green pastures and waving harvest-fields outside the wall, with flowers and orchards and vineyards within?

It was in a remote corner of the beautiful gardens of the monastery that a young monk, Father Palemon, was humbly at work one morning some years ago amid the lettuces and onions and fast-growing potatoes. The sun smote the earth with the fierce heat of departing June; and pausing to wipe the thick bead of perspiration from his forehead, he rested a moment, breathing heavily. His powerful legs were astride a row of the succulent shoots, and his hands clasped the handle of the hoe that

gave him a staff-like support in front.   He was dressed
in the sacred garb of his order.   His heavy sabots crushed the clods in the furrows.   His cream-colored serge
cowl, the long skirt of which would have touched the
ground, had been folded up to his knees and tied with
hempen cords.   The wide sleeves, falling away, showed
up to the elbows the superb muscles of his bronzed
arms ; and the calotte, pushed far back from his head,
revealed the outlines of his neck, full, round, like a column.   Nearly a month had passed since the convent
barber had sheared his poll, and his yellow hair was
just beginning to enrich his temples with a fillet of thick
curling locks.   Had Father Palemon's hair been per-
mitted to grow, it would have fallen down on each side
in masses shining like flax and making the ideal head
of a saint.   But his face was not the face of a saint.   It
had in it no touch of the saint's agony—none of those
fine subtle lines that are the material net-work of intense
spirituality brooding within.   Scant vegetarian diet and
the deep shadows of cloistral life had preserved in his
complexion the delicate hues of youth, noticeable still
beneath the tan of recent exposure to the summer sun.
His calm, steady blue eyes, also, had the open look
peculiar to self-unconscious childhood ; so that as he
stood thus, tall, sinewy, supple, grave, bareheaded under the open sky, clad in spotless white, a singular
union of strength, manliness, and unawakened innocence, he was a figure startling to come upon.

As he rested, he looked down and discovered that the
hempen cords fastening the hem of his cowl were becoming untied, and walking to the border of grass which
ran round the garden just inside the monastery wall, he
sat down to secure the loosened threads.   He was very

tired. He had come forth to work before the first gray
of dawn. His lips were parched with thirst. Save the
little cup of cider and a slice of black bread with which
he had broken his fast after matins, he had not tasted
food since the frugal meal of the previous noon. Both
weary and faint, therefore, he had hardly sat down before, in the weakness of his flesh, a sudden powerful impulse came upon him to indulge in a moment's repose.
His fingers fell away from the untied cords, his body
sank backward against the trunk of the gnarled apple-tree
by which he was shaded, and closing his eyes, he drank
in eagerly all the sweet influences of the perfect day.

For Nature was in an ecstasy. The sunlight never
fell more joyous upon the unlifting shadows of human
life. The breeze that cooled his sweating face was
heavy with the odor of the wonderful monastery roses.
In the dark green canopy overhead two piping flame-
colored orioles drained the last bright dew-drop from
the chalice of a leaf. All the liquid air was slumbrous
with the minute music of insect life, and from the honeysuckles clambering over the wall at his back came
the murmur of the happy, happy bees.

But what power have hunger and thirst and momentary weariness over the young? Father Palemon was
himself part of the pure and beautiful nature around
him. His heart was like some great secluded crimson
flower that is ready to burst open in a passionate seeking of the sun. As he sat thus in the midst of Nature's
joyousness and irrepressible unfoldings, and peaceful
consummations, he forgot hunger and thirst and weariness in a feeling of delicious languor. But beneath
even this, and more subtle still, was the stir of restlessness and the low fever of vague desire for something

wholly beyond his experience. He sighed and opened his eyes. Right before them, on the spire beyond the gardens, was the ancient cross to which he was consecrated. On his shoulders were the penitential wounds · he had that morning inflicted with the knotted scourge. In his ears was the faint general chorus of saints and martyrs, echoing backward ever more solemnly to the very passion of Christ. While Nature was everywhere clothing itself with living greenness, around his gaunt body and muscular limbs—over his young head and his coursing hot blood—he had wrapped the dead white cowl of centuries gone as the winding-sheet of his humanity. These were not clear thoughts in his mind, but the vaguest suggestions of feeling, which of late had come to him at times, and now made him sigh more deeply as he sat up and bent over again to tie the hempen cords. As he did so, his attention was arrested by the sound of voices just outside the monastery wall, which was low here, so that in the general stillness they became entirely audible.

II.

Outside the wall was a long strip of woodland which rose gently to the summit of a ridge half a mile away. This woodland was but little used. Into it occasionally a lay-brother drove the gentle monastery cows to pasture, or here a flock sheltered itself beneath forest oaks against the noontide summer heat. Beyond the summit lay the homestead of a gentleman farmer. As one descended this slope towards the abbey, he beheld it from the most picturesque side, and visitors at the homestead usually came to see it by this secluded approach.

If Father Palemon could have seen beyond the wall, he would have discovered that the voices were those of a young man and a young woman—the former a slight, dark cripple, and invalid. He led the way along a footpath up quite close to the wall, and the two sat down beneath the shade of a great tree. Father Palemon, listening eagerly, unconsciously, overheard the following conversation :

"I should like to take you inside the abbey wall, but, of course, that is impossible, as no woman is allowed to enter the grounds. So we shall rest here a while. I find that the walk tires me more than it once did, and this tree has become a sort of outside shrine to me on my pilgrimages."

"Do you come often ?"

"Oh yes. When we have visitors, I am appointed their guide, probably because I feel more interest in the place than any one else. If they are men, I take them over the grounds inside ; and if they are women, I bring them thus far and try to describe the rest."

"As you will do for me now ?"

"No ; I am not in the mood for describing. Even when I am, my description always disappoints me. How is one to describe such human beings as these monks ? Sometimes, during the long summer days, I walk over here alone and lie for hours under this tree, until the influences of the place have completely possessed me and I feel wrought up to the point of description. The sensation of a chill comes over me. Look up at these Kentucky skies ! You have never seen them before. Are there any more delicate and tender ? Well, at such times, where they bend over this abbey, they look as hard and cold as a sky of Landseer's. The sun seems no longer

to warm the pale cross on the spire yonder, the great
drifting white clouds send a shiver through me as though
uplifted snow-banks were passing over my head. I fancy
that if I were to go inside I should see the white but-
terflies dropping down dead from the petals of the white
roses, finding them stiff with frost, and that the white
rabbits would be limping trembling through the frozen
grass, like the hare in 'The Eve of St. Agnes.' Everything becomes cold to me—cold, cold, cold ! The bleak
and rugged old monks themselves, in their hoary cowls,
turn to personifications of perpetual winter ; and if I
were in the chapel, I should expect to meet in one of
them Keats's very beadsman—patient, holy man, meagre, wan—whose fingers were numb while he told his
rosary, and his breath frosted as it took flight for
heaven. Ugh ! I am cold now. My blood must be
getting very thin."

"No ; you make *me* shiver also."

"At least the impression is a powerful one. I have
watched these old monks closely. Whether it is from
the weakness of vigils and fasts or from positive cold,
they all tremble—perpetually tremble. I fancy that
their souls ache as well. Are not their cowls the grave-
clothes of a death in life ?"

"You seem to forget, Austin, that faith warms them."

"By extinguishing the fires of nature ! Why should
not faith and nature grow strong together ? I have spent
my life on the hill-side back yonder, as you know, and
I have had leisure enough for studying these monks. I
have tried to do them justice. At different times I have
almost lived with St. Benedict at Subiaco, and St. Pat-
rick on the mountain, and St. Anthony in the desert.
and St. Thomas in the cell. I understand and value

the elements of truth and beauty in the lives of the
ancient solitaries.   But they belong so inalienably to
the past.   We have outgrown the ideals of antiquity.
How can a man now look upon his body as his evil ten-
ement of flesh?   How can he believe that he approaches
sainthood by destroying his manhood?   The highest
type of personal holiness is said to be attained in the
cloister.   That is not true.   The highest type of personal holiness is to be attained in the thick of the
world's temptations.   Then it becomes sublime.   It
seems to me that the heroisms worth speaking of now-
adays are active, not meditative.   But why should I
say this to you, who as much as any one else have
taught me to think thus—I who myself am able to do
nothing?   But though I can do nothing, I can at least
look upon the monastic ideal of life as an empty, dead,
husk, into which no man with the largest ideas of duty
will ever compress his powers.   Even granting that it
develops personal holiness, this itself is but one element in the perfect character, and not even the greatest one."

"But do you suppose that these monks have delib-
erately and freely chosen their vocation?   You know
perfectly well that often there are almost overwhelming
motives impelling men and women to hide themselves
away from the world—from its sorrows, its dangers,
its temptations."

"You are at least orthodox.   I know that such motives exist, but are they sufficient?   Of course there was
a time when the cloister was a refuge from dangers.
Certainly that is not true in this country now.   And as
for the sorrows and temptations, I say that they must
be met in the world.   There is no sorrow *befalling* a man

in the world that he should not *bear* in the world—bear it as well for the sake of his own character as for the sake of helping others who suffer like him. This way lie moral heroism and martyrdom. This way, even, lies the utmost self-sacrifice, if one will only try to see it. No, I have but little sympathy with such cases. The only kind of monk who has all my sympathy is the one that is produced by early training and education. Take a boy whose nature has nothing in common with the scourge and the cell. Immure him. Never let him get from beneath the shadow of convent walls or away from the sound of masses and the waving of crucifixes. Bend him, train him, break him, until he turns monk despite nature's purposes, and ceases to be a man without becoming a saint. I have sympathy for *him.* Sympathy! I do not know of any violation of the law of personal liberty that gives me so much positive suffering."

"But why suffer over imaginary cases? Such constraint belongs to the past."

"On the contrary, it is just such an instance of constraint that has colored my thoughts of this abbey. It is this that has led me to haunt the place for years from a sort of sad fascination. Men find their way to this valley from the remotest parts of the world. No one knows from what inward or outward stress they come. They are hidden away here and their secret histories are buried with them. But the history of one of these fathers is known, for he has grown up here under the shadow of these monastery walls. You may think the story one of mediæval flavor, but I believe its counterpart will here and there be found as long as monasteries rise and human beings fall.

"He was an illegitimate child. Who his father was,

no one ever so much as suspected. When his mother died he was left a homeless waif in one of the Kentucky towns. But some invisible eye was upon him. He was soon afterwards brought to the boarding-school for poor boys which is taught by the Trappist fathers here. Perhaps this was done by his father, who wished to get him safely out of the world. Well, he has never left this valley since then. The fathers have been his only friends and advisers. He has never looked on the face of a woman since he looked into his mother's when a child. He knows no more of the modern world—except what the various establishments connected with the abbey have taught him—than the most ancient hermit. While he was in the Trappist school, during afternoons and vacations he worked in the monastery fields with the lay-brothers. With them he ate and slept. When his education was finished he became a lay-brother himself. But amid such influences the rest of the story is foreseen; in a few years he put on the brown robe and leathern girdle of a brother of the order, and last year he took final vows, and now wears the white cowl and black scapular of a priest."

"But if he has never known any other life, he, most of all, should be contented with this. It seems to me that it would be much harder to have known human life and then renounce it."

"That is because you are used to dwell upon the good, and strive to better the evil. No; I do not believe that he is happy. I do not believe nature is ever thwarted without suffering, and nature in him never cried out for the monkish life, but against it. His first experience with the rigors of its discipline proved nearly fatal. He was prostrated with long illness. Only

by special indulgence in food and drink was his health
restored. His system even now is not inured to the
cruel exactions of his order. You see, I have known
him for years. I was first attracted to him as a lonely
little fellow with the sad lay-brothers in the fields. As I
would pass sometimes, he would eye me with a boy's
unconscious appeal for the young and for companion-
ship. I have often gone into the abbey since then, to
watch and study him. He works with a terrible pent-
up energy. I know his type among the young Kentuckians. They make poor monks. Time and again
they have come here to join the order. But all have
soon fallen away. Only Father Palemon has ever per-
severed to the taking of the vows that bind him until
death. My father knew his mother and says that he is
much like her—an impulsive, passionate, trustful, beautiful creature, with the voice of a seraph. Father Palemon himself has the richest voice in the monks' choir.
Ah, to hear him, in the dark chapel, sing the *Salve Re-
gina!* The others seem to moderate their own voices,
that his may rise clear and uncommingled to the vaulted
roof. But I believe that it is only the music he feels.
He puts passion and an outcry for human sympathy into
every note. Do you wonder that I am so strongly
drawn towards him? I can give you no idea of his appearance. I shall show you his photograph, but that
will not do it. I have often imagined you two together
by the very law of contrast. I think of you at home in
New York City, with your charities, your missions, your
energetic, untiring beneficence. You stand at one ex-
treme. Then I think of him at the other—doing nothing, shut up in this valley, spending his magnificent
manhood in a never-changing, never-ending routine of

10

sterile vigils and fasts and prayers. Oh, we should change places, he and I ! I should be in there and he out here. He should be lying here by your side, looking up into your face, loving you as I have loved you, and winning you as I never can. Oh, Madeline, Madeline, Madeline !"

The rapid, broken utterance suddenly ceased.

In the deep stillness that followed, Father Palemon heard the sound of a low sob and a groan.

He had sat all this time rivetted to the spot, and as though turned into stone. He had hardly breathed. A bright lizard gliding from out a crevice in the wall had sunned itself in a little rift of sunshine between his feet. A bee from the honeysuckles had alighted unnoticed upon his hand. Others sounds had died away from his ears, which were strained to catch the last echoes of these strange voices from another world.

Now all at once across the gardens came the stroke of a bell summoning to instant prayer. Why had it suddenly grown so loud and terrible? He started up. He forgot priestly gravity and ran—fairly ran, head-long and in a straight course, heedless of the tender plants that were being crushed beneath his feet. From another part of the garden an aged brother, his eye attracted by the sunlight glancing on a bright moving object, paused while training a grape-vine and watched with amazement the disorderly figure as it fled. As he ran on, the skirts of his cowl, which he had forgotten to tie up, came down. When at last he reached the door of the chapel and stooped to unroll them, he discovered that they had been draggled over the dirt and stained against the bruised weeds until they were

hardly recognizable as having once been spotless white.
A pang of shame and alarm went through him.   It was
the first stain.   ·

III.

Every morning the entire Trappist brotherhood meet
in a large room for public confession and accusation.
High at one end sits the venerable abbot; beside him,
but lower, the prior ; while the fathers in white and the
brothers in brown range themselves on benches placed
against the wall on each side.

It was near the close of this impressive ceremony
that Father Palemon arose, and, pushing the hood far
back from his face, looked sorrowfully around upon the
amazed company.   A thrill of the tenderest sympathy
shot through them.   He was the youngest by far of
their number and likeliest therefore to go astray; but
never had any one found cause to accuse him, and never had he condemned himself.   Many a head wearing
its winter of age and worldly scars had been lifted in
that sacred audience-chamber of the soul confessing to
secret sin.   But not he.   So awful a thing is it for a
father to accuse himself, that in utter self-abasement his
brethren throw themselves prone to the floor when he
rises.   It was over the prostrate forms of his brethren
that Father Palemon now stood up erect, alone.   Unearthly spectacle !   He began his confession.   In the
hushed silence of the great bare chamber his voice
awoke such echoes as might have terrified the soul had
one gone into a vast vault and harangued the shrouded
dead.   But he went on, sparing not himself and laying
bare his whole sin—the yielding to weariness in the

garden ; the listening to the conversation ; most of all, the harboring of strange doubts and desires since then. Never before had the word "woman" been breathed at this confessional of devoted celibates.   More than one hooded, faded cheek blushed secret crimson at the sound.   The circumstances attending Father Palemon's temptation invested it with an ancient horror.   The scene, a garden ; the tempter, a woman.   It was like some modern Adam confessing his fall.

His penance was severe.   For a week he was not to leave his cell, except at brief seasons.   Every morning he must scourge himself on his naked back until the blood came.   Every noon he must go about the re- fectory on his knees, begging his portion of daily bread, morsel by morsel, from his brethren, and must eat it sitting before them on the floor.   This repast was re- duced in quantity one half.   An aged deaf monk took his place in the garden.

His week of penance over, Father Palemon came forth too much weakened to do heavy work, and was sent to relieve one of the fathers in the school.   Edu- cated there himself, he had often before this taught its round of familiar duties.

The school is situated outside the abbey wall on a hill-side several hundred yards away.   Between it and the abbey winds the road which enters the valley above and goes out below, connecting two country highways. Where it passes the abbey it offers slippery, unsafe footing on account of a shelving bed of rock which rises on each side as a steep embankment, and is kept moist by overhanging trees and by a small stream that issues from the road-side and spreads out over the whole pass. The fathers are commanded to cross this road at a quick gait, the hood drawn completely over the face, and the eyes bent on the ground.

One sultry afternoon, a few days later, Father Palemon had sent away his little group of pious pupils, and seated himself to finish his work. The look of unawakened innocence had vanished from his eyes. They were full of thought and sorrow. A little while and, as though weighed down with heaviness, his head sank upon his arms, which were crossed over the desk. But he soon lifted it with alarm. One of the violent storms which gather and pass so quickly in the Kentucky skies was rushing on from the south. The shock of distant thunder sent a tremor through the building. He walked to the window and stood for a moment watching the rolling edge of the low storm-cloud with its plumes of white and gray and ominous dun-green colors. Suddenly his eyes were drawn to the road below. Around a bend a horse came running at full speed, uncontrolled by the rider. He clasped his hands and breathed a prayer. Just ahead was the slippery, dangerous footing. Another moment and horse and rider disappeared behind the embankment. Then the horse reappeared on the other side, without saddle or rider, rushing away like a forerunner of the tempest.

He ran down. When he reached the spot he saw lying on the road-side the form of a woman—the creature whom his priestly vows forbade him ever to approach. Her face was upturned, but hidden under a great wave of her long, loosened, brown hair. He knelt down and, lifting the hair aside, gazed down into it.

"*Ave Maria!*—Mother of God!" The disjointed exclamations were instinctive. The first sight of beautiful womanhood had instantly lifted his thought to the

utmost height of holy associations. Indeed, no sweet
face had he ever looked on but the Virgin's picture.
Many a time in the last few years had he, in moments
of restlessness, drawn near and studied it with a sudden rush of indefinable tenderness and longing. But
beauty, such as this seemed to him, he had never dreamed of. He bent over it, reverential, awe-stricken. Then,
as naturally as the disciple John might have succored
Mary, finding her wounded and fainting by the way-
side, he took the unconscious sufferer in his arms and
bore her to the school-room for refuge from the bursting storm. There he quickly stripped himself of his
great soft cowl, and, spreading it on the bare floor, laid
her on it, and with cold water and his coarse monk's
handkerchief bathed away the blood that flowed from
a little wound on her temple.

A few moments and she opened her eyes. He was
bending close over her, and his voice sounded as sweet
and sorrowful as a vesper bell :

" Do you suffer ? Are you much hurt ? Your horse
must have fallen among the rocks. The girth was
broken."

She sat up bewildered, and replied slowly:

" I think I am only stunned. Yes, my horse fell. I
was hurrying home out of the storm. He took fright at
something and I lost control of him. What place is
this ?"

"This is the school of the abbey. The road passes
just below. I was standing at the window when your
horse ran past, and I brought you here."

" I must go home at once. They will be anxious
about me. I am visiting at a place not more than a
mile away."

He shook his head and pointed to the window. A
sudden gray blur of rain had effaced the landscape.
The wind shook the building.

"You must remain here until the storm is over. It
will last but a little while."

During this conversation she had been sitting on the
white cowl, and he, with the frankness of a won-
dering, innocent child, had been kneeling quite close
beside her. Now she got up and walked to one of
the windows, looking out upon the storm, while he
retired to another window at the opposite end of the
room.

What was the tempest-swept hill outside to the wild,
swift play of emotions in him? A complete revulsion
of feeling quickly succeeded his first mood. What if
she was more beautiful—far more beautiful—than the
sweet Virgin's picture in the abbey? She was a devil,
a beautiful devil. Her eyes, her hair, which had blown
against his face and around his neck, were the Devil's
implements; her form, which he had clasped in his
arms, was the Devil's subtlest hiding-place. She had
brought sin into the world. She had been the curse of
man ever since. She had tempted St. Anthony. She
had ruined many a saint, sent many a soul to purgatory,
many a soul to hell. Perhaps she was trying to send
his soul to hell now—now while he was alone with her
and under her influence. It was this same woman who
had broken into the peace of his life two weeks before,
for he had instantly recognized the voice as the one
that he had heard in the garden and that had been the
cause of his severe penance. Amid all his scourgings,
fasts, and prayers that voice had never left him. It
made him ache to think of what penance he must now

do again on her account; and with a sudden impulse
he walked across the room, and, standing before her
with arms folded across his breast, said in a voice of
the simplest sorrow:

"Why have you crossed my path-way, thus to tempt
me?"

She looked at him with eyes that were calm but full
of natural surprise.

"I do not understand how I have tempted you."

"You tempt me to believe that woman is not the
devil she is."   ,

She was silent with confusion. The whole train of
his thought was unknown to her. It was difficult, be-
wildering. A trivial answer was out of the question,
for he hung upon her expected reply with a look of
pitiable eagerness. She took refuge in the didactic.

"I have nothing to say about the nature of woman.
It is vague, contradictory; it is anything, everything.
But I *can* speak to you of the lives of women; that is a
definite subject. Some women may be what you call
devils. But some are not. I thought that you recognized the existence of saintly women within the memories and the present pale of your church."

"True. It is the women of the world who are the
devils."

"You know so well the women of the world?"

"I have been taught. I have been taught that if
Satan were to appear to me on my right hand and a
beautiful woman of the world on my left, I should flee
to Satan from the arms of my greater enemy. You
tempt me to believe that this is not true—to believe
that the fathers have lied to me. You tempt me to believe that Satan would not dare to appear in your pres-

ence. Is it because you are yourself a devil that you tempt me thus?"

"Should you ask me? I am a woman of the world. I live in a city of more than a million souls—in the company of thousands of these women-devils. I see hundreds of them daily. I may be one myself. If you think I am a devil, you ought not to ask me to tell you the truth. You should not listen to me or believe me."

She felt the cruelty of this. It was like replying logically to a child who had earnestly asked to be told something that might wreck its faith and happiness.

The storm was passing. In a few minutes this strange interview would end: he back to his cell again; she back to the world. Already it had its deep influence over them both. She, more than he, felt its almost tragical gravity, and was touched by its pathos. These two young human souls, true and pure, crossing each other's path-way in life thus strangely, now looked into each other's eyes, as two travellers from opposite sides of the world meet and salute and pass in the midst of the desert.

"I shall believe whatever you tell me," he said, with tremulous eagerness.

The occasion lifted her ever-serious nature to the extraordinary; and trying to cast the truth that she wished to teach into the mould which would be most familiar to him, she replied:

"Do you know who are most like you monks in consecration of life? It is the women—the good women of the world. What are your great vows? Are they not poverty, labor, self-denial, chastity, prayer? Well, there is not one of these but is kept in the hearts of good women. Only, you monks keep your vows for

your own sakes, while women keep them as well for the
sakes of others. For the sake of others they live and
die poor. Sometimes they even starve. You never do
that. They work for others as you have never worked;
they pray for others as you have never prayed. In
sickness and weariness, day and night, they deny themselves and sacrifice themselves for others as you have
never done—never can do. You keep yourselves pure.
They keep themselves pure and make others pure. If
you are the best examples of personal holiness that
may be found in the world apart from temptation, they
are the higher types of it maintained amid temptations
that never cease. You are content to pray for the
world, they also work for it. If you wish to see, in the
most nearly perfect form that is ever attained in this
world, love and sympathy and forgiveness; if you wish
to find vigils and patience and charity—go to the good
women of the world. They are all through the world,
of which you know nothing — in homes, and schools,
and hospitals; with the old, the suffering, the dying.
Sometimes they are clinging to the thankless, the dissolute, the cruel; sometimes they are ministering to the
weary, the heart-broken, the deserted. No, no! Some
women may be what you call them, devils—"

  She blushed all at once with recollection of her earnestness. It was the almost elemental simplicity of
her listener that had betrayed her into it. Meantime,
as she had spoken, his quickly changing mood had re-
gained its first pitch. She seemed to rise higher—to be
arraigning him and his ideals of duty. In his own sight
he seemed to grow smaller, shrink up, become despicable;
and when she suddenly ceased speaking, he lifted his
eyes to her, alas! too plainly now betraying his heart.

" And you are one of these good women ?"

" I have nothing to say of myself; I spoke of others.
I may be a devil."

For an instant through the scattering clouds the sunlight had fallen in through the window, lighting up her
head as with a halo.   It fell upon the cowl also, which
lay on the floor like a luminous heap.   She went to it,
and, lifting it, said to him :

" Will you leave me now?   They must pass here soon
looking for me.   I shall see them from the window.   I
do not know what should have happened to me but for
your kindness.   And I can only thank you very grate-
fully."

He took the hand that she gave him in both of his,
and held it closely a while as his eyes rested long and
intently upon her face.   Then, quickly muffling up his
own in the folds of his cowl, he turned away and left
the room.   She watched him disappear behind the embankment below and then reappear on the opposite
side, striding rapidly towards the abbey.

IV.

All that night the two aged monks whose cells were
one on each side of Father Palemon's heard him tossing
in his sleep.   At the open confessional next morning he
did not accuse himself.   The events of the day before
were known to none.   There were in that room but
two who could have testified against him.   One was
Father Palemon himself; the other was a small dark-
red spot on the white bosom of his cowl, just by his
heart.   It was a blood-stain from the wounded head

that had lain on his breast. Through the dread examination and the confessions Father Palemon sat motionless, his face shadowed by his hood, his arms crossed over his bosom, hiding this scarlet stain. What nameless foreboding had blanched his cheek when he first beheld it? It seemed to be a dead weight over his heart, as those earth-stains on the hem had begun to clog his feet.

That day he went the round of his familiar duties faultlessly but absently. Without heeding his own voice, he sang the difficult ancient offices of the Church in a full volume of tone, that was heard above the rich unison of the unerring choir. When, at twilight, he lay down on his hard, narrow bed, with the leathern cincture about his gaunt waist, he seemed girt for some lonely spiritual conflict of the midnight hours. Once, in the sad tumult of his dreams, his out-stretched arms struck sharply against some object and he awoke; it was the crucifix that hung against the bare wall at his head.

He sat up. The bell of the monastery tolled twelve. A new day was beginning. A new day for him? In two hours he would set his feet, as evermore, in the small circle of ancient monastic exactions. Already the westering moon poured its light through the long windows of the abbey and flooded his cell. He arose softly and walked to the open casement, looking out upon the southern summer midnight. Beneath the window lay the garden of flowers. Countless white roses, as though censers swung by unseen hands, waved up to him their sweet incense. Some dreaming bird awoke its happy mate with a note prophetic of the coming dawn. From the bosom of the stream below, white trailing shapes rose ethereal through

the moonlit air, and floated down the valley as if jour-
neying outward to some mysterious bourn. On the dim
horizon stood the domes of the forest trees, marking the
limits of the valley—the boundary of his life. He pressed his hot head against the cold casement and groaned
aloud, seeming to himself, in his tumultuous state, the
only thing that did not belong to the calm and holy
beauty of the scene. Disturbed by the sound, an old
monk sleeping a few feet distant turned in his cell and
prayed aloud :

*"Seigneur! Seigneur! Oubliez la faiblesse de ma jeunesse!
Vive Jésus! Vive sa Croix!"*

The prayer smote him like a warning. Conscience
was still torturing this old man—torturing him even
in his dreams on account of the sinful fevers that
had burned up within him half a century ago. On
the very verge of the grave he was uplifting his hands
to implore forgiveness for the errors of his youth.
Ah! and those other graves in the quiet cemetery
garth below—the white-cowled dust of his brethren,
mouldering till the resurrection morn. They, too, had
been sorely tempted — had struggled and prevailed,
and now reigned as saints in heaven, whence they
looked sorrowfully and reproachfully down upon him,
and upon their sinful heaps of mortal dust, which had
so foiled the immortal spirit.

Miserably, piteously, he wrestled with himself. Even
conscience was divided in twain and fought madly on
both sides. His whole training had left him obedient
to ideas of duty. To be told what to do always had
been for him to do it. But hitherto his teachers had
been the fathers. Lately two others had appeared—a
man and a woman of the world, who had spoken of life

and of duty as he had never thought of them. The pale, dark hunchback, whom he had often seen haunting the monastery grounds and hovering around him at his work, had unconsciously drawn aside for him the curtains of the world and a man's nobler part in it. The woman, whom he had addressed as a devil, had come in his eyes to be an angel. Both had made him blush for his barren life, his inactivity. Both had shown him which way duty lay.

Duty? Ah! it was not duty. It was the woman, the woman! The old tempter! It was the sinful passion of love that he was responding to; it was the recollection of that sweet face against which his heart had beat—of the helpless form that he had borne in his arms. Duty or love, he could not separate them. The great world, on the boundaries of which he wished to set his feet, was a dark, formless, unimaginable thing, and only the light from the woman's face streamed across to him and beckoned him on. It was she who made his priestly life wretched—made even the wearing of his cowl an act of hypocrisy that was the last insult to Heaven. Better anything than this. Better the renunciation of his sacred calling, though it should bring him the loss of earthly peace and eternal pardon.

The clock struck half-past one. He turned back to his cell. The ghastly beams of the setting moon suffused it with the pallor of a death-scene. God in heaven! The death-scene was there—the crucifixion! The sight pierced him afresh with the sharpest sorrow, and taking the crucifix down, he fell upon his knees and covered it with his kisses and his tears. There was the wound in the side, there were the drops of blood and the thorns on the brow, and the divine face still serene and victorious in the last agony of self-renunciation. Self-renunciation!

"Lord, is it true that I cannot live to Thee alone? And Thou didst sacrifice Thyself to the utmost for me! Consider me, how I am made! Have mercy, have mercy! If I sin, be Thou my witness that I do not know it!—Thou, too, didst love her well enough to die for her!"

In that hour, when he touched the highest point that nature ever enabled him to attain, Father Palemon, looking into his conscience and into the divine face, took his final resolution. He was still kneeling in steadfast contemplation of the cross when the moon withdrew its last ray and over it there rushed a sudden chill and darkness. He was still immovable before it when, at the resounding clangor of the bell, all the spectral figures of his brethren started up from their couches like ghosts from their graves, and in a long, shadowy line wound noiselessly downward into the gloom of the chapel, to begin the service of matins and lauds.

V.

He did not return with them when at the close of day they wound upward again to their solemn sleep. He slipped unseen into the windings of a secret passage-way, and hastening to the reception-room of the abbey sent for the abbot.

It was a great bare room. A rough table and two plain chairs in the middle were the only furniture. Over the table there swung from the high ceiling a single low, lurid point of light, that failed to reach the shad-

ows of the recesses. The few poor pictures of saints
and martyrs on the walls were muffled in gloom. The
air was dank and noisome, and the silence was that of
a vault.

Standing half in light and half in darkness, Father
Palemon awaited the coming of his august superior. It
was an awful scene. His face grew whiter than his
cowl, and he trembled till he was ready to sink to the
floor. A few moments, and through the dim door-way
there softly glided in the figure of the aged abbot, like
a presence rather felt than seen. He advanced to the
little zone of light, the iron keys clanking at his girdle,
his delicate fingers interlaced across his breast, his gray
eyes filled with a look of mild surprise and displeasure.

"You have disturbed me in my rest and medita-
tions. The occasion must be extraordinary. Speak!
Be brief!"

"The occasion *is* extraordinary. I shall be brief.
Father Abbot, I made a great mistake in ever becoming a monk. Nature has not fitted me for such a life.
I do not any longer believe that it is my duty to live it.
I have disturbed your repose only to ask you to receive
the renunciation of my priestly vows and to take back
my cowl: I will never put it on again."

As he spoke he took off his cowl and laid it on the
table between them, showing that he wore beneath the
ordinary dress of a working-man.

Under the flickering spark the face of the abbot had
at first flushed with anger and then grown ashen with
vague, formless terror. He pushed the hood back from
his head and pressed his fingers together until the jew-
elled ring cut into the flesh.

"You are a priest of God, consecrated for life. Con-

sider the sin and folly of what you say. You have made
no mistake. It would be too late to correct it, if you
had."

"I shall do what I can to correct it as soon as possible. I shall leave the monastery to-night."

"To-night you confess what has led you to harbor
this suggestion of Satan. To-night I forgive you. To-
night you sleep once more at peace with the world and
your own soul. Begin! Tell me everything that has
happened—everything!"

"It were better untold. It could only pain—only
shock you."

"Ha! You say this to me, who stand to you in
God's stead?"

"Father Abbot, it is enough that Heaven should
know my recent struggles and my present purposes.
It does know them."

"And it has not smitten you? It is merciful."

"It is also just."

"Then do not deny the justice you receive. Did you
not give yourself up to my guidance as a sheep to a
shepherd? Am I not to watch near you in danger and
lead you back when astray? Do you not realize that I
may not make light of the souls committed to my
charge, as my own soul shall be called into judgment
at the last day? Am I to be pushed aside—made
naught of—at such a moment as this?"

Thus urged, Father Palemon told what had recently
befallen him, adding these words:

"Therefore I am going—going now. I cannot expect your approval: that pains me. But have I not a
claim upon your sympathy? You are an old man, Father Abbot. You are nearer heaven than this earth.

11

But you have been young; and I ask you, is there not
in the past of your own buried life the memory of some
one for whom you would have risked even the peace
and pardon of your own soul?"

The abbot threw up his hands with a gesture of sudden anguish, and turned away into the shadowy dis-
tances of the room.

When he emerged again, he came up close to Father
Palemon in the deepest agitation.

"I tell you this purpose of yours is a suggestion of
the Evil Spirit. Break it against the true rock of the
Church. You should have spoken sooner. Duty, hon-
or, gratitude, should have made you speak. Then I
could have made this burden lighter for you. But,
heavy as it is, it will pass. You suffer now, but it will
pass, and you will be at peace again—at perfect peace
again."

"Never! Never again at peace here! My place is
in the world. Conscience tells me that. Besides, have
I not told you, Father Abbot, that I love her, that I
think of her day and night? Then I am no priest.
There is nothing left for me but to go out into the
world."

"The world! What do you know of the world? If
I could sum up human life to you in an instant of time,
I might make you understand into what sorrow this ca-
price of restlessness and passion is hurrying you."

Sweetness had forsaken the countenance of the aged
shepherd. His tones rung hoarse and hollow, and
the muscles of his face twitched and quivered as he
went on:

"Reflect upon the tranquil life that you have spent
here, preparing your soul for immortality. All your

training has been for the solitude of the cloister. All
your enemies have been only the spiritual foes of your
own nature. You say that you are not fitted for this
life. Are you then prepared for a life in the world?
Foolish, foolish boy! You exchange the terrestrial solitude of heaven for the battle-field of hell. Its coarse,
foul atmosphere will stifle and contaminate you. It has
problems that you have not been taught to solve. It
has shocks that you would never withstand. I see you
in the world? Never, never! See you in the midst of
its din and sweat of weariness, its lying and dishonor?
You say that you love this woman. Heaven forgive
you this sin! You would follow her. Do you not know
that you may be deluded, trifled with, disappointed?
She may love another. Ah! you are a child—a simple
child!"

"Father Abbot, it is time that I were becoming a man."

But the abbot did not hear or pause, borne on now
by a torrent of ungovernable feelings:

"Your parents committed a great sin." He suddenly lifted the cross from his bosom to his lips, which
moved rapidly for an instant in silent prayer. "It has
never been counted against you here, as it will never
be laid to your charge in heaven. But the world will
count it against you. It will make you feel its jeers
and scorn. You have no father," again he bent over
and passionately kissed his cross, "you have no name.
You are an illegitimate child. There is no place for
you in the world—in the world that takes no note of
sin unless it is discovered. I warn you—I warn you
by all the years of my own experience, and by all the
sacred obligations of your holy order, against this fatal
step."

"Though it be fatal, I must and will take it."

"I implore you! God in heaven, dost thou punish me thus? See! I am an old man. I have but a few years to live. You are the only tie of human tenderness that binds me to my race. My heart is buried in yours. I have watched over you since you were brought here, a little child. I have nursed you through months of sickness. I have hastened the final assumption of your vows, that you might be safe within the fold. I have stayed my last days on earth with the hope that when I am dead, as I soon shall be, you would perpetuate my spirit among your brethren, and in time come to be a shepherd among them, as I have been. Do not take this solace from me. The Church needs you—most of all needs you in this age and in this country. I have reared you within it that you might be glorified at last among the saints and martyrs. No, no! You will not go away!"

"Father Abbot, what better can I do than heed the will of Heaven in my own conscience?"

"I implore you!"

"I must go."

"I warn you, I say."

"Oh, my father! You only make more terrible the anguish of this moment. Bless me, and let me go in peace."

"*Bless* you?" almost shrieked the abbot, starting back with horror, his features strangely drawn, his uplifted arms trembling, his whole body swaying. "*Bless* you? Do this, and I will hurl upon you the awful curse of the everlasting Church!"

As though stricken by the thunderbolt of his own imprecation, he fell into one of the chairs and buried his head in his arms upon the table. Father Palemon had staggered backward, as though the curse had struck him in the forehead. These final words he had never thought of—never foreseen. For a moment the silence of the great chamber was broken only by his own quick breathing and by the convulsive agitation of the abbot. Then with a rapid movement Father Palemon came forward, knelt, and kissed the hem of the abbot's cowl, and, turning away, went out.

Love—duty—the world; in those three words lie all the human, all the divine, tragedy.

VI.

Years soon pass away in the life of a Trappist priest.

For shade to shade will come too drowsily,
And drown the wakeful anguish of the soul.

Another June came quickly into the lonely valley of the Abbey of Gethsemane. Again the same sweet monastery bells in the purple twilights, and the same midnight masses. Monks again at work in the gardens, their cowls well tied up with hempen cords. Monks once more teaching the pious pupils in the school across the lane. The gorgeous summer came and passed beyond the southern horizon, like a mortal vision of beauty never to return. There were few changes to note. Only the abbot seemed to have grown much feebler. His hand trembled visibly now as he lifted the crosier, and he walked less than of yore among his brethren while they busied themselves with the duties of the waning autumn. But he was oftener seen pacing to and fro where the leaves fell sadly from the moaning choir of English elms.   Or at times he would take a little foot-path that led across the brown November fields, and, having gained a crest on the boundary of the valley, would stand looking far over the outward landscape into imaginary spaces, limitless and unexplored.

But Father Palemon, where was he?   Amid what splendors of the great metropolis was he bursting Joy's grape against his palate fine?   What of his dreams of love and duty, and a larger, more modern stature of manhood?

Late one chill, cloud-hung afternoon in November there came into the valley of Gethsemane the figure of a young man. He walked slowly along the road towards the abbey, with the air of one who is weary and forgetful of his surroundings.   His head dropped heavily forward on his breast, and his empty hands hung listlessly down.   At the iron gate of the porter's lodge entrance was refused him; the abbey was locked in repose for the night. Urging the importance of his seeing the abbot, he was admitted.   He erased a name from a card ` and on it wrote another, and waited for the interview.

Again the same great dark room, lighted by a flickering spark.   He did not stand half in light and half in shadow, but hid himself away in one of the darkest recesses.   In a few moments the abbot entered, holding the card in his hand and speaking with tremulous haste:

"'Father Palemon?'—who wrote this name, 'Father Palemon?'"

Out of the darkness came a low reply:

"I wrote it."

" I do not know you."

" I am Father Palemon."

The calm of a great sadness was in the abbot's voice, as he replied, musingly:

" There — *is* — no — Father Palemon: he died long ago."

"Oh, my father! Is this the way you receive me?"

He started forward and came into the light. Alas! No; it was not Father Palemon. His long hair was unkempt and matted over his forehead; his face pinched and old with suffering, and ashen gray except for the red spots on his cheeks. Deep shadows lay under his hollow eyes, which were bloodshot and restless and burning.

" I have come back to lead the life of a monk. Will you receive me?"

" Twice a monk, no monk. Receive you for what time? Until next June?"

" Until death."

" I have received you once already until death. How many times am I to receive you until death?"

" I beseech you do not contest in words with me. It is too much. I am ill. I am in trouble."

He suddenly checked his passionate utterance, speaking slowly and with painful self-control:

" I cannot endure now to tell you all that has befallen me since I went away. The new life that I had begun in the world has come to an end. Father Abbot, she is dead. I have just buried her and my child in one grave. Since then the one desire I have had has been to return to this place. God forgive me! I have no heart now for the duties I had undertaken. I had not measured my strength against this calamity. It has left

me powerless for good to any human creature. My
plans were wrecked when she died. My purposes have
gone to pieces. There is no desire in me but for peace
and solitude and prayer. All that I can do now is to
hide my poor, broken, ineffectual life here, until by
God's will, sooner or later, it is ended."

"You speak in the extremity of present suffering.
You are young. Nearly all your life lies yet before you.
In time Nature heals nearly all the wounds that she in-
flicts. In a few years this grief which now unmans you
—which you think incurable—will wear itself out. You
do not believe this. You think me cruel. But I speak
the truth. Then you may be happy again—happier than
you have ever been. Then the world will resume its hold
upon you. If the duties of a man's life have appealed
to your conscience, as I believe they have, they will
then appeal to it with greater power and draw you with
a greater sense of their obligations. Moreover, you may
love again—ah! Hush! Hear me through! You think
this is more unfeeling still. But I must speak, and speak
now. It is impossible to seclude you here against all
temptation. Some day you may see another woman's
face—hear another woman's voice. You may find your
priestly vows intolerable again. Men who once break
their holiest pledges for the sake of love will break them
again, if they love again. No, no! If you were unfit
for the life of a monk once, much more are you unfit
now. Now that you are in the world, better to remain
there."

"In Heaven's name, will you deny me? I tell you
that this is the only desire left to me. The world is as
dead to me as though it never existed, because my
heart is broken. You misunderstood me then. You

misunderstand me now.   Does experience count for
nothing in preparing a man for the cloister?"

"I did misunderstand you once; I thought that you
were fitted for the life of a monk. I understand you
now: I do not make the same mistake twice."

"This is the home of my childhood, and you turn me
away?"

"You went away yourself, in the name of conscience
and of your own passion."

"This is the house of God, and you close its doors
against me?"

"You burst them open of your own self-will."

Hitherto the abbot had spoken for duty, for his
church, for the inviolable sanctity of his order.   Against
these high claims the pent-up tenderness of his heart
had weighed as nothing. But now as the young man,
having fixed a long look upon his face, turned silently away towards the door, with out-stretched arms
he tottered after him, and cried out in broken tones:
"Stop! Stop, I pray you! You are ill. You are free
to remain here a guest. No one was ever refused shelter. Oh, my God! what have I done?"

Father Palemon had reeled and fallen fainting in the
door-way.

In this life, from earliest childhood, we are trained by
merciful degrees to brave its many sorrows. We begin
with those of infancy, which, Heaven knows, at the
time seem grievous enough to be borne. As we grow
older we somehow also grow stronger, until through the
discipline of many little sufferings we are enabled to
bear up under those final avalanches of disaster that
rush down upon us in maturer years. Even thus forti-

fied, there are some of us on whom these fall only to
overwhelm.

But Father Palemon. Unnaturally shielded by the
cloister up to that period of young manhood when feeling is deepest and fortitude least, he had suddenly appeared upon the world's stage only to enact one of the
greatest scenes in the human tragedy—that scene where-
in the perfect ecstasy of love by one swift, mortal transition becomes the perfect agony of loss. What wonder
if he had staggered blindly, and if, trailing the habili-
ments of his sorrow, he had sought to return to the only
place that was embalmed in his memory as a peaceful
haven for the shipwrecked? But even this quiet port
was denied him.

Into the awful death-chamber of the abbey they bore
him one midnight some weeks later. The tension of
physical powers during the days of his suspense and
suffering, followed by the shock of his rejection, had
touched those former well-nigh fatal ravages that had
prostrated him during the period of his austere novitiate.
He was dying. The delirium of his fever had passed
away, and with a clear, dark, sorrowful eye he watched
them prepare for the last agony.

On the bare floor of the death-chamber they sprinkled
consecrated ashes in the form of a cross. Over these
they scattered straw, and over the straw they drew a
coarse serge cloth. This was his death-bed—a sign
that in the last hour he was admitted once more to the
fellowship of his order. From the low couch on which
he lay he looked at it. Then he made a sign to the
abbot, in the mute language of the brotherhood. The
abbot repeated it to one of the attendant fathers, who

withdrew and soon returned, bringing a white cowl. Lifting aside the serge cloth, he spread the cowl over the blessed cinders and straw. Father Palemon's request had been that he might die upon his cowl, and on this they now stretched his poor emaciated body, his cold feet just touching the old earth-stains upon its hem. He lay for a little while quite still, with closed eyes. Then he turned them upon the abbot and the monks, who were kneeling in prayer around him, and said, in a voice of great and gentle dignity:

" My father—my brethren, have I your full forgiveness ?"

With sobs they bowed themselves around him. After this he received the crucifix, tenderly embracing it, and then lay still again, as if awaiting death. But finally he turned over on one side, and raising himself on one forearm, sought with the hand of the other among the folds of his cowl until he found a small blood-stain now faint upon its bosom. Then he lay down again, pressing his cheek against it ; and thus the second time a monk, but even in death a lover, he breathed out his spirit with a faint whisper—" Madeline !"

And as he lay on the floor, so now he lies in the dim cemetery garth outside, wrapped from head to foot in his cowl, with its stains on the hem and the bosom.

SISTER DOLOROSA.

Sister Dolorosa.

1.

WHEN Sister Dolorosa had reached the summit of a low hill on her way to the convent she turned and stood for a while looking backward. The landscape stretched away in a rude, unlovely expanse of gray fields, shaded in places by brown stubble, and in others lightened by pale, thin corn—the stunted reward of necessitous husbandry. This way and that ran wavering lines of low fences, some worm-eaten, others rotting beneath over-clambering wild rose and blackberry. About the horizon masses of dense and rugged woods burned with sombre fires as the westering sun smote them from top to underbrush. Forth from the edge of one a few long-horned cattle, with lowered heads, wound meekly homeward to the scant milking. The path they followed led towards the middle background of the picture, where the weather-stained and sagging roof of a farm-house rose above the tops of aged cedars. Some of the branches, broken by the sleet and snow of winters, trailed their burdens from the thinned and desolated crests —as sometimes the highest hopes of the mind, after being beaten down by the tempests of the world, droop around it as memories of once transcendent aspirations.

Where she stood in the dead autumn fields few sounds broke in upon the pervasive hush of the declining day.

Only a cricket, under the warm clod near by, shrilled
sturdily with cheerful forethought of drowsy hearth-
stones ; only a lamb, timid of separation from the fold,
called anxiously in the valley beyond the crest of the
opposite hill; only the summoning whistle of a quail
came sweet and clear from the depths of a neighboring
thicket.   Through all the air floated that spirit of vast
loneliness which at seasons seems to steal like a human
mood over the breast of the great earth and leave her
estranged from her transitory children.   At such an
hour the heart takes wing for home, if any home it have;
or when, if homeless, it feels the quick stir of that yearning for the evening fireside with its half-circle of trusted
faces young and old, and its bonds of love and marriage, those deepest, most enchanting realities to the
earthly imagination.   The very landscape, barren and
dead, but framing the simple picture of a home, spoke
to the beholder the everlasting poetry of the race.

But Sister Dolorosa, standing on the brow of the hill
whence the whole picture could be seen, yet saw nothing
of it.   Out of the western sky there streamed an indescribable splendor of many-hued light, and far into the
depths of this celestial splendor her steadfast eyes were
gazing.

She seemed caught up to some august height of holy
meditation.   Her motionless figure was so lightly poised
that her feet, just visible beneath the hem of her heavy
black dress, appeared all but rising from the dust of the
path-way ; her pure and gentle face was upturned, so
that the dark veil fell away from her neck and shoulders; her lips were slightly parted ; her breath came
and went so imperceptibly that her hands did not appear to rise and fall as they clasped the cross to her

bosom. Exquisite hands they were—most exquisite—
gleaming as white as lilies against the raven blackness
of her dress; and with startling fitness of posture, the
longest finger of the right hand pointed like a marble
index straight towards a richly embroidered symbol
over her left breast—the mournful symbol of a crimson
heart pierced by a crimson spear. Whether attracted
by the lily-white hands or by the red symbol, a butterfly, which had been flitting hither and thither in search
of the gay races of the summer gone, now began to
hover nearer, and finally lighted unseen upon the glowing spot. Then, as if disappointed not to find it the
bosom of some rose, or lacking hope and strength for
further quest—there it rested, slowly fanning with its
white wings the tortured emblem of the divine despair.

Lower sank the sun, deeper and more wide-spread the
splendor of the sky, more rapt and radiant the expression of her face. A painter of the angelic school, seeing her standing thus, might have named the scene the
transfiguration of angelic womanhood. What but heavenly images should she be gazing on ; or where was
she in spirit but flown out of the earthly autumn fields
and gone away to sainted vespers in the cloud-built
realm of her own fantasies ? Perhaps she was now entering yon vast cathedral of the skies, whose white
spires touched blue eternity ; or toiling devoutly up yon
gray mount of Calvary, with its blackened crucifix falling from the summit.

Standing thus towards the close of the day, Sister
Dolorosa had not yet passed out of that ideal time
which is the clear white dawn of life. She was still
within the dim, half-awakened region of womanhood,

12

whose changing mists are beautiful illusions, whose
shadows about the horizon are the mysteries of poetic
feeling, whose purpling east is the palette of the imagination, and whose upspringing skylark is blithe aspiration that has not yet felt the weight of the clod it soars
within.   Before her still was the full morning of reality
and the burden of the mid-day hours.

But if the history of any human soul could be perfectly known, who would wish to describe this passage
from the dawn of the ideal to the morning of the real—
this transition from life as it is imagined through hopes
and dreams to life as it is known through action and
submission ?   It is then that within the country of the
soul occur events too vast, melancholy, and irreversible
to be compared to anything less than the downfall of
splendid dynasties, or the decay of an august religion.
It is then that there leave us forever bright, aerial spirits of the fancy, separation from whom is like grief for
the death of the beloved.

The moment of this transition had come in the life
of Sister Dolorosa, and unconsciously she was taking
her last look at the gorgeous western clouds from the
hill-tops of her chaste life of dreams.

A flock of frightened doves sped hurtling low over
her head, and put an end to her reverie.   Pressing the rosary to her lips, she turned and walked on towards the
convent, not far away.   The little foot-path across the
fields was well trodden and familiar, running as it did
between the convent and the farm-house behind her
in which lived old Ezra and Martha Cross; and as she
followed its windings, her thoughts, as is likely to be
true of the thoughts of nuns, came home from the
clouds to the humblest concerns of the earth, and she

began to recall certain incidents of the visit from which she was returning.

The aged pair were well known to the Sisters. Their daughters had been educated at the convent; and, although these were married and scattered now, the tie then formed had since become more close through their age and loneliness. Of late word had come to the Mother Superior that old Martha was especially ailing, and Sister Dolorosa had several times been sent on visits of sympathy. For reasons better to be understood later on, these visits had had upon her the effect of an April shower on a thirsting rose. Her missions of mercy to the aged couple over, for a while the white taper of ideal consecration to the Church always burned in her bosom with clearer, steadier lustre, as though lit afresh from the Light eternal. But to-day she could not escape the conviction that these visits were becoming a source of disquietude; for the old couple, forgetting the restrictions which her vows put upon her very thoughts, had spoken of things which it was trying for her to hear — love-making, marriage, and children. In vain had she tried to turn away from the proffered share in such parental confidences. The old mother had even read aloud a letter from her eldest son, telling them of his approaching marriage and detailing the hope and despair of his wooing. With burning cheeks and downcast eyes Sister Dolorosa had listened till the close and then risen and quickly left the house.

The recollection of this returned to her now as she pursued her way along the foot-path which descended into the valley; and there came to her, she knew not whence or why, a piercing sense of her own separation from all but the divine love. The cold beauty of un-

fallen spirituality which had made her august as she
stood on the hill-top died away, and her face assumed a
tenderer, more appealing loveliness, as there crept over
it, like a shadow over snow, that shy melancholy under
which those women dwell who have renounced the great
drama of the heart.   She resolved to lay her trouble
before the Mother Superior to-night, and ask that some
other Sister be sent hereafter in her stead.   And yet
this resolution gave her no peace, but a throb of painful renunciation ; and since she was used to the most
scrupulous examination of her conscience, to detect the
least presence of evil, she grew so disturbed by this
state of her heart that she quite forgot the windings of
the path-way along the edge of a field of corn, and was
painfully startled when a wounded bird, lying on the
ground a few feet in front of her, flapped its wings in a
struggle to rise.   Love and sympathy were the strongest principles of her nature, and with a little outcry she
bent over and took it up ; but scarce had she done so,
when, with a final struggle, it died in her hand.   A single drop of blood oozed out and stood on its burnished
breast.

She studied it—delicate throat, silken wings, wounded bosom—in the helpless way of a woman, unwilling
to put it down and leave it, yet more unwilling to
take it away.   Many a time, perhaps, she had watched
this very one flying to and fro among its fellows in the
convent elms.   Strange that any one should be hunting
in these fields, and she looked quickly this way and
that.   Then, with a surprised movement of the hands
that caused her to drop the bird at her feet, Sister Dolorosa discovered, standing half hidden in the edge of
the pale-yellow corn a few yards ahead, wearing a hunt-

ing-dress, and leaning on the muzzle of his gun, a young man who was steadfastly regarding her. For an instant they stood looking each into the other's face, taken so unprepared as to lose all sense of convention. Their meeting was as unforeseen as another far overhead, where two white clouds, long shepherded aimlessly and from opposite directions across the boundless pastures by the unreasoning winds, touched and melted into one. Then Sister Dolorosa, the first to regain self-possession, gathered her black veil closely about her face, and advancing with an easy, rapid step, bowed low with downcast eyes as she passed him, and hurried on towards the convent.

She had not gone far before she resolved to say nothing about the gossip to which she had listened. Of late the Mother Superior had seemed worn with secret care and touched with solicitude regarding her. Would it be kind to make this greater by complaining like a weak child of a trivial annoyance? She took her conscience proudly to task for ever having been disturbed by anything so unworthy. And as for this meeting in the field, even to mention that would be to give it a certain significance, whereas it had none whatever. A stranger had merely crossed her path a moment and then gone his way. She would forget the occurrence herself as soon as she could recover from her physical agitation.

II.

The Convent of the Stricken Heart is situated in that region of Kentucky which early became the great field of Catholic immigration. It was established in the first years of the present century, when mild Dominicans, starving Trappists, and fiery Jesuits hastened into the green wildernesses of the West with the hope of turning them into religious vineyards. Then, accordingly, derived from such sources as the impassioned fervor of Italy, the cold, monotonous endurance of Flanders, and the dying sorrows of ecclesiastical France, there sprang up this new flower of faith, unlike any that ever bloomed in pious Christendom. From the meagrest beginning, the order has slowly grown rich and powerful, so that it now has branches in many States, as far as the shores of the Pacific Ocean.

The convent is situated in a retired region of country, remote from any village or rural highway. The very peace of the blue skies seems to descend upon it. Around the walls great elms stand like tranquil sentinels, or at a greater distance drop their shadows on the velvet verdure of the artificial lawns. Here, when the sun is hot, some white veiled novice may be seen pacing soft-footed and slow, while she fixes her sad eyes upon pictures drawn from the literature of the Dark Ages, or fights the first battle with her young heart, which would beguile her to heaven by more jocund path-ways. Drawn by the tranquillity of this retreat—its trees and flowers and dews—all singing-birds of the region come here to build and brood. No other sounds than their pure cadences disturb the echoless

air except the simple hymns around the altar, the vesper bell, the roll of the organ, the deep chords of the
piano, or the thrum of the harp. It may happen, indeed, that some one of the Sisters, climbing to the observatory to scan the horizon of her secluded world,
will catch the faint echoes of a young ploughman in a
distant field lustily singing of the honest passion in his
heart, or hear the shouts of happy harvesters as they
move across the yellow plains. The population scattered around the convent domain are largely of the
Catholic faith, and from all directions the country is
threaded by foot-paths that lead to the church as a
common shrine. It was along one of these that Sister
Dolorosa, as has been said, hastened homeward through
the falling twilight.

When she reached the convent, instead of seeking
the Mother Superior as heretofore with news from old
Martha, she stole into the shadowy church and knelt
for a long time in wordless prayer—wordless, because
no petition that she could frame appeared inborn and
quieting. An unaccountable remorse gnawed the heart
out of language. Her spirit seemed parched, her will
was deadened as by a blow. Trained to the most rig-
orous introspection, she entered within herself and pen-
etrated to the deepest recesses of her mind to ascertain
the cause. The bright flame of her conscience thus
employed was like the turning of a sunbeam into a
darkened chamber to reveal the presence of a floating
grain of dust. But nothing could be discovered. It
was the undiscovered that rebuked her as it often re-
bukes us all—the undiscovered evil that has not yet
linked itself to conscious transgression. At last she
rose with a sigh and, dejected, left the church.

Later, the Mother Superior, noiselessly entering her room, found her sitting at the open window, her hands crossed on the sill, her eyes turned outward into the darkness.

"Child, child," she said, hurriedly, "how uneasy you have made me! Why are you so late returning?"

"I went to the church when I came back, Mother," replied Sister Dolorosa, in a voice singularly low and composed. "I must have returned nearly an hour ago."

"But even then it was late."

"Yes, Mother; I stopped on the way back to look at the sunset. The clouds looked like cathedrals. And then old Martha kept me. You know it is difficult to get away from old Martha."

The Mother Superior laughed slightly, as though her anxiety had been removed. She was a woman of commanding presence, with a face full of dignity and sweetness, but furrowed by lines of difficult resignation.

"Yes; I know," she answered. "Old Martha's tongue is like a terrestrial globe; the whole world is mapped out on it, and a little movement of it will show you a continent. How is her rheumatism?"

"She said it was no worse," replied Sister Dolorosa, absently.

The Mother Superior laughed again. "Then it must be better. Rheumatism is always either better or worse."

"Yes, Mother."

This time the tone caught the Mother Superior's ear.

"You seem tired. Was the walk too long?"

"I enjoyed the walk, Mother. I do not feel tired."

They had been sitting on opposite sides of the room.

The Mother Superior now crossed, and, laying her hand softly on Sister Dolorosa's head, pressed it backward and looked fondly down into the upturned eyes.

"Something troubles you.   What has happened?"

There is a tone that goes straight to the hearts of women in trouble.   If there are tears hidden, they gather in the eyes.   If there is any confidence to give, it is given then.

A tremor, like that of a child with an unspent sob, passed across Sister Dolorosa's lips, but her eyes were tearless.

"Nothing has happened, Mother.   I do not know why, but I feel disturbed and unhappy."   This was the only confidence that she had to give.

The Mother Superior passed her hand slowly across the brow, white and smooth like satin.   Then she sat down, and as Sister Dolorosa slipped to the floor beside her she drew the young head to her lap and folded her aged hands upon it.   What passionate, barren loves haunt the hearts of women in convents!   Between these two there existed a tenderness more touching than the natural love of mother and child.

"You must not expect to know at all times," she said, with grave gentleness.   "To be troubled without any visible cause is one of the mysteries of our nature. As you grow older you will understand this better.   We are forced to live in conscious possession of all faculties, all feelings, whether or not there are outward events to match them.   Therefore you must expect to have anxiety within when your life is really at peace without; to have moments of despair when no failure threatens; to have your heart wrung with sympathy when no object of sorrow is nigh ; to be spent with the need of

loving when there is no earthly thing to receive your
love. This is part of woman's life, and of all women,
especially those who, like you, must live not to stifle the
tender, beautiful forces of nature, but to ennoble and
unite them into one divine passion. Do not think,
therefore, to escape these hours of heaviness and pain.
No saint ever walked this earth without them. Perhaps the lesson to be gained is this : that we may feel
things before they happen, so that if they do happen
we shall be disciplined to bear them."

The voice of the Mother Superior had become low
and meditative; and, though resting on the bowed
head, her eyes seemed fixed on events long past. After the silence of a few moments she continued in a
brighter tone :

"But, my child, I know the reason of *your* unhappiness. I have warned you that excessive ardor would
leave you overwrought and nervous; that you were being carried too far by your ideals. You live too much
in your sympathies and your imagination. Patience,
my little St. Theresa! No saint was ever made in a
day, and it has taken all the centuries of the Church to
produce its martyrs. Only think that your life is but
begun ; there will be time enough to accomplish everything. I have been watching, and I know. This is
why I send *you* to old Martha. I want you to have the
rest, the exercise, the air of the fields. Go again to-
morrow, and take her the ointment. I found it while
you were gone to-day. It has been in the Church for
centuries, and you know this bottle came from blessed
Loretto in Italy. It may do her some good. And,
for the next few days, less reading and study."

"Mother !" Sister Dolorosa spoke as though she had

not been listening. "What would become of me if I should ever—if any evil should ever befall me?"

The Mother Superior stretched her hands out over the head on her knees as some great, fierce, old, gray eagle, scarred and strong with the storms of life, might make a movement to shield its imperilled young. The tone in which Sister Dolorosa had spoken startled her as the discovered edge of a precipice. It was so quiet, so abrupt, so terrifying with its suggestion of an abyss. For a moment she prayed silently and intensely.

"Heaven mercifully shield you from harm!" she then said, in an awe-stricken whisper. "But timid lamb, what harm can come to you?"

Sister Dolorosa suddenly rose and stood before the Mother Superior.

"I mean," she said, with her eyes on the floor and her voice scarcely audible—"I mean—if I should ever fail, would you cast me out?"

"My child!—Sister!—Sister Dolorosa!—Cast you out!"

The Mother Superior started up and folded her arms about the slight, dark figure, which at once seemed to be standing aloof with infinite loneliness. For some time she sought to overcome this difficult, singular mood.

"And now, my daughter," she murmured at last, "go to sleep and forget these foolish fears. I am near you!" There seemed to be a fortress of sacred protection and defiance in these words; but the next instant her head was bowed, her upward-pointing finger raised in the air, and in a tone of humble self-correction she added: "Nay, not I; the Sleepless guards you! Good-night."

Sister Dolorosa lifted her head from the strong shoulder and turned her eyes, now luminous, upon the troubled face.

"Forgive me, Mother!" she said, in a voice of scornful resolution. "Never—never again will I disturb you with such weakness as I have shown to-night. I *know* that no evil can befall me! Forgive me, Mother. Good-night."

While she sleeps learn her history. Pauline Cambron was descended from one of those sixty Catholic families of Maryland that formed a league in 1785 for the purpose of emigrating to Kentucky without the rending of social ties or separation from the rites of their ancestral faith. Since then the Kentucky branch of the Cambrons has always maintained friendly relations with the Maryland branch, which is now represented by one of the wealthy and cultivated families of Baltimore. On one side the descent is French; and, as far back as this can be traced, there runs a tradition that some of the most beautiful of its women became barefoot Carmelite nuns in the various monasteries of France or on some storm-swept island of the Mediterranean Sea.

The first of the Kentucky Cambrons settled in that part of the State in which nearly a hundred years later lived the last generation of them—the parents of Pauline. Of these she was the only child, so that upon her marriage depended the perpetuation of the Kentucky family. It gives to the Protestant mind a startling insight into the possibilities of a woman's life and destiny in Kentucky to learn the nature of the literature by which her sensitive and imaginative character was from the first impressed. This literature covers a field wholly unknown to the ordinary student of Kentucky history. It is not to be found in well-known works, but in the letters, reminiscences, and lives of foreign priests, and in the kindling and heroic accounts of the establishment of Catholic missions. It abounds in such stories as those of a black friar fatally thrown from a wild horse in the pathless wilderness; of a gray friar torn to pieces by a saw-mill; of a starving white friar stretched out to die under the green canopy of an oak ; of priests swimming half-frozen rivers with the sacred vestments in their teeth; of priests hewing logs for a hut in which to celebrate the mass; of priests crossing and recrossing the Atlantic and traversing Italy and Belgium and France for money and pictures and books; of devoted women laying the foundation of powerful convents in half-ruined log-cabins, shivering on beds of straw sprinkled on the ground, driven by poverty to search in the wild woods for dyes with which to give to their motley worldly apparel the hue of the cloister, and dying at last, to be laid away in pitiless burial without coffin or shroud.

Such incidents were to her the more impressive since happening in part in the region where lay the Cambron estate ; and while very young she was herself repeatedly taken to visit the scenes of early religious tragedies. Often, too, around the fireside there was proud reference to the convent life of old France and to the saintly zeal of the Carmelites ; and once she went with her parents to Baltimore and witnessed the taking of the veil by a cousin of hers—a scene that afterwards burned before her conscience as a lamp before a shrine.

Is it strange if under such influences, living in a country place with few associates, reading in her father's

library books that were to be had on the legends of the
monastic orders and the lives of the saints—is it strange
if to the young Pauline Cambron this world before long
seemed little else than the battle-field of the Church,
the ideal man in it a monk, the ideal woman a nun, the
human heart a solemn sacrifice to Heaven, and human
life a vast, sad pilgrimage to the shrine eternal?

Among the places which had always appealed to her
imagination as one of the heroic sites of Kentucky history was the Convent of the Stricken Heart, not far
away. Whenever she came hither she seemed to be
treading on sacred ground. Happening to visit it one
summer day before her education was completed, she
asked to be sent hither for the years that remained.
When these were past, here, with the difficult consent
of her parents, who saw thus perish the last hope of the
perpetuation of the family, she took the white veil.
Here at last she hid herself beneath the black. Her
whole character at this stage of its unfolding may be
understood from the name she assumed—Sister Dolorosa. With this name she wished not merely to extin-
guish her worldly personality, but to clothe herself with
a life-long expression of her sympathy with the sorrows
of the world. By this act she believed that she would
attain a change of nature so complete that the black
veil of Sister Dolorosa would cover as in a funeral urn
the ashes which had once been the heart of Pauline
Cambron. And thus her conventual life began.

But for those beings to whom the span on the sum-
mer-evening cloud is as nothing compared with that
fond arch of beauty which it is a necessity of their nature to hang as a bow of promise above every beloved
hope—for such dreamers the sadness of life lies in the

dissipation of mystery and the disillusion of truth. When she had been a member of the order long enough to see things as they were, Sister Dolorosa found herself living in a large, plain, comfortable brick convent, situated in a retired and homely region of Southern Kentucky. Around her were plain nuns with the invincible contrariety of feminine temperament. Before her were plain duties. Built up around her were plain restrictions. She had rushed with out-stretched arms towards poetic mysteries, and clasped prosaic reality.

As soon as the lambent flame of her spirit had burned over this new life, as a fire before a strong wind rushes across a plain, she one day surveyed it with that sense of reality which sometimes visits the imaginative with such appalling vividness. Was it upon this dreary waste that her soul was to play out its drama of ideal womanhood?

She answered the question in the only way possible to such a nature as hers. She divided her life in twain. Half, with perfect loyalty, she gave out to duty; the other, with equal loyalty, she stifled within. But perhaps this is no uncommon lot — this unmating of the forces of the mind, as though one of two singing-birds should be released to fly forth under the sky, while the other—the nobler singer—is kept voiceless in a darkened chamber.

But the Sisters of the Stricken Heart are not cloistered nuns. Their chief vow is to go forth into the world to teach. Scarcely had Sister Dolorosa been intrusted with work of this kind before she conceived an aspiration to become a great teacher of history or literature, and obtained permission to spend extra hours in the convent library on a wider range of sacred reading.

Here began a second era in her life. Books became
the avenues along which she escaped from her present
into an illimitable world. Her imagination, beginning
to pine, now took wing and soared back to the remote,
the splendid, the imperial, the august. Her sympathies,
finding nothing around her to fix upon, were borne afar
like winged seed and rooted on the colossal ruins of the
centuries. Her passion for beauty fed on holy art. She
lived at the full flood of life again.

If in time revulsion came, she would live a shy, exquisite, hidden life of poetry in which she herself played
the historic roles. Now she would become a powerful
abbess of old, ruling over a hundred nuns in an impreg-
nable cloister. To the gates, stretched on a litter,
wounded to death, they bore a young knight of the
Cross. She had the gates opened. She went forth
and bent over him; heard his dying message; at his
request drew the plighted ring from his finger to send
to another land. How beautiful he was! How many
masses—how many, many masses—had she not ordered
for the peace of his soul! Now she was St. Agatha,
tortured by the proconsul; now she lay faint and cold
in an underground cell, and was visited by Thomas à
Kempis, who read to her long passages from the *Imitation*. Or she would tire of the past, and making
herself an actor in her own future, in a brief hour live
out the fancied drama of all her crowded years.

But whatever part she took in this dream existence
and beautiful passion-play of the soul, nothing attracted her but the perfect. For the commonplace she felt
a guileless scorn.

Thus for some time these unmated lives went on—
the fixed outward life of duty, and the ever-wandering

inner life of love. In mid-winter, walking across the
shining fields, you have come to some little frost-locked
stream. How mute and motionless! You set foot
upon it, the ice is broken, and beneath is musical running water. Thus under the chaste, rigid numbness of
convent existence the heart of Sister Dolorosa murmured unheard and hurried away unseen to plains
made warm and green by her imagination. But the old
may survive upon memories; the young cannot thrive
upon hope. Love, long reaching outward in vain, returns to the heart as self-pity. Sympathies, if not supported by close realities, fall in upon themselves like
the walls of a ruined house. At last, therefore, even
the hidden life of Sister Dolorosa grew weary of the
future and the past, and came home to the present.

The ardor of her studies and the rigor of her duties
combined—but more than either that wearing away of
the body by a restless mind—had begun to affect her
health. Both were relaxed, and she was required to
spend as much time as possible in the garden of the
convent. It was like lifting a child that has become
worn out with artificial playthings to an open window
to see the flowers. With inexpressible relief she turned
from mediæval books to living nature; and her beautiful
imagination, that last of all faculties to fail a human
being in an unhappy lot, now began to bind nature to
her with fellowships which quieted the need of human
association. She had long been used to feign corres-
pondences with the fathers of the Church; she now established intimacies with dumb companions, and poured
out her heart to them in confidence.

The distant woods slowly clothing themselves in
green; the faint perfume of the wild rose, running riot
13

over some rotting fence; the majestical clouds about
the sunset; the moon dying in the spectral skies; the
silken rustling of doves' wings parting the soft foliage
of the sentinel elms; landscapes of frost on her win-
dow-pane; crumbs in winter for the sparrows on the
sill; violets under the leaves in the convent garden;
myrtle on the graves of the nuns—such objects as these
became the means by which her imprisoned life was released. On the sensuous beauty of the world she spent
the chaste ravishments of her virginal heart.   Her love
descended on all things as in the night the dew fills
and bends down the cups of the flowers.

A few of these confidences—written on slips of paper, and no sooner written than cast aside—are given
here.   They are addressed severally to a white violet,
an English sparrow, and a butterfly.

"I have taken the black veil, but thou wearest the
white, and thou dwellest in dim cloisters of green leaves
—in the domed and many-pillared little shrines that
line the dusty road-side, or seem more fitly built in the
depths of holy woodlands. How often have I drawn
near with timid steps, and, opening the doors of thy tiny
oratories, found thee bending at thy silent prayers—
bending so low that thy lips touched the earth, while
the slow wind rang thine Angelus! Wast thou blooming anywhere near when He came into the wood of the
thorn and the olive? Didst thou press thy cool face
against his bruised feet? Had I been thou, I would
have bloomed at the foot of the cross, and fed his failing lungs with my last breath. Time never destroys
thee, little Sister, or stains thy whiteness; and thou wilt
be bending at thy prayers among the green graves on
the twilight hill-side ages after I who lie below have

finished mine. Pray for me then, pray for thine erring sister, thou pure-souled violet!"

"How cold thou art! Shall I take thee in and warm thee on my bosom? Ah, no! For I know who thou art! Not a bird, but a little brown mendicant friar, begging barefoot in the snow. And thou livest in a cell under the convent eaves opposite my window. What ugly feet thou hast, little Father! And the thorns are on thy toes instead of about thy brow. That is a bad sign for a saint. I saw thee in a brawl the other day with a mendicant brother of thine order, and thou drovest him from roof to roof and from icy twig to twig, screaming and wrangling in a way to bring reproach upon the Church. Thou shouldst learn to defend a thesis more gently. Who is it that visits thy cell so often? A penitent to confess? And dost thou shrive her freely? I'd never confess to thee, thou cross little Father! Thou'dst have no mercy on me if I sinned, as sin I must since human I am. The good God is very good to thee that he keeps thee from sinning while he leaves me to do wrong. Ah, if it were but natural for me to be perfect! But that, little Father, is my idea of heaven. In heaven it will be natural for me to be perfect. I'll feed thee no longer than the winter lasts, for then thou'lt be a monk no longer, but a bird again. And canst thou tell me why? Because, when the winter is gone, thou'lt find a mate, and wert thou a monk thou'dst have none. For thou knowest perfectly well, little Father, that monks do not wed."

"No fitting emblem of my soul art thou, fragile Psyche, mute and perishable lover of the gorgeous earth. For my soul has no summer, and there is no earthly object of beauty that it may fly to and rest upon

as thou upon the beckoning buds. It is winter where I
live.   All things are cold and white, and my soul flies
only above fresh fields of flowerless snow. But no blast
can chill its wings, no mire bedraggle, or rude touch
fray.   I often wonder whether thou art mute, or the divine framework of winged melodies.   Thy very wings
are shaped like harps for the winds to play upon.   So,
too, my soul is silent never, though none can hear its
music.   Dost thou know that I am held in exile in this
world that I inhabit?   And dost thou know the flower
that I fly ever towards and cannot reach?   It is the white
flower of eternal perfection that blooms and waits for
the soul in Paradise.   Upon that flower I shall some
day rest my wings as thou foldest thine on a faultless
rose."

Harmonizing with this growing passion for the beauty
of the world—a passion that marked her approach to
riper womanhood—was the care she took of her person.
The coarse, flowing habit of the order gave no hint of
the curves and symmetry of the snow-white figure throb-
bing with eager life within; but it could not conceal an
air of refinement and movements of the most delicate
grace. There was likewise a suggestion of artistic study
in the arrangement of her veil, and the sacred symbol
on her bosom was embroidered with touches of elabo-
ration.

It was when she had grown weary of books, of the
imaginary drama of her life, and the loveliness of Nature, that Sister Dolorosa was sent by the Mother Superior on those visits of sympathy to old Martha Cross;
and it was during her return from one of them that
there befell her that adventure which she had deemed
too slight to mention.

III.

Her outward history was that night made known to
Gordon Helm by old Martha Cross. When Sister
Dolorosa passed him he followed her at a distance until she entered the convent gates. It caused him subtle
pain to think what harm might be lurking to insnare
her innocence. But subtler pain shot through him as
he turned away, leaving her housed within that inaccessible fold.

Who was she, and from what mission returning alone
at such an hour across those darkening fields? He had
just come to the edge of the corn and started to follow
up the path in quest of shelter for the night, when he
had caught sight of her on the near hill-top, outlined
with startling distinctness against the jasper sky and
bathed in a tremulous sea of lovely light. He had held
his breath as she advanced towards him. He had
watched the play of emotions in her face as she paused
a few yards off, and her surprise at the discovery of him
—the timid start; the rounding of the fawn-like eyes;
the vermeil tint overspreading the transparent purity of
her skin: her whole nature disturbed like a wind-
shaken anemone. All this he now remembered as he
returned along the foot-path. It brought him to the
door of the farm-house, where he arranged to pass the
night.

"You are a stranger in this part of the country," said
the old housewife an hour later.

When he came in she had excused herself from rising
from her chair by the chimney-side; but from that moment her eyes had followed him—those eyes of the old

which follow the forms of the young with such despair-
ing memories. By the chimney-side sat old Ezra, powerful, stupid, tired, silently smoking, and taking little notice of the others. Hardly a chill was in the air, but
for her sake a log blazed in the cavernous fireplace
and threw its flickering light over the guest who sat in
front.

He possessed unusual physical beauty—of the type
sometimes found in the men of those Kentucky families
that have descended with little admixture from English
stock; body and limbs less than athletic, but formed for
strength and symmetry; hair brown, thick, and slightly
curling over the forehead and above the ears; complexion blond, but mellowed into rich tints from sun
and open air; eyes of dark gray-blue, beneath brows
low and firm; a mustache golden-brown, thick, and
curling above lips red and sensuous; a neck round and
full, and bearing aloft a head well poised and moulded.
The irresistible effect of his appearance was an impression of simple joyousness in life. There seemed to
be stored up in him the warmth of the sunshine of his
land; the gentleness of its fields; the kindness of its
landscapes. And he was young—so young! To study
him was to see that he was ripe to throw himself heedless into tragedy; and that for him, not once but nightly, Endymion fell asleep to be kissed in his dreams by
encircling love.

"You are a stranger in this part of the country,"
said the old housewife, observing the elegance of his
hunting-dress and his manner of high breeding.

"Yes; I have never been in this part of Kentucky
before." He paused; but seeing that some account of
himself was silently waited for, and as though wishing

at once to despatch the subject, he added : " I am from the blue-grass region, about a hundred miles north-ward of here. A party of us were on our way farther south to hunt. On the train we fell in with a gentle-man who told us he thought there were a good many birds around here, and I was chosen to stop over to as-certain. We might like to try this neighborhood as we return, so I left my things at the station and struck out across the country this afternoon. I have heard birds in several directions, but had no dog. However, I shot a few doves in a cornfield."

" There are plenty of birds close around here, but most of them stay on the land that is owned by the Sisters, and they don't like to have it hunted over. All the land between here and the convent belongs to them except the little that's mine." This was said somewhat dryly by the old man, who knocked the ashes off his pipe without looking up.

" I am sorry to have trespassed ; but I was not ex-pecting to find a convent out in the country, although I believe I have heard that there is an abbey of Trap-pist monks somewhere down here."

" Yes ; the abbey is not far from here."

" It seems strange to me. I can hardly believe I am in Kentucky," he said, musingly, and a solemn look came over his face as his thoughts went back to the sunset scene.

The old housewife's keen eyes pierced to his secret mood.

" You ought to go there."

" Do they receive visitors at the convent ?" he asked, quickly.

" Certainly ; the Sisters are very glad to have stran-

gers visit the place. It's a pity you hadn't come sooner. One of the Sisters was here this afternoon, and you
might have spoken to her about it."

This intelligence threw him into silence, and again
her eyes fed upon his firelit face with inappeasable
hunger. She was one of those women, to be met with
the world over and in any station, who are remarkable
for a love of youth and the world, which age, sickness,
and isolation but deepen rather than subdue; and his
sudden presence at her fireside was more than grateful.
Not satisfied with what he had told, she led the talk
back to the blue-grass country, and got from him other
facts of his life, asking questions in regard to the features of that more fertile and beautiful land. In return
she sketched the history of her own region, and dwelt
upon its differences of soil, people, and religion—chiefly
the last. It was while she spoke of the Order of the
Stricken Heart that he asked a question he had long
reserved.

"Do you know the history of any of these Sisters?"

"I know the history of all of them who are from
Kentucky. I have known Sister Dolorosa since she
was a child."

"Sister Dolorosa!" The name pierced him like a
spear.

"The nun who was here to-day is called Sister Dolorosa. Her real name was Pauline Cambron."

The fire died away. The old man left the room on
some pretext and did not return. The story that followed was told with many details not given here—traced
up from parentage and childhood with that fine tracery
of the feminine mind which is like intricate embroidery,
and which leaves the finished story wrought out on the

mind like a complete design, with every point fastened to the sympathies.

As soon as she had finished he rose quickly from a desire to be alone. So well had the story been knit to his mind that he felt it an irritation, a binding pain. He was bidding her good-night when she caught his hand. Something in his mere temperament drew women towards him.

"Are you married?" she asked, looking into his eyes in the way with which those who are married sometimes exchange confidences.

He looked quickly away, and his face flushed a little fiercely.

"I am not married," he replied, withdrawing his hand.

She threw it from her with a gesture of mock, pleased impatience; and when he had left the room, she sat for a while over the ashes.

"If she were not a nun"—then she laughed and made her difficult way to her bed. But in the room above he sat down to think.

Was this, then, not romance, but life in his own State? Vaguely he had always known that farther south in Kentucky a different element of population had settled, and extended into the New World that mighty cord of ecclesiastical influence which of old had braided every European civilization into an iron tissue of faith. But this knowledge had never touched his imagination. In his own land there were no rural Catholic churches, much less convents, and even among the Catholic congregations of the neighboring towns he had not many acquaintances and fewer friends.

To descend as a gay bird of passage, therefore, upon

these secluded, sombre fields, and find himself in the
neighborhood of a powerful Order—to learn that a girl,
beautiful, accomplished, of wealth and high social posi-
tion, had of her own choice buried herself for life within
its bosom—gave him a startling insight into Kentucky
history as it was forming in his own time.   Moreover
—and this touched him especially—it gave him a deeper insight into the possibilities of woman's nature; for
a certain narrowness of view regarding the true mission
of woman in the world belonged to him as a result of
education.   In the conservative Kentucky society by
which he had been largely moulded the opinion prevailed
that woman fulfilled her destiny when she married well
and adorned a home.   All beauty, all accomplishments,
all virtues and graces, were but means for attaining this
end.

As for himself he came of a stock which throughout
the generations of Kentucky life, and back of these along
the English ancestry, had stood for the home; a race
of men with the fireside traits : sweet-tempered, patient,
and brave; well-formed and handsome; cherishing towards women a sense of chivalry; protecting them fiercely and tenderly; loving them romantically and quickly
for the sake of beauty; marrying early, and sometimes
at least holding towards their wives such faith, that
these had no more to fear from all other women in the
world than from all other men.

Descended from such a stock and moulded by the social ideals of his region, Helm naturally stood for the
home himself.   And yet there was a difference.   In a
sense he was a product of the new Kentucky.   His infancy had been rocked on the chasm of the Civil War;
his childhood spent amid its ruins; his youth ruled by

two contending spirits—discord and peace : and earliest manhood had come to him only in the morning of the new era. It was because the path of his life had thus run between light and shade that his nature was joyous and grave; only joy claimed him entirely as yet, while gravity asserted itself merely in the form of sympathy with anything that suffered, and a certain seriousness touching his own responsibility in life.

Reflecting on this responsibility while his manhood was yet forming, he felt the need of his becoming a better, broader type of man, matching the better, broader age. His father was about his model of a gentleman; but he should be false to the admitted progress of the times were he not an improvement on his father. And since his father had, as judged by the ideals of the old social order, been a blameless gentleman of the rural blue-grass kind, with farm, spacious homestead, slaves, leisure, and a library—to all of which, except the slaves, he would himself succeed upon his father's death—his dream of duty took the form of becoming a rural blue-grass gentleman of the newer type, reviving the best traditions of the past, but putting into his relations with his fellow-creatures an added sense of helpfulness, a broader sense of justice, and a certain energy of leadership in all things that made for a purer, higher human life. It will thus be seen that he took seriously not only himself, but the reputation of his State ; for he loved it, people and land, with broad, sensitive tenderness, and never sought or planned for his future apart from civil and social ends.

It was perhaps a characteristic of him as a product of the period that he had a mind for looking at his life somewhat abstractedly and with a certain thought-out

plan ; for this disposition of mind naturally belongs to
an era when society is trembling upon the brink of new
activities and forced to the discovery of new ideals. But
he cherished no religious passion, being committed by
inheritance to a mild, unquestioning, undeviating Prot-
estantism.   His religion was more in his conduct than
in his prayers, and he tried to live its precepts instead
of following them from afar.   Still, his make was far
from heroic. He had many faults ; but it is less impor-
tant to learn what these were than to know that, as far
as he was aware of their existence, he was ashamed of
them, and tried to overcome them.

Such, in brief, were Pauline Cambron and Gordon
Helm : coming from separate regions of Kentucky, descended from unlike pasts, moulded by different influences, striving towards ends in life far apart and hos-
tile.   And being thus, at last they slept that night.

When she had been left alone, and had begun to prepare herself for bed, across her mind passed and re-
passed certain words of the Mother Superior, stilling
her spirit like the waving of a wand of peace : " To be
troubled without any visible cause is one of the mysteries of our nature."   True, before she fell asleep there
rose all at once a singularly clear recollection of that
silent meeting in the fields ; but her prayers fell thick
and fast upon it like flakes of snow, until it was chaste-
ly buried from the eye of conscience ; and when she
slept, two tears, slowly loosened from her brain by some
repentant dream, could alone have told that there had
been trouble behind her peaceful eyes.

IV.

Sister Dolorosa was returning from her visit to old Martha on the following afternoon. When she awoke that morning she resolutely put away all thought of what had happened the evening before. She prayed oftener than usual that day. She went about all duties with unwonted fervor. When she set out in the afternoon, and reached the spot in the fields where the meeting had taken place, it was inevitable that a nature sensitive and secluded like hers should be visited by some question touching who he was and whither he had gone ; for it did not even occur to her that he would ever cross her path again. Soon she reached old Martha's ; and then—a crippled toad with a subtile tongue had squatted for an hour at the ear of Eve, and Eve, beguiled, had listened. And now she was again returning across the fields homeward. Homeward?

Early that afternoon Helm had walked across the country to the station, some two miles off, to change his dress, with the view of going to the convent the next day. As he came back, he followed the course which he had taken the day before, and this brought him into the same foot-path across the fields.

Thus they met the second time. When she saw him, had she been a bird, with one sudden bound she would have beaten the air down beneath her frightened wings and darted high over his head straight to the convent. But his step grew slower and his look expectant. When they were a few yards apart he stepped out of the path into the low, gray weeds of the field, and seemed ready

to pause; but she had instinctively drawn her veil close,
and was passing on. Then he spoke quickly.

"I beg your pardon, but are strangers allowed to visit
the convent?"

There was no mistaking the courtesy of the tone.
But she did not lift her face towards him. She merely
paused, though seeming to shrink away. He saw the
fingers of one hand lace themselves around the cross.
Then a moment later, in a voice very low and gentle,
she replied, "The Mother Superior is glad to receive
visitors at the convent," and, bowing, moved away.

He stood watching her with a quick flush of disappointment. Her voice, even more than her garb, had
at once waved off approach. In his mind he had
crossed the distance from himself to her so often that
he had forgotten the actual abyss of sacred separation.
Very thoughtfully he turned at last and took his way
along the foot-path.

As he was leaving the farm-house the next day to go
to the convent, Ezra joined him, merely saying that he
was going also. The old man had few thoughts; but
with that shrewd secretiveness which is sometimes found
in the dull mind he kept his counsels to himself. Their
walk was finished in silence, and soon the convent stood
before them.

Through a clear sky the wan light fell upon it as lifeless as though sent from a dead sun. The air hung
motionless. The birds were gone. Not a sound fell
upon the strained ear. Not a living thing relieved the
eye And yet within what tragedies and conflicts, what
wounds and thorns of womanhood! Here, then, she
lived and struggled and soared. An unearthly quietude
came over him as he walked up the long avenue of

elms, painfully jarred on by the noise of Ezra's shuffling feet among the dry leaves.   Joyous life had retired to infinite remoteness; and over him, like a preternatural chill in the faint sunlight, crept the horror of this death in life.   Strangely enough he felt at one and the same time a repugnance to his own nature of flesh and a triumphant delight in the possession of bodily health, liberty—the liberty of the world—and a mind unfettered by tradition.

A few feet from the entrance an aged nun stepped from behind a hedge-row of shrubbery and confronted them.

"Will you state your business?" she said, coldly, glancing at Helm and fixing her eyes on Ezra, who for reply merely nodded to Helm.

" I am a stranger in this part of the country, and heard that I would be allowed to visit the convent."

" Are you a Catholic?"

"No; I am a Protestant."

" Are you acquainted with any of the young ladies in the convent?"

" I am not."

She looked him through and through.   He met her scrutiny with frank unconsciousness.

"Will you come in?   I will take your name to the Mother Superior."

They followed her into a small reception-room, and sat for a long time waiting.   Then an inner door opened, and another aged nun, sweet-faced and gentle, entered and greeted them pleasantly, recognizing Ezra as an acquaintance.

" Another Sister will be sent to accompany us," she said, and sat down to wait, talking naturally the while

to the old man. Then the door opened again, and the
heart of Helm beat violently; there was no mistaking
the form, the grace. She crossed to the Sister, and
spoke in an undertone.

"Sister Generose is engaged. Mother sent me in her
place, Sister." Then she greeted Ezra and bowed to
Helm, lifting to him an instant, but without recognition,
her tremulous eyes. Her face had the whiteness of al-
abaster.

"We will go to the church first," said the Sister, addressing Helm, who placed himself beside her, the others
following.

When they entered the church he moved slowly
around the walls, trying to listen to his guide and to fix
his thoughts upon the pictures and the architecture.
Presently he became aware that Ezra had joined them,
and as soon as pretext offered he looked back. In a
pew near the door through which they had entered he
could just see the kneeling form and bowed head of
Sister Dolorosa. There she remained while they made
the circuit of the building, and not until they were quit-
ting it did she rise and again place herself by the side
of Ezra. Was it her last prayer before her temptation?

They walked across the grounds towards the old-fashioned flower-garden of the convent. The Sister opened
the little latticed gate, and the others passed in. The
temptation was to begin in the very spot where Love
had long been wandering amid dumb companions.

"Ezra!" called the aged Sister, pausing just inside
the gate and looking down at some recently dug bulbs,
"has Martha taken up her tender bulbs? The frost
will soon be falling." The old man sometimes helped
at the convent in garden work.

"Who is this young man?" she inquired carelessly a few moments later.

But Ezra was one of those persons who cherish a faint dislike of all present company. Moreover, he knew the good Sister's love of news. So he began to resist her with the more pleasure that he could at least evade her questions.

"I don't know," he replied, with a mysterious shake of the head.

"Come this way," she said beguilingly, turning aside into another walk, "and look at the chrysanthemums. How did you happen to meet him?"

When Sister Dolorosa and Helm found themselves walking slowly side by side down the garden-path—this being what he most had hoped for and she most had feared—there fell upon each a momentary silence of preparation. Speak she must; if only in speaking she might not err. Speak he could; if only in speaking he might draw from her more knowledge of her life, and in some becoming way cause her to perceive his interest in it.

Then she, as his guide, keeping her face turned towards the border of flowers, but sometimes lifting it shyly to his, began with great sweetness and a little hurriedly, as if fearing to pause:

"The garden is not pretty now. It is full of flowers, but only a few are blooming. These are daffodils. They bloomed in March, long ago. And here were spring beauties. They grow wild, and do not last long. The Mother Superior wished some cultivated in the garden, but they are better if let alone to grow wild. And here are violets, which come in April. And here

14

is Adam and Eve, and tulips. They are gay flowers, and
bloom together for company. You can see Adam and
Eve a long way off, and they look better at a distance.
These were the white lilies, but one of the Sisters died,
and we made a cross. That was in June. Jump-up-
Johnnies were planted in this bed, but they did not do
well. It has been a bad year. A storm blew the holly-
hocks down, and there were canker-worms in the roses.
That is the way with the flowers : they fail one year, and
they succeed the next. They would never fail if they
were let alone. It is pleasant to see them starting out
in the Spring to be perfect each in its own way. It is
pleasant to water them and to help. But some will be
perfect, and some will be imperfect, and no one can alter
that. They are like the children in the school; only
the flowers would all be perfect if they had their way,
and the children would all be wrong if they had theirs
—the poor, good children ! This is touch-me-not. Perhaps you have never heard of any such flower. And
there, next to it, is love-lies-bleeding. We have not
much of that; only this one little plant." And she
bent over and stroked it.

His whole heart melted under the white radiance of
her innocence. He had thought her older; now his
feeling took the form of the purest delight in some exquisite child nature. And therefore, feeling thus towards her, and seeing the poor, dead garden with only
common flowers, which nevertheless she separately
loved, oblivious of their commonness, he said with sudden warmth, holding her eyes with his :

"I wish you could see my mother's garden and the
flowers that bloom in it." And as he spoke there came
to him a vision of her as she might look in a certain

secluded corner of it, where ran a trellised walk ; over-clambering roses pale-golden, full-blown or budding, and bent with dew ; the May sun golden in the heavens ; far and near birds singing and soaring in ecstasy ; the air lulling the sense with perfume, quickening the blood with freshness ; and there, within that frame of roses, her head bare and shining, her funereal garb forever laid aside for one that matched the loveliest hue of living nature around, a flower at her throat, flowers in her hand, sadness gone from her face, there the pure and radiant incarnation of a too-happy world, this exquisite child-nature, advancing towards him with eyes of love.

Having formed this picture, he could not afterwards destroy it ; and as they resumed their walk he began very simply to describe his mother's garden, she listen-ing closely because of her love for flowers, which had become companions to her, and merely saying dreamily, half to herself and with guarded courtesy half to him, " It must be beautiful."

"The Mother Superior intends to make the garden larger next year, and to have fine flowers in it, Ezra. It has been a prosperous year in the school, and there will be money to spare. This row of lilacs is to be dug up, and the fence set back so as to take in the onion patch over there. When does he expect to go away?" The aged Sister had not made rapid progress.

" I haven't heard him say," replied the old man.

" Perhaps Martha has heard him say."

Ezra only struck the toe of his stout boot with his staff.

" The Mother Superior will want *you* to dig up the lilacs, Ezra. You can do it better than any one else."

The old man shook his head threateningly at the bushes. " I can settle them," he said.

" Better than any one else. Has Martha heard him say when he is going away ?"

" To-morrow," he replied, conceding something in return for the lilacs.

" These are the chrysanthemums.   They are white, but some are perfect and some are imperfect, you see. Those that are perfect are the ones to feel proud of, but the others are the ones to love."

" If all were perfect would you no longer love them ?" he said gently, thinking how perfect she was and how easy it would be to love her.

" If all were perfect, I could love all alike, because none would need to be loved more than others."

" And when the flowers in the garden are dead, what do you find to love then ?" he asked, laughing a little and trying to follow her mood.

" It would not be fair to forget them because they are dead.   But they are not dead ; they go away for a season, and it would not be fair to forget them because they have gone away."   This she said simply and seriously as though her conscience were dealing with human virtues and duties.

" And are you satisfied to love things that are not present ?" he asked, looking at her with sudden earnestness.

" The Mother Superior will wish him to take away a favorable impression of the convent," said the Sister. " Young ladies are sometimes sent to us from that region."   And now, having gotten from Ezra the information she desired and turned their steps towards the others, she looked at Helm with greater interest.

"Should you like to go upon the observatory?" she meekly asked, pointing to the top of the adjacent building. "From there you can see how far the convent lands extend. Besides, it is the only point that commands a view of the whole country."

The scene of the temptation was to be transferred to the pinnacle of the temple.

"It is not asking too much of you to climb so far for my pleasure?"

"It is our mission to climb," she replied, wearily; "and if our strength fails, we rest by the way."

Of herself she spoke literally; for when they came to the topmost story of the building, from which the observatory was reached by a short flight of steps, she sank into a seat placed near as a resting-place.

"Will you go above, Sister?" she said feebly. "I will wait here."

On the way up, also, the old man had been shaking his head with a stupid look of alarm and muttering his disapproval.

"There is a high railing, Ezra," she now said to him. "You could not fall." But he refused to go farther; he suffered from vertigo.

The young pair went up alone.

For miles in all directions the landscape lay shimmering in the autumnal sunlight—a poor, rough, homely land, with a few farm·houses of the plainest kind. Briefly she traced for him the boundary of the convent domain. And then he, thinking proudly of his own region, now lying heavy in varied autumnal ripeness and teeming with noble, gentle animal life; with rolling past-

ures as green as May under great trees of crimson and
gold; with flashing streams and placid sheets of water,
and great secluded homesteads—he, in turn, briefly described it; and she, loving the sensuous beauty of the
world, listened more dreamily, merely repeating over
and over, half to herself, and with more guarded courtesy
half to him, "It must be very beautiful."

But whether she suddenly felt that she had yielded
herself too far to the influence of his words and wished
to counteract this, or whether she was aroused to offset
his description by another of unlike interest, scarcely
had he finished when she pointed towards a long
stretch of woodland that lay like a mere wavering band
of brown upon the western horizon.

"It was through those woods," she said, her voice
trembling slightly, "that the procession of Trappists
marched behind the cross when they fled to this country from France. Beyond that range of hills is the
home of the Silent Brotherhood. In this direction,"
she continued, pointing southward, "is the creek which
used to be so deep in winter that the priests had to
swim it as they walked from one distant mission to another in the wilderness, holding above the waves the
crucifix and the sacrament. Under that tree down
there the Father who founded this convent built with
his own hands the cabin that was the first church, and
hewed out of logs the first altar. It was from those
trees that the first nuns got the dyes for their vestments.
On the floor of that cabin they sometimes slept in mid-
winter with no other covering than an armful of straw.
Those were heroic days."

If she had indeed felt some secret need to recover
herself by reciting the heroisms of local history, she

seemed to have succeeded. Her face kindled with emotion; and as he watched it he forgot even her creed in this revelation of her nature, which touched in him also something serious and exalted. But as she ceased he asked, with peculiar interest:

"Are there any Kentuckians among the Trappist Fathers?"

"No," she replied, after a momentary silence, and in a voice lowered to great sadness. "There was one a few years ago. His death was a great blow to the Fathers. They had hoped that he might some day become the head of the order in Kentucky. He was called Father Palemon."

For another moment nothing was said. They were standing side by side, looking towards that quarter of the horizon which she had pointed out as the site of the abbey. Then he spoke meditatively, as though his mind had gone back unawares to some idea that was very dear to him:

"No, this does not seem much like Kentucky; but, after all, every landscape is essentially the same to me if there are homes on it. Poor as this country is, still it is history; it is human life. Here are the eternal ties and relations. Here are the eternal needs and duties; everything that keeps the world young and the heart at peace. Here is the unchanging expression of our common destiny, as creatures who must share all things, and bear all things, and be bound together in life and death."

"Sister!" called up the nun waiting below, "is not the wind blowing? Will you not take cold?"   —

"The wind is not blowing, Sister, but I am coming."

They turned their faces outward upon the landscape

once more. Across it wound the little foot-path towards the farm-house in the distance. By a common
impulse their eyes rested upon the place of their first
meeting. He pointed to it.

"I shall never forget that spot," he said, impulsively.

"Nor I!"

Her words were not spoken. They were not uttered
within. As unexpectedly and silently as in the remotest
profound of the heavens at midnight some palest little
star is loosened from its orbit, shoots a brief span, and
disappears, this confession of hers traced its course
across the depths of her secret consciousness; but,
having made it to herself, she kept her eyes veiled, and
did not look at him again that day.

"I think you have now seen everything that could be
of any interest," the aged Sister said, doubtfully, when
they stood in the yard below.

"The place is very interesting to me," he answered,
looking around that he might discover some way of pro-
longing his visit.

"The graveyard, Sister. We might go there." The
barely audible words were Sister Dolorosa's. The scene
of the temptation was to be transferred for the third
time.

They walked some distance down a sloping hill-side,
and stepped softly within the sacred enclosure. A
graveyard of nuns! O Mother Earth, all-bearing, pas-
sion-hearted mother! Thou that sendest love one for
another into thy children, from the least to the greatest, as thou givest them life! Thou that livest by their
loves and their myriad plightings of troth and myriad
marriages! With what inconsolable sorrow must thou
receive back upon thy bosom the chaste dust of lorn

virgins, whose bosoms thou didst mould for a lover's arms and a babe's slumbers! As marble vestals of the ancient world, buried and lost, they lie, chiselled into a fixed attitude of prayer through the silent centuries.

The aspect and spirit of the place : the simple graves placed side by side like those of the nameless poor or of soldiers fallen in an unfriendly land ; the rude wood-en cross at the head of each, bearing the sacred name of her who was dust below; the once chirruping nests of birds here and there in the grass above the song-less lips ; the sad desolation of this unfinished end—all were the last thing needed to wring the heart of Helm with dumb pity and an ungovernable anguish of re-bellion. This, then, was to be her portion. His whole nature cried aloud against it. His ideas of human life, civilization, his age, his country, his State, rose up in protest. He did not heed the words of the Sister be-side him. His thoughts were with Sister Dolorosa, who followed with Ezra in a silence which she had but once broken since her last words to him. He could have caught her up and escaped back with her into the liberty of life, into the happiness of the world.

Unable to endure the place longer, he himself led the way out. At the gate the Sister fell behind with Ezra.

" He seems deeply impressed by his visit," she said, in an undertone, "and should bear with him a good ac-count of the convent. Note what he says, Ezra. The order wants friends in Kentucky, where it was born and has flourished ;" and looking at Sister Dolorosa and Helm, who were a short distance in front, she add-ed to herself:

" In her, more than in any other one of us, he will

behold the perfect spiritual type of the convent. By her he will be made to feel the power of the order to consecrate women, in America, in Kentucky, to the service of the everlasting Church."

Meantime, Sister Dolorosa and Helm walked side by side in a silence that neither could break. He was thinking of her as a woman of Kentucky—of his own generation—and trying to understand the motive that had led her to consecrate herself to such a life. His own ideal of duty was so different.

"I have never thought," he said, at length, in a voice lowered so as to reach her ear alone—"I have never thought that my life would not be full of happiness. I have never supposed I could help being happy if I did my duty."

She made no reply, and again they walked on in silence and drew near the convent building. There was so much that he wished to say, but scarcely one of his thoughts that he dared utter. At length he said, with irrepressible feeling :

"I wish your life did not seem to me so sad. I wish, when I go away to-morrow, that I could carry away, with my thoughts of this place, the thought that you are happy. As long as I remember it I wish I could remember you as being happy."

"You have no right to remember me at all," she said, quickly, speaking for the nun and betraying the woman.

"But I cannot help it," he said.

"Remember me, then, not as desiring to be happy, but as living to become blessed."

This she said, breaking the long silence which had followed upon his too eager exclamation. Her voice had become hushed into unison with her meek and pa-

tient words.   And then she paused, and, turning, waited
for the Sister to come up beside them.   Nor did she
even speak to him again, merely bowing without lifting
her eyes when, a little later, he thanked them and took
his leave.

In silence he and the old man returned to the farm-
house, for his thoughts were with her.   In the garden
she had seemed to him almost as a child, talking art-
lessly of her sympathies and ties with mute playthings;
then on the heights she had suddenly revealed herself
as the youthful transcendent devotee; and finally, amid
the scenes of death, she had appeared a woman too
quickly aged and too early touched with resignation.
He did not know that the effect of convent life is to
force certain faculties into maturity while others are repressed into unalterable unripeness; so that in such
instances as Sister Dolorosa's the whole nature resem-
bles some long, sloping mountain-side, with an upper
zone of ever-lingering snow for childhood, below this a
green vernal belt for maidenhood, and near the foot
fierce summer heats and summer storms for womanhood.
Gradually his plan of joining his friends the next day
wavered for reasons that he could hardly have named.

And Sister Dolorosa—what of her when the day was
over?   Standing that night in a whitewashed, cell-like
room, she took off the heavy black veil and hood which
shrouded her head from all human vision, and then un-
fastening at waist and throat the heavier black vestment of the order, allowed it to slip to the floor, reveal-
ing a white under-habit of the utmost simplicity of
design.   It was like the magical transformation of a
sorrow-shrouded woman back into the shape of her
own earliest maidenhood.

Her hair, of the palest gold, would, if unshorn, have
covered her figure in a soft, thick golden cloud; but
shorn, it lay about her neck and ears in large, lustrous
waves that left defined the contour of her beautiful
head, and gave to it the aerial charm that belongs to
the joyousness of youth. Her whole figure was relaxed
into a posture slightly drooping; her bare arms, white
as the necks of swans, hung in forgotten grace at her
sides; her eyes, large, dark, poetic, and spiritual, were
bent upon the floor, so that the lashes left their shadows
on her cheeks, while the delicate, overcircling brows
were arched high with melancholy. As the nun's funereal robes had slipped from her person had her mind
slipped back into the past, that she stood thus, all the
pure oval of her sensitive face stilled to an expression
of brooding pensiveness? On the urn which held the
ashes of her heart had some legend of happy shapes
summoned her fondly to return?—some garden? some
radiant playfellow of childhood summers, already dim
but never to grow dimmer?

Sighing deeply, she stepped across the dark circle on
the floor which was the boundary of her womanhood.
As she did so her eyes rested on a small table where
lay a rich veil of white that she had long been embroid-
ering for a shrine of the Virgin. Slowly, still absently,
she walked to it, and, taking it up, threw it over her
head, so that the soft fabric enveloped her head and
neck and fell in misty folds about her person; she
thinking the while only of the shrine; she looking down
on this side and on that, and wishing only to judge
how well this design and that design, patiently and
prayerfully wrought out, might adorn the image of the
Divine Mother in the church of the convent.

But happening to be standing quite close to the white wall of the room with the lamp behind her, when she raised her eyes she caught sight of her shadow, and with a low cry clasped her hands, and for an instant, breathless, surveyed it.   No mirrors are allowed in the convent.   Since entering it Sister Dolorosa had not seen a reflection of herself, except perhaps her shadow in the sun or her face in a troubled basin of water. Now, with one overwhelming flood of womanly self-consciousness, she bent forward, noting the outline of her uncovered head, of her bared neck and shoulders and arms.   Did this accidental adorning of herself in the veil of a bride, after she had laid aside the veil of the Church, typify her complete relapse of nature?   And was this the lonely marriage-moment of her betrayed heart?

For a moment, trembling, not before the image on the wall, but before that vivid mirror which memory and fancy set before every woman when no real mirror is nigh, she indulged her self-surrender to thoughts that covered her, on face and neck, with a rosy cloud more maidenly than the white mist of the veil.   Then, as if recalled by some lightning stroke of conscience, with fearful fingers she lifted off the veil, extinguished the lamp, and, groping her way on tiptoe to the bedside, stood beside it, afraid to lie down, afraid to pray, her eyes wide open in the darkness.

V.

Sleep gathers up the soft threads of passion that have been spun by us during the day, and weaves them into a tapestry of dreams on which we see the history of our own characters.   We awake to find our wills more inextricably caught in the tissues of their own past; we stir, and discover that we are the heirs to our dead selves of yesterday, with a larger inheritance of transmitted purpose.

When Gordon awoke the next morning among his first thoughts was the idea of going on to join his friends that day, and this thought now caused him unexpected depression. Had he been older, he might have accepted this unwillingness to go away as the best reason for leaving; but, young, and habitually self-indulgent towards his desires when they were not connected with vice, he did not trouble himself with any forecast of consequences.

"You ought not to go away to-day," the old housewife said to him in the morning, wishing to detain him through love of his company. "To-morrow will be Sunday, and you ought to go to vespers and hear Sister Dolorosa sing. There is not such another voice in any convent in Kentucky."

"I will stay," he replied, quickly; and the next afternoon he was seated in the rear of the convent church, surrounded by rural Catholic worshippers who had assembled from the neighborhood. The entire front of the nave on one side was filled with the black-veiled Sisters of the order; that on the other with the white-veiled novices—two far-journeying companies of consecrated souls who reminded him in the most solemn way how remote, how inaccessible, was that young pilgrim among them of whom for a long time now he had been solely thinking. With these two companies of sacrificial souls before him he understood her character in a new light.

He beheld her much as a brave, beautiful boy volun-

teer, who, suddenly waving a bright, last adieu to gay
companions in some gay-streeted town, from motives of
the loftiest heroism, takes his place in the rear of passing soldiery, marching to misguided death; who, from
the rear, glowing with too impetuous ardor, makes his
way from rank to rank ever towards the front; and
who, at last, bearing the heavy arms and wearing the
battle-stained uniform of a veteran, steps forward to the
van at the commander's side and sets his fresh, pure
face undaunted towards destruction. As he thought of
her thus, deeper forces stirred within his nature than
had ever been aroused by any other woman. In comparison every one that he had known became for the
moment commonplace, human life as he was used to it
gross and uninspiring, and his own ideal of duty a
dwarfish mixture of selfishness and luxurious triviality.
Impulsive in his recognition of nobleness of nature
wherever he perceived it, for this devotedness of purpose he began to feel the emotion which of all that ever
visit the human heart is at once the most humbling, the
most uplifting, and the most enthralling—the hero-wor-
ship of a strong man for a fragile woman.

The service began. As it went on he noticed here
and there among those near him such evidences of
restlessness as betray in a seated throng high-wrought
expectancy of some pleasure too long deferred. But at
last these were succeeded by a breathless hush, as,
from the concealed organ-loft above, a low, minor pre-
lude was heard, groping and striving nearer and nearer
towards the concealed motive, as a little wave creeps
farther and farther along a melancholy shore. Suddenly, beautiful and clear, more tender than love, more
sorrowful than death, there floated out upon the still

air of the church the cry of a woman's soul that has offended, and that, shrinking from every prayer of speech, pours forth its more intense, inarticulate, and suffering need through the diviner faculty of song.

At the sound every ear was strained to listen. Hitherto the wont had been to hear that voice bear aloft the common petition as calmly as the incense rose past the altar to the roof; but now it quivered over troubled depths of feeling, it rose freighted with the burden of self-accusal. Still higher and higher it rose, borne triumphantly upward by love and aspiration, until the powers of the singer's frame seemed spending themselves in one superhuman effort of the soul to make its prayer understood to the divine forgiveness. Then, all at once, at the highest note, as a bird soaring towards the sun has its wings broken by a shot from below, it too broke, faltered, and there was a silence. But only for a moment: another voice, poor and cold, promptly finished the song; the service ended; the people poured out of the church.

When Gordon came out there were a few groups standing near the door talking; others were already moving homeward across the grounds. Not far off he observed a lusty young countryman, with a frank, winning face, who appeared to be waiting, while he held a child that had laid its bright head against his tanned, athletic neck. Gordon approached him, and said with forced calmness:

"Do you know what was the matter in the church?"

"My wife has gone to see," he replied, warmly. "Wait; she'll be here in a minute. Here she is now."

The comely, Sunday-dressed young wife came up and took the child, who held out its arms, fondly smiling.

"She hadn't been well, and they didn't want her to sing to-day; but she begged to sing, and broke down." Saying this, the young mother kissed her child, and slipping one hand into the great brown hand of her husband, which closed upon it, turned away with them across the lawn homeward.

When Sister Dolorosa, who had passed a sleepless, prayerless night, stood in the organ-loft and looked across the church at the scene of the Passion, at the shrine of the Virgin, at the white throng of novices and the dark throng of the Sisters, the common prayer of whom was to be borne upward by her voice, there came upon her like a burying wave a consciousness of how changed she was since she had stood there last. Thus at the moment when Gordon, sitting below, reverently set her far above him, as one looks up to a statue whose feet are above the level of his head, she, thinking of what she had been and had now become, seemed to herself as though fallen from a white pedestal to the miry earth. But when, to a nature like hers, absolute loyalty to a sinless standard of character is the only law of happiness itself, every lapse into transgression is followed by an act of passionate self-chastisement and by a more passionate outburst of love for the wronged ideal; and therefore scarce had she begun to sing, and in music to lift up the prayer she had denied herself in words, before the powers of her body succumbed, as the strings of an instrument snap under too strenuous a touch of the musician.

Gordon walked out of the grounds beside the rustic young husband and wife, who plainly were lovers still.

"The Sister who sang has a beautiful voice," he said.

15

"None of them can sing like her," replied the wife.
"I love her better than any of the others."

"I tin sing!" cried the little girl, looking at Gordon,
resentfully, as though he had denied her that accom-
plishment.

"But you'll never sing in a convent, missy," cried
the father, snatching her from her mother. "You'll
sing for some man till he marries you as your mother
did me. I was going to join the Trappist monks, but
my wife said I was too good a sweetheart to spoil, and
she had made up her mind to have me herself," he
added, turning to Gordon with a laugh.

"I'd have been a Sister long ago if you hadn't
begged and begged me not," was the reply, with the
coquettish toss of a pretty head.

"I doin' be Tap monk," cried the little girl, looking
at Gordon still more assertively, but joining in the laugh
that followed with a scream of delight at the wisdom of
her decision.

Their paths here diverged, and Gordon walked slowly on alone, but not without turning to watch the retreating figures, his meeting with whom at such a moment formed an episode in the history of that passion
under the influence of which he was now rapidly passing. For as he had sat in the church his nature, which
was always generous in its responsiveness, had lent itself wholly to the solicitations of the service; and for a
time the stillness, the paintings portraying the divine
sorrow, the slow procession of nameless women, the ta-
pers, the incense, the hoary antiquity of the ceremonial,
had carried him into a little known region of his religious feeling. But from this he had been sharply recalled by the suggestion of a veiled personal tragedy

close at hand in that unfinished song. His mood again became one of vast pity for her; and issuing from the church with this feeling, there, near the very entrance, he had come upon a rustic picture of husband, wife, and child, with a sharpness of transition that had seemed the return of his spirit to its own world of flesh and blood. There to him was the poetry and the religion of life—the linked hands of lovers; the twining arms of childhood; health and joyousness; and a quiet walk over familiar fields in the evening air from peaceful church to peaceful home. And so, thinking of this as he walked on alone and thinking also of her, the two thoughts blended, and her image stood always before him in the path-way of his ideal future.

The history of the next several days may soon be told. He wrote to his friends, stating that there was no game in the neighborhood, and that he had given up the idea of joining them and would return home. He took the letter to the station, and waited for the train to pass southward, watching it rush away with a subtle pleasure at being left on the platform, as though the bridges were now burned behind him. Then he returned to the farm-house, where Ezra met him with that look of stupid alarm which was natural to him whenever his few thoughts were agitated by a new situation of affairs.

Word had come from the convent that he was wanted there to move a fence and make changes in the garden, and, proud of the charge, he wished to go; but certain autumnal work in his own orchard and garden claimed his time, and hence the trouble. But Gordon, who henceforth had no reason for tarrying with the old couple, threw himself eagerly upon this opportunity to

do so, and offered his aid in despatching the tasks.
So that thus a few days passed, during which he unconsciously made his way as far as any one had ever
done into the tortuous nature of the old man, who began to regard him with blind trustfulness.

But they were restless, serious days. One after another passed, and he heard nothing of Sister Dolorosa.
He asked himself whether she were ill, whether her
visits to old Martha had been made to cease ; and he
shrank from the thought of bearing away into his life
the haunting pain of such uncertainty. But some inner
change constrained him no longer to call her name. As
he sat with the old couple at night the housewife renewed her talks with him, speaking sometimes of the
convent and of Sister Dolorosa, the cessation of whose
visits plainly gave her secret concern ; but he listened
in silence, preferring the privacy of his own thoughts.
Sometimes, under feint of hunting, he would take his
gun in the afternoon and stroll out over the country;
but always the presence of the convent made itself felt
over the landscape, dominating it, solitary and impreg-
nable, like a fortress. It began to draw his eyes with
a species of fascination. He chafed against its asser-
tion of barriers, and could have wished that his own
will might be brought into conflict with it. It appeared
to watch him; to have an eye at every window; to
see in him a lurking danger. At other times, borne
to him across the darkening fields would come the
sweet vesper bell, and in imagination he would see
her entering the church amid the long procession
of novices and nuns, her hands folded across her
breast, her face full of the soft glories of the lights
that streamed in through the pictured windows. Over

the fancied details of her life more and more fondly he lingered.

And thus, although at first he had been interested in her wholly upon general grounds, believing her secretly unhappy, thus by thinking always of her, and watching for her, and walking often beside her in his dreams, with the folly of the young, with the romantic ardor of his race, and as part of the never-ending blind tragedy of the world, he came at last to feel for her, among women, that passionate pain of yearning to know which is to know the sadness of love.

Sleepless one night, he left the house after the old couple were asleep. The moon was shining, and unconsciously following the bent of his thoughts, he took the foot-path that led across the fields. He passed the spot where he had first met her, and absorbed in recollection of the scene, he walked on until before him the convent towered high in light and shadow. He had reached the entrance to the long avenue of elms. He traversed it, turned aside into the garden, and, following with many pauses around its borders, lived over again the day when she had led him through it. The mere sense of his greater physical nearness to her inthralled him. All her words came back: "These are daffodils. They bloomed in March, long ago. . . . And here are violets, which come in April." After awhile, leaving the garden, he walked across the lawn to the church and sat upon the steps, trying to look calmly at this whole episode in his life, and to summon resolution to bring it to an end. He dwelt particularly upon the hopelessness of his passion; he made himself believe that if he could but learn that she were not ill and suffering—if he could but see her once more, and be

very sure—he would go away, as every dictate of reason urged.

Across the lawn stood the convent building. There
caught his eye the faint glimmer of a light through a
half-opened window, and while he looked he saw two
of the nuns moving about within. Was some one dying?
Was this light the taper of the dead? He tried to
throw off a sudden weight of gloomy apprehension, and
resolutely got up and walked away; but his purpose
was formed not to leave until he had intelligence of her.

One afternoon, a few days days later, happening to
come to an elevated point of the landscape, he saw her
figure moving across the fields in the distance below
him. Between the convent and the farm-house, in one
of the fields, there is a circular, basin-like depression;
and it was here, hidden from distant observation, with
only the azure of the heavens above them, that their
meeting took place.

On the day when she had been his guide he had told
her that he was going away on the morrow, and as she
walked along now it might have been seen that she
thought herself safe from intrusion. Her eyes were
bent on the dust of the path-way. One hand was passing bead by bead upward along her rosary. Her veil
was pushed back, so that between its black border and
the glistening whiteness of her forehead there ran, like
a rippling band of gold, the exposed edges of her shining hair. In the other hand she bore a large cluster
of chrysanthemums, whose snow-white petals and green
leaves formed a strong contrast with the crimson symbol that they partly framed against her sable bosom.

He had come up close before the noise of his feet
in the stubble drew her attention. Then she turned

and saw him. But certain instincts of self-preservation act in women with lightning quickness. She did not recognize him, or give him time to recognize her. She merely turned again and walked onward at the same pace. But the chrysanthemums were trembling with the beating of her heart, and her eyes had in them that listening look with which one awaits the oncoming of danger from behind.

But he had stopped. His nature was simple and trustful, and he had expected to renew his acquaintanceship at the point where it had ceased. When, therefore, she thus reminded him, as indeed she must, that there was no acquaintanceship between them, and that she regarded herself as much alone as though he were nowhere in sight, his feelings were arrested as if frozen by her coldness. Still, it was for this chance that he had waited all these days. Another would not come; and whatever he wished to say to her must be said now. A sensitiveness wholly novel to his nature held him back, but a moment more and he was walking beside her.

"I hope I do not intrude so very far," he said, in a tone of apology, but also of wounded self-respect.

It was a difficult choice thus left to her. She could not say "Yes" without seeming unpardonably rude; she could not say "No" without seeming to invite his presence. She walked on for a moment, and then, pausing, turned towards him.

"Is there anything that you wished to ask me in regard to the convent?" This she said in the sweetest tone of apologetic courtesy, as though in having thought only of herself at first she had neglected some larger duty.

If he had feared that he would see traces of physical suffering on her face, he was mistaken. She had forgotten to draw her veil close, and the sunlight fell upon its loveliness. Never had she been to him half so beautiful. Whatever the expression her eyes had worn before he had come up, in them now rested only inscrutable calmness.   •

"There is one thing I have wished very much to know," he answered, slowly, his eyes resting on hers. "I was at the church of the convent last Sunday and heard you sing. They said you were not well. I have hoped every day to hear that you were better. I have not cared to go away until I knew this."

Scarcely had he begun when a flush dyed her face, her eyes fell, and she stood betrayed by the self-consciousness of what her own thoughts had that day been. One hand absently tore to pieces the blooms of the chrysanthemums, so that the petals fell down over her dark habit like snowflakes. But when he finished, she lifted her eyes again.

"I am well now, thank you," she said ; and the first smile that he had ever seen came forth from her soul to her face. But what a smile! It wrung his heart more than the sight of her tears could have done.

"Then I shall hope to hear you sing again to-morrow," he said, quickly, for she seemed on the point of moving away.

"I shall not sing to-morrow," she replied a little hurriedly, with averted face, and again she started on. But he walked beside her.

"In that case I have still to thank you for the pleasure I have had. I imagine that one would never do wrong if he could hear you sing whenever he is tempted," he said, looking sidewise at her with a quiet, tentative smile.

"It is not my voice," she replied more hurriedly. "It is the music of the service. Do not thank me. Thank God."

"I have heard the service before. It was your voice that touched me."

She drew her veil about her face and walked on in silence.

"But I have no wish to say anything against your religion," he continued, his voice deepening and trembling. "If it has such power over the natures of women, if it lifts them to such ideals of duty, if it develops in them such characters, that merely to look into their faces, to be near them, to hear their voices, is to make a man think of a better world, I do not know why I should say anything against it."

How often, without meaning it, our words are like a flight of arrows into another's heart. What he said but reminded her of her unfaithfulness. And therefore while she revolved how with perfect gentleness she might ask him to allow her to continue her way alone, she did what she could: she spoke reverently, though all but inaudibly, in behalf of her order.

"Our vows are perfect and divine. If they ever seem less, it is the fault of those of us who dishonor them."

The acute self-reproach in her tone at once changed his mood.

"On the other hand, I have also asked myself this question: Is it the creed that makes the natures of you women so beautiful, or it is the nature of woman that gives the beauty to the creed? It is not so with

any other idea that women espouse? with any other
cause that they undertake? Is it not so with anything
that they spend their hearts upon, toil for, and sacrifice
themselves for? Do I see any beauty in your vows except such as your life gives to them? I can believe it.
I can believe that if you had never taken those vows
your life would still be beautiful. I can believe that
you could change them for others and find yourself
more nearly the woman that you strive to be—that you
were meant to be!" He spoke in the subdued voice
with which one takes leave of some hope that brightens
while it disappears.

"I must ask you," she said, pausing—" I must ask
you to allow me to continue my walk alone;" and her
voice quivered.

He paused, too, and stood looking into her eyes in
silence with the thought that he should never see her
again. The color had died out of his face.

"I can never forgive your vows," he said, speaking
very slowly and making an effort to appear unmoved.
"I can never forgive your vows that they make it a sin
for me to speak to you. I can never forgive them that
they put between us a gulf that I cannot pass. Remember, I owe you a great deal. I owe you higher
ideas of a woman's nature and clearer resolutions regarding my own life. Your vows perhaps make it even
a sin that I should tell you this. But by what right?
By what right am I forbidden to say that I shall remember you always, and that I shall carry away with
me into my life—"

"Will you force me to turn back?" she asked in
greater agitation; and though he could not see her face,
he saw her tears fall upon her hands.

" No," he answered sadly; " I shall not force you to turn back. I know that I have intruded. But it seemed that I could not go away without seeing you again, to be quite sure that you were well. And when I saw you, it seemed impossible not to speak of other things. Of course this must seem strange to you—stranger, perhaps, than I may imagine, since we look at human relationships so differently. My life in this world can be of no interest to you. You cannot, therefore, understand why yours should have any interest for me. Still, I hope you can forgive me," he added abruptly, turning his face away as it flushed and his voice faltered.

She lifted her eyes quickly, although they were dim. " Do not ask me to forgive anything. There is nothing to be forgiven. It is I who must ask—only leave me !"

" Will you say good-bye to me?" And he held out his hand.

She drew back, but, overborne by emotion, he stepped forward, gently took her hand from the rosary, and held it in both his own.

" Good-bye ! But, despite the cruel barriers that they have raised between us, I shall always—"

She foresaw what was coming. His manner told her that. She had not withdrawn her hand. But at this point she dropped the flowers that were in her other hand, laid it on her breast so that the longest finger pointed towards the symbol of the transfixed heart, and looked quickly at him with indescribable warning and distress. Then he released her, and she turned back towards the convent.

" Mother," she said, with a frightened face, when she reached it, " I did not go to old Martha's. Some one was hunting in the fields, and I came back. Do not send me again, Mother, unless one of the Sisters goes with me." And with this half-truth on her lips and full remorse for it in her heart, she passed into that deepening imperfection of nature which for the most of us makes up the inner world of reality.

Gordon wrote to her that night. He had not foreseen his confession. It had been drawn from him under the influences of the moment; but since it was made, a sense of honor would not have allowed him to stop there, even had feeling carried him no further. Moreover, some hope had been born in him at the moment of separation, since she had not rebuked him, but only reminded him of her vows.

His letter was full of the confidence and enthusiasm of youth, and its contents may be understood by their likeness to others. He unfolded the plan of his life— the life which he was asking her to share. He dwelt upon its possibilities, he pointed out the field of its aspirations. But he kept his letter for some days, unable to conceive a way by which it might be sent to its destination. At length the chance came in the simplest of disguises.

Ezra was starting one morning to the convent. As he was leaving the room, old Martha called to him. She sat by the hearthstone, with her head tied up in red flannel, and her large, watery face flushed with pain, and pointed towards a basket of apples on the window sill.

"Take them to Sister Dolorosa, Ezra," she said "Mind that you see *her*, and give them to her with your own hands. And ask her why she hasn't been to see me, and when she is coming." On this point her mind seemed more and more troubled. "But what's the use

of asking *you* to find out for me?" she added, flashing
out at him with heroic anger.

The old man stood in the middle of the room, dry
and gnarled, his small eyes kindling into a dull rage at
a taunt made in the presence of a guest whose good
opinion he desired. But he took the apples in silence
and left the room.

As Gordon followed him beyond the garden, noting
how his mind was absorbed in petty anger, a simple
resolution came to him.

" Ezra," he said, handing him the letter, " when you
give the Sister the apples, deliver this. And we do not
talk about business, you know, Ezra."

The old man took the letter and put it furtively into
his pocket, with a backward shake of his head towards
the house.

" Whatever risks I may have to run from other
quarters, he will never tell *her*," Gordon said to himself.

When Ezra returned in the evening he was absorbed,
and Gordon noted with relief that he was also un
suspicious. He walked some distance to meet the old
man the next two days, and his suspense became almost
unendurable, but he asked no questions. The third
day Ezra drew from his pocket a letter, which he delivered, merely saying :

" The Sister told me to give you this."

Gordon soon turned aside across the fields, and having reached a point screened from observation he
opened the letter and read as follows :

" I have received your letter. I have read it. But
how could I listen to your proposal without becoming

false to my vows?   And if you knew that I had proved
false to what I held most dear and binding, how could
you ever believe that I would be true to anything else ?
Ah, no!   Should you unite yourself to one who for your
sake had been faithless to the ideal of womanhood which
she regarded as supreme, you would soon withdraw
from her the very love that she had sacrificed even her
hopes of Heaven to enjoy.

"But it seems possible that in writing to me you believe my vows no longer precious to my heart and .
sacred to my conscience.   You are wrong.   They are
more dear to me at this moment than ever before, because at this moment, as never before, they give me a
mournful admonition of my failure to exhibit to the
world in my own life the beauty of their ineffable holiness.   For had there not been something within me to
lead you on—had I shown to you the sinless nature
which it is their office to create—you would never have
felt towards me as you do.   You would no more have
thought of loving me than of loving an angel of God.

"The least reparation I can make for my offense is to
tell you that in offering me your love you offer me the
cup of sacred humiliation, and that I thank you for re-
minding me of my duty, while I drain it to the dregs.

"After long deliberation I have written to tell you
this ; and if it be allowed me to make one request, I
would entreat that you will never lay this sin of mine to
the charge of my religion and my order.

"We shall never meet again.   Although I may not
listen to your proposal, it is allowed me to love you as
one of the works of God.   And since there are exalted
women in the world who do not consecrate themselves
to the Church, I shall pray that you may find one of

these to walk by your side through life. I shall pray that she may be worthy of you; and perhaps you will teach her sometimes to pray for one who will always need her prayers.

"I only know that God orders our lives according to his goodness. My feet he set in one path of duty, yours in another, and he had separated us forever long before he allowed us to meet. If, therefore, having thus separated us, he yet brought us together only that we should thus know each other and then be parted, I cannot believe that there was not in it some needed lesson for us both. At least, if he will deign to hear the ceaseless, fervent petition of one so erring, he will not leave you unhappy on account of that love for me, which in this world it will never be allowed me to return. Farewell!"

The first part of this letter awakened in Gordon keen remorse and a faltering of purpose, but the latter filled him with a joy that excluded every other feeling.

"She loves me!" he exclaimed; and, as though registering a vow, he added aloud, "And nothing— God help me!—nothing shall keep us apart."

Walking to a point of the landscape that commanded a view of the convent, he remained there while the twilight fell, revolving how he was to surmount the remaining barriers between them, for these now seemed hardly more than cobwebs to be brushed aside by his hand; and often, meanwhile, he looked towards the convent, as one might look longingly towards some forbidden shrine, which the coming night would enable him to approach.

VI.

A night for love it was. The great sun at setting had looked with steadfast eye at the convent standing lonely on its wide landscape, and had then thrown his final glance across the world towards the east ; and the moon had quickly risen and hung about it the long silvery twilight of her heavenly watchfulness. The summer, too, which had been moving southward, now came slowly back, borne on warm airs that fanned the convent walls and sighed to its chaste lattices with the poetry of dead flowers and vanished songsters. But sighed in vain. With many a prayer, with many a cross on pure brow and shoulder and breast, with many a pious kiss of crucifix, the convent slept. Only some little novice, lying like a flushed figure of Sleep on a couch of snow, may have stirred to draw one sigh, as those zephyrs, toying with her warm hair, broke some earthly dream of too much tenderness. Or they may merely have cooled the feverish feet of a withered nun, who clasped her dry hands in ecstasy, as on her cavernous eyes there dawned a vision of the glories and rewards of Paradise. But no , not all slept. At an open window on the eastern side of the convent stood the sleepless one, looking out into the largeness of the night like one who is lost in the largeness of her sorrow.

Across the lawn, a little distance off, stood the church of the convent. The moonlight rested on it like a smile of peace, the elms blessed it with tireless arms, and from the zenith of the sky down to the horizon there rested on outstretched wings, rank above rank

and pinion brushing pinion, a host of white, angelic
cloud-shapes, as though guarding the sacred portal.

But she looked at it with timid yearning. Greater
and greater had become the need to pour into some
ear a confession and a prayer for pardon. Her peace
was gone. She had been concealing her heart from
the Mother Superior. She had sinned against her
vows. She had impiously offended the Divine Mother.
And to-day, after answering his letter in order that she
might defend her religion, she had acknowledged to
her heart that she loved him. But they would never
meet again. To-morrow she would make a full confession of what had taken place. Beyond that miserable
ordeal she dared not gaze into her own future.

Lost in the fears and sorrows of such thoughts, long
she stood looking out into the night, stricken with a
sense of alienation from human sympathy. She felt
that she stood henceforth estranged from the entire
convent—Mother Superior, novice, and nun—as an object of reproach, and of suffering into which no one of
them could enter.

Sorer yet grew her need, and a little way across the
lawn stood the church, peaceful in the moonlight. Ah,
the divine pity! If only she might steal first alone to the
shrine of her whom most she had offended, and to an ear
gracious to sorrow make confession of her frailty. At
length, overcome with this desire and gliding noiselessly out of the room, she passed down the moonlit hall,
on each side of which the nuns were sleeping. She
descended the stairway, took from the wall the key of
the church, and then softly opening the door, stepped
out into the night. For a moment she paused, icy and
faint with physical fear; then, passing like a swift
16

shadow across the silvered lawn, she went round to the side entrance of the church, unlocked the door, and, entering quickly, locked herself inside. There she stood for some time with hands pressed tightly to her fluttering heart, until bodily agitation died away before the recollection of her mission; and there came upon her that calmness with which the soul enacts great tragedies. Then slowly, very slowly, hidden now, and now visible where the moonlight entered the long, gothic windows, she passed across the chancel towards the shrine of one whom ancestral faith had taught her to believe divine; and before the image of a Jewish woman—who herself in full humanity loved and married a carpenter nearly two thousand years ago, living beside him as blameless wife and becoming blameless mother to his children—this poor child, whose nature was unstained as snow on the mountain-peaks, poured out her prayer to be forgiven the sin of her love.

To the woman of the world, the approaches of whose nature are defended by the intricacies of willfulness and the barriers of deliberate reserve; to the woman of the world, who curbs and conceals that feeling to which she intends to yield herself in the end, it may seem incredible that there should have rooted itself so easily in the breast of one of her sex this flower of a fatal passion. But it should be remembered how unbefriended that bosom had been by any outpost of feminine self-consciousness; how exposed it was through very belief in its unearthly consecration; how like some 'unwatched vase that had long been collecting the sweet dews and rains of heaven, it had been silently filling with those unbidden intimations that are shed from above as the best gifts of womanhood. Moreover, her life was unspeakably isolate. In the monotony of its routine a trifling event became an epoch; a fresh impression stirred within the mind material for a chapter of history. Lifted far above commonplace psychology of the passions, however, was the planting and the growth of an emotion in a heart like hers.

Her prayer began. It began with the scene of her first meeting with him in the fields, for from that moment she fixed the origin of her unfaithfulness. Of the entire hidden life of poetic reverie and unsatisfied desires which she had been living before, her innocent soul took no account. Therefore, beginning with that afternoon, she passed in review the history of her thoughts and feelings. The moon outside, flooding the heavens with its beams, was not so intense a lamp as memory, now turned upon the recesses of her mind. Nothing escaped detection. His words, the scenes with him in the garden, in the field—his voice, looks, gestures—his anxiety and sympathy—his passionate letter— all were now vividly recalled, that they might be forgotten; and their influence confessed, that it might forever be renounced. Her conscience stood beside her love as though it were some great fast-growing deadly plant in her heart, with deep-twisted roots and strangling tendrils, each of which to the smallest fibre must be uptorn so that not a germ should be left.

But who can describe the prayer of such a soul! It is easy to ask to be rid of ignoble passions. They come upon us as momentary temptations and are abhorrent to our better selves; but of all tragedies enacted within the theatre of the human mind what one is so pitiable as that in which a pure being prays to be forgiven the one feeling of nature that is the revelation of

beauty, the secret of perfection, the solace of the world,
and the condition of immortality?

The passing of such a tragedy scars the nature of the
penitent like the passing of an age across a mountain
rock. If there had lingered thus long on Sister Dolorosa's nature any upland of childhood snows, these
vanished in that hour ; if any vernal belt of maidenhood,
it felt the hot breath of that experience of the world
and of the human destiny which quickly ages whatever
it does not destroy. So that while she prayed there
seemed to rise from within her and take flight forever
that spotless image of herself as she once had been,
and in its place to stand the form of a woman, older,
altered, and set apart by sorrow.

At length her prayer ended and she rose. It had
not brought her the peace that prayer brings to women ;
for the confession of her love before the very altar—
the mere coming into audience with the Eternal to renounce it—had set upon it the seal of irrevocable truth.
It is when the victim is led to the altar of sacrifice that
it turns its piteous eyes upon the sacrificing hand and
utters its poor dumb cry for life ; and it was when Sister
Dolorosa bared the breast of her humanity that it might
be stabbed by the hand of her religion, that she, too,
though attempting to bless the stroke, felt the last pangs
of that deep thrust.

With such a wound she turned from the altar, walked
with bowed head once more across the church, unlocked
the door, stepped forth and locked it. The night had
grown more tender. The host of seraphic cloud-forms
had fled across the sky; and as she turned her eyes
upward to the heavens, there looked down upon her
from their serene, untroubled heights only the stars,

that never falter or digress from their forewritten courses.
The thought came to her that never henceforth should
she look up to them without being reminded of how
her own will had wandered from its orbit. The moon
rained its steady beams upon the symbol of the sacred
heart on her bosom, until it seemed to throb again
with the agony of the crucifixion. Never again should
she see it without the remembrance that *her* sin also
had pierced it afresh.

With what loneliness that sin had surrounded her!
As she had issued from the damp, chill atmosphere of
the church, the warm airs of the south quickened within
her long-sleeping memories; and with the yearning of
stricken childhood she thought of her mother, to whom
she had turned of yore for sympathy; but that mother's
bosom was now a mound of dust. She looked across
the lawn towards the convent where the Mother Superior and the nuns were sleeping. To-morrow she would
stand among them a greater alien than any stranger.
No; she was alone; among the millions of human beings on the earth of God there was not one on whose
heart she could have rested her own. Not one save
him—him—whose love had broken down all barriers
that it might reach and infold her. And him she had
repelled. A joy, new and indescribable, leaped within
her that for him and not for another she suffered and
was bound in this tragedy of her fall.

Slowly she took her way along the side of the church
towards the front entrance, from which a paved walk
led to the convent building. She reached the corner,
she turned, and then she paused as one might pause
who had come upon the beloved dead, returned to life.

For he was sitting on the steps of the church, leaning

against one of the pillars, his face lifted upward so that
the moonlight fell upon it.   She had no time to turn
back before he saw her.   With a low cry of surprise
and joy he sprang up and followed along the side of
the church; for she had begun to retrace her steps to
the door, to lock herself inside.   When he came up beside her, she paused.   Both were trembling; but when
he saw the look of suffering on her face, acting upon
the impulse which had always impelled him to stand
between her and unhappiness, he now took both of her
hands.

" Pauline !"

He spoke with all the pleading love, all the depth of
nature, that was in him.

She had attempted to withdraw her hands; but at the
sound of that once-familiar name, she suddenly bowed
her head as the wave of memories and emotions passed
over her; then he quickly put his arms around her,
drew her to him, and bent down and kissed her.

VII.

For hours there lasted an interview, during which he,
with the delirium of hope, she with the delirium of despair, drained at their young lips that cup of life which
is full of the first confession of love.

In recollections so overwhelming did this meeting
leave Gordon on the next morning, that he was un-
mindful of everything beside; and among the consequences of absent-mindedness was the wound that he
gave himself by the careless handling of his gun.

When Ezra had set out for the convent that morning

he had walked with him, saying that he would go to
the station for a daily paper, but chiefly wishing to escape the house and be alone. They had reached in
the fields a rotting fence, on each side of which grew
briers and underwood. He had expected to climb this
fence, and as he stood beside it speaking a few parting
words to Ezra he absently thrust his gun between two
of the lower rails, not noticing that the lock was
sprung. Caught in the brush on the other side, it was
discharged, making a wound in his left leg a little below the thigh. He turned to a deadly paleness, looked
at Ezra with that stunned, bewildered expression seen
in the faces of those who receive a wound, and fell.

By main strength the old man lifted and bore him to
the house and hurried off to the station, near which the
neighborhood physician and surgeon lived. But the
latter was away from home; several hours passed before he came; the means taken to stop the hemorrhage
had been ineffectual; the loss of blood had been very
great; certain foreign matter had been carried into the
wound; the professional treatment was unskilful; and
septic fever followed, so that for many days his life
hung upon a little chance. But convalescence came
at last, and with it days of clear, calm thinking. For
he had not allowed news of his accident to be sent
home or to his friends; and except the old couple, the
doctor, and the nurse whom the latter had secured, he
had no company but his thoughts.

No tidings had come to him of Sister Dolorosa since
his accident; and nothing had intervened to remove
that sad image of her which had haunted him through
fever and phantasy and dream since the night of their
final interview. For it was then that he had first real-

ized in how pitiless a tragedy her life had become entangled, and how conscience may fail to govern a woman's heart in denying her the right to love, but may still
govern her actions in forbidding her to marry. To
plead with her had been to wound only the more deeply a nature that accepted even this pleading as a further proof of its own disloyalty, and was forced by it
into a state of more poignant humiliation. What wonder, therefore, if there had been opened in his mind
from that hour a certain wound which grew deeper and
deeper, until, by comparison, his real wound seemed
painless and insignificant.

Nevertheless, it is true that during this interview he
had not been able to accept her decision as irreversible. The spell of her presence over him was too complete; even his wish to rescue her from a lot, henceforth unhappier still, too urgent; so that in parting he
had clung to the secret hope that little by little he
might change her conscience, which now interposed
the only obstacle between them.

Even the next day, when he had been wounded and
life was rapidly flowing from him, and earthly ties
seemed soon to be snapped, he had thought only of
this tie, new and sacred, and had written to her. Poor
boy!—he had written, as with his heart's blood, his
brief, pathetic appeal that she would come and be
united to him before he died. In all ages of the world
there have been persons, simple in nature and simple
in their faith in another life, who have forgotten everything else in the last hour but the supreme wish to
grapple to them those they love, for eternity, and at
whatever cost. Such simplicity of nature and faith belonged to him; for although in Kentucky the unrest

of the century touching belief in the supernatural, and the many phases by which this expresses itself, are not, unknown, they had never affected him. He believed as his fathers had believed, that to be united in this world in any relation is to be united in that relation, mysteriously changed yet mysteriously the same, in another.

But this letter had never been sent. There had been no one to take it at the time; and when Ezra returned with the physician he had fainted away from loss of blood.

Then had followed the dressing of the wound, days of fever and unconsciousness, and then the assurance that he would get well. Thus, nearly a month had passed, and for him a great change had come over the face of nature and the light of the world. With that preternatural calm of mind which only an invalid or a passionless philosopher ever obtains, he now looked back upon an episode which thus acquired fictitious remoteness. So weak that he could scarcely lift his head from his pillow, there left his heart the keen, joyous sense of human ties and pursuits. He lost the key to the motives and forces of his own character. But it is often the natural result of such illness that while the springs of feeling seem to dry up, the conscience remains sensitive, or even burns more brightly, as a star through a rarer atmosphere. So that, lying thus in the poor farm-house during dreary days, with his life half-gone out of him and with only the sad image of her always before his eyes, he could think of nothing but his cruel folly in having broken in upon her peace; for perfect peace of some sort she must have had in comparison with what was now left her.

Beneath his pillow he kept her letter, and as he often read it over he asked himself how he could ever have hoped to change the conscience which had inspired such a letter as that. If her heart belonged to him, did not her soul belong to her religion; and if one or the other must give way, could it be doubtful with such a nature as hers which would come out victorious? Thus he said to himself that any further attempt to see her could but result in greater suffering to them both, and that nothing was left him but what she herself had urged—to go away and resign her to a life, from which he had too late found out that she could never be divorced.

As soon as he had come to this decision, he began to think of her as belonging only to his past. The entire episode became a thing of memory and irreparable incompleteness; and with the conviction that she was lost to him her image passed into that serene, reverential sanctuary of our common nature, where all the highest that we have grasped at and missed, and all the beauty that we have loved and lost, take the forms of statues around dim walls and look down upon us in mournful, never-changing perfection.

As he lay one morning revolving his altered purpose, Ezra came quietly into the room and took from a table near the foot of the bed a waiter on which were a jelly-glass and a napkin.

"*She* said I'd better take these back this morning," he observed, looking at Gordon for his approval, and motioning with his head towards that quarter of the house where Martha was supposed to be.

"Wait awhile, will you, Ezra?" he replied, looking at the old man with the dark, quiet eye of an invalid. "I think I ought to write a few lines this morning to thank them for their kindness. Come back in an hour, will you?"

The things had been sent from the convent; for, from the time that news had reached the Mother Superior of the accident of the young stranger who had visited the convent some days before, there had regularly come to him delicate attentions which could not have been supplied at the farm-house. He often asked himself whether they were not inspired by *her;* and he thought that when the time came for him to write his thanks, he would put into the expression of them something that would be understood by her alone—something that would stand for gratitude and a farewell.

When Ezra left the room, with the thought of now doing this another thought came unexpectedly to him. By the side of the bed there stood a small table on which were writing materials and a few books that had been taken from his valise. He stretched out his hand and opening one of them took from it a letter which bore the address, "Sister Dolorosa." It contained those appealing lines that he had written her on the day of his accident; and with calm, curious sadness he now read them over and over, as though they had never come from him. From the mere monotony of this exercise sleep overtook him, and he had scarcely restored the letter to the envelope and laid it back on the table before his eyelids closed.

While he still lay asleep, Ezra came quietly into the room again, and took up the waiter with the jelly-glass and the napkin. Then he looked around for the letter that he was to take. He was accustomed to carry Gordon's letters to the station, and his eye now rested on

the table where they were always to be found.   Seeing
one on it, he walked across, took it up and read the
address, "Sister Dolorosa," hesitated, glanced at Gordon's closed eyes, and then, with an intelligent nod to
signify that he could understand without further in-
struction, he left the room and set out briskly for the
convent.

Sister Dolorosa was at the cistern filling a bucket
with water when he came up and, handing her the letter, passed on to the convent kitchen.   She looked at
it with indifference; then she opened and read it; and
then in an instant everything whirled before her eyes,
and in her ears the water sounded loud as it dropped
from the chain back into the cistern.   And then she
was gone—gone with a light, rapid step, down the avenue of elms, through the gate, across the meadows, out
into the fields—bucket and cistern, Mother Superior
and sisterhood, vows and martyrs, zeal of Carmelite,
passion of Christ, all forgotten.

When, nearly a month before, news had reached the
Mother Superior of the young stranger's accident, in
accordance with the rule which excludes from the convent worldly affairs, she had not made it known except
to those who were to aid in carrying out her kindly
plans for him.   To Sister Dolorosa, therefore, the accident had just occurred, and now—now as she hastened to him—he was dying.

During the intervening weeks she had undergone by
insensible degrees a deterioration of nature.   Prayer
had not passed her lips.   She believed that she had no
right to pray.   Nor had she confessed.   From such a
confession as she had now to make, certain new-born
instincts of womanhood bade her shrink more deeply

into the privacy of her own being. And therefore she had become more scrupulous, if possible, of outward duties, that no one might be led to discover the paralysis of her spiritual life. But there was that change in her which soon drew attention; and thenceforth, in order to hide her heart, she began to practice with the Mother Superior little acts of self-concealment and evasion, and by-and-by other little acts of pretense and feigning, until — God pity her! — being most sorely pressed by questions, when sometimes she would be found in tears or sitting listless with her hands in her lap like one who is under the spell of mournful phantasies, these became other little acts of positive deception. But for each of them remorse preyed upon her the more ruthlessly, so that she grew thin and faded, with a shadow of fear darkening always her evasive eyes.

What most held her apart, and most she deemed put upon her the angry ban of Heaven, was the consciousness that she still loved him, and that she was even bound to him the more inseparably since the night of their last meeting. For it was then that emotions had been awakened which drew her to him in ways that love alone could not have done. These emotions had their source in the belief that she owed him reparation for the disappointment which she had brought upon his life. The recollection of his face when she had denied him hope rose in constant reproach before her; and since she held herself blamable that he had loved her, she took the whole responsibility of his unhappiness.

It was this sense of having wronged him that cleft even conscience in her and left her struggling. But how to undo the wrong—this she vainly pondered; for he was gone, bearing away into his life the burden of enticed and baffled hope.

On the morning when she was at the cistern—for the Sisters of the Order have among them such interchange of manual offices—if, as she read the letter that Ezra gave her, any one motive stood out clear in the stress of that terrible moment, it was, that having been false to other duties she might at least be true to this. She felt but one desire—to atone to him by any sacrifice of herself that would make his death more peaceful. Beyond this everything was void and dark within her as she hurried on, except the consciousness that by this act she separated herself from her Order and terminated her religious life in utter failure and disgrace.

The light, rapid step with which she had started soon brought her across the fields. As she drew near the house, Martha, who had caught sight of her figure through the window, made haste to the door and stood awaiting her. Sister Dolorosa merely approached and said :

"Where is he?"

For a moment the old woman did not answer. Then she pointed to a door at the opposite end of the porch, and with a sparkle of peculiar pleasure in her eyes she saw Sister Dolorosa cross and enter it. A little while longer she stood, watching the key-hole furtively, but then went back to the fireside, where she sat upright and motionless with the red flannel pushed back from her listening ears.

The room was dimly lighted through half-closed shutters. Gordon lay asleep near the edge of the bed, with his face turned towards the door. It might well have been thought the face of one dying. Her eyes rested on it a moment, and then with a stifled sob and moan she glided across the room and sank on her knees at the bedside. In the utter self-forgetfulness of her remorse, pity, and love, she put one arm around his neck, she buried her face close beside his.

He had awaked, bewildered, as he saw her coming towards him. He now took her arm from around his neck, pressed her hand again and again to his lips, and then laying it on his heart crossed his arms over it, letting one of his hands rest on her head. For a little while he could not trust himself to speak ; his love threatened to overmaster his self-renunciation. But then, not knowing why she had come unless from some great sympathy for his sufferings, or perhaps to see him once more since he was now soon to go away, and not understanding any cause for her distress but the tragedy in which he had entangled her life—feeling only sorrow for her sorrow and wishing only by means of his last words to help her back to such peace as she still might win, he said to her with immeasurable gentleness :

" I thought you would never come ! I thought I should have to go away without seeing you again ! They tell me it is not yet a month since the accident, but it seems to me so *long*—a lifetime ! I have lain here day after day thinking it over, and I see things differently now—so differently ! That is why I wanted to see you once more. I wanted you to understand that I felt you had done right in refusing—in refusing to marry me. I wanted to ask you never to blame yourself for what has happened — never to let any thought of having made *me* unhappy add to the sorrow of your life. It is my fault, not yours. But I meant it—God *knows*, I meant it!—for the happiness of us both! I believed that your life was not suited to you I meant to make you happy! But since you *cannot* give up your life, I have only been unkind. And since you think it wrong to give it up, I am glad that you are so true to it! If you *must* live it, Heaven only knows how glad I am that you will live it heroically. And Heaven keep me equally true to the duty in mine, that I also shall not fail in it! If we never meet again, we can always think of each other as living true to ourselves and to one another. Don't deny me this! Let me believe that your thoughts and prayers will always follow me. Even your vows will not deny me this! It will always keep us near each other, and it will bring us together where they cannot separate us."

He had spoken with entire repression of himself, in the slow voice of an invalid, and on the stillness of the room each word had fallen with hard distinctness. But now, with the thought of losing her, by a painful effort he moved closer to the edge of the bed, put his arms around her neck, drew her face against his own, and continued :

"But do not think it is easy to tell you this! Do not think it is easy to give you up! Do not think that I do not love you! Oh Pauline—not in *another* life, but in *this—in this!*" He could say no more ; and out of his physical weakness tears rose to his eyes and fell drop by drop upon her veil.

VIII.

Sister Dolorosa had been missed from the convent. There had been inquiry growing ever more anxious, and search growing ever more hurried. They found her bucket overturned at the cistern, and near it the print of her feet in the moist earth. But she was gone. They sought her in every hidden closet, they climbed to the observatory and scanned the surrounding fields. Work was left unfinished, prayer unended, as the news spread through the vast building; and as time went by and nothing was heard of her, uneasiness became alarm, and alarm became a vague, immeasurable foreboding of ill. Each now remembered how strange of late had been Sister Dolorosa's life and actions, and no one had the heart to name her own particular fears to any other or to read them in any other's eyes. Time passed on and discipline in the convent was forgotten. They began to pour out into the long corridors, and in tumultuous groups passed this way and that, seeking the Mother Superior. But the Mother Superior had gone to the church with the same impulse that in all ages has brought the human heart to the altar of God when stricken by peril or disaster; and into the church they also gathered. Into the church likewise came the white flock of the novices, who had burst from their isolated quarter of the convent with a sudden contagion of fear. When, therefore, the Mother Superior rose from where she had been kneeling, turned, and in the dark church saw them assembled close around her, pallid, anxious, disordered, and looking with helpless

17

dependence to her for that assurance for which she
had herself in helpless dependence looked to God, so
unnerved was she by the spectacle that strength failed
her and she sank upon the steps of the altar, stretching out her arms once more in voiceless supplication
towards the altar of the Infinite helpfulness.

But at that moment a little novice, whom Sister Dolorosa loved and whom she had taught the music of the
harp, came running into the church, wringing her hands
and crying. When she was half-way down the aisle,
in a voice that rang through the building, she called
out:

"Oh, Mother, she is coming! Something has happened to her! Her veil is gone!" and, turning again,
she ran out of the church.

They were hurrying after her when a note of com-
mand, inarticulate but imperious, from the Mother
Superior arrested every foot and drew every eye in that
direction. Voice had failed her, but with a gesture
full of dignity and reproach she waved them back, and
supporting her great form between two of the nuns,
she advanced slowly down the aisle of the church and
passed out by the front entrance. But they forgot to
obey her and followed; and when she descended the
steps to the bottom and made a sign that she would
wait there, on the steps behind they stood grouped
and crowded back to the sacred doors.

Yes, she was coming—coming up the avenue of elms
—coming slowly, as though her strength were almost
gone. As she passed under the trees on one side of the
avenue she touched their trunks one by one for support.
She walked with her eyes on the ground and with the
abstraction of one who has lost the purpose of walking.

When she was perhaps half-way up the avenue, as she paused by one of the trees and supported herself against it, she raised her eyes and saw them all waiting to receive her on the steps of the church. For a little while she stood and surveyed the scene; the Mother Superior standing in front, her sinking form supported between two Sisters, her hands clasping the crucifix to her bosom; behind her the others, step above step, back to the doors; some looking at her with frightened faces; others with their heads buried on each other's shoulders; and hiding somewhere in the throng, the little novice, only the sound of whose sobbing revealed her presence. Then she took her hand from the tree, walked on quite steadily until she was several yards away, and paused again.

She had torn off her veil and her head was bare and shining. She had torn the sacred symbol from her bosom, and through the black rent they could see the glistening whiteness of her naked breast. Comprehending them in one glance, as though she wished them all to listen, she looked into the face of the Mother Superior, and began to speak in a voice utterly forlorn, as of one who has passed the limits of suffering.

" Mother!—"

" Mother !—"

She passed one hand slowly across her forehead, to brush away some cloud from her brain, and for the third time she began to speak:

" Mother !—"

Then she paused, pressed both palms quickly to her temples, and turned her eyes in bewildered appeal towards the Mother Superior. But she did not fall. With a cry that might have come from the heart of the boundless pity the Mother Superior broke away from the restraining arms of the nuns and rushed forward and caught her to her bosom.

IX.

The day had come when Gordon was well enough to go home. As he sat giving directions to Ezra, who was awkwardly packing his valise, he looked over the books, papers, and letters that lay on the table near the bed.

"There is one letter missing," he said, with a troubled expression, as he finished his search. Then he added quickly, in a tone of helpless entreaty:

"You couldn't have taken it to the station and mailed it with the others, could you, Ezra? It was not to go to the station. It was to have gone to the convent."

The last sentence he uttered rather to his own thought than for the ear of his listener.

"I *took* it to the convent," said Ezra, stoutly, raising himself from over the valise in the middle of the floor. "I didn't *take* it to the station!"

Gordon wheeled on him, giving a wrench to his wound which may have caused the groan that burst from him, and left him white and trembling.

"You took it *to the convent!* Great God, Ezra! When?"

"The day you *told* me to take it," replied Ezra, simply. "The day the Sister came to see you."

"Oh, *Ezra!*" he cried piteously, looking into the rugged, faithful countenance of the old man, and feeling that he had not the right to censure him.

Now for the first time he comprehended the whole significance of what had happened. He had never certainly known what motive had brought her to him that day. He had never been able to understand why, having come, she had gone away with such abruptness. Scarcely had he begun to speak to her when she had strangely shrunk from him ; and scarcely had he ceased speaking when she had left the room without a word, and without his having so much as seen her face.

Slowly now the sad truth forced itself upon his mind that she had come in answer to his entreaty. She must have thought his letter just written, himself just wounded and dying. It was as if he had betrayed her into the utmost expression of her love for him and in that moment had coldly admonished her of her duty. For him she had broken what was the most sacred obligation of her life, and in return he had given her an exhortation to be faithful to her vows.

He went home to one of the older secluded country-places of the Blue-grass Region not far from Lexington. His illness served to account for a strange gravity and sadness of nature in him. When the winter had passed and spring had come, bringing perfect health again, this sadness only deepened. For health had brought back the ardor of life. The glowing colors of the world returned ; and with these there flowed back into his heart, as waters flow back into a well that has gone dry, the perfect love of youth and strength with which he had loved her and tried to win her at first. And with this love of her came back the first complete realization that he had lost her ; and with this pain, that keenest pain of having been most unkind to her when he had striven to be kindest.

He now looked back upon his illness, as one who
has gained some clear headland looks down upon a
valley so dark and overhung with mist that he cannot
trace his own course across it. He was no longer in
sympathy with that mood of self-renunciation which
had influenced him in their last interview. He charged
himself with having given up too easily; for might he
not, after all, have won her? Might he not, little by
little, have changed her conscience, as little by little he
had gained her love? Would it have been possible, he
asked himself again and again, for her ever to have
come to him as she had done that day, had not her
conscience approved? Of all his torturing thoughts,
none cost him greater suffering than living over in imagination what must have happened to her since then—
the humiliation, perhaps public exposure; followed by
penalties and sorrows of which he durst not think, and
certainly a life more unrelieved in gloom and desolation.

In the summer his father's health began to fail and
in the autumn he died. The winter was passed in settling the business of the estate, and before the spring
passed again Gordon found himself at the head of affairs, and stretching out before him, calm and clear,
the complete independence of his new-found manhood.
His life was his own to make it what he would. As
fortunes go in Kentucky he was wealthy, his farm being
among the most beautiful of the beautiful ones which
make up that land, and his homestead being dear
through family ties and those intimations of fireside
peace which lay closest the heart of his ideal life.
But amid all his happiness, that one lack which made
the rest appear lacking—that vacancy within which
nothing would fill! The beauty of the rich land hence.

forth brought him the dream-like recollection of a rough, poor country a hundred miles away. Its quiet homesteads, with the impression they create of sweet and simple lives, reminded him only of a convent standing lonely and forbidding on its wide landscape. The calm liberty of woods and fields, the bounding liberty of life, the enlightened liberty of conscience and religion, which were to him the best gifts of his State, his country, and his time, forced on him perpetual contrast with the ancient confinement in which she languished.

Still he threw himself resolutely into his duties. In all that he did or planned he felt a certain sacred, uplifting force added to his life by that high bond through which he had sought to link their sundered path-ways. But, on the other hand, the haunting thought of what might have befallen her since became a corrosive care, and began to eat out the heart of his resolute purposes.

So that when the long, calm summer had passed and autumn had come, bringing him lonelier days in the brown fields, lonelier rides on horseback through the gorgeous woods, and lonelier evenings beside his re-kindled hearth-stones, he could bear the suspense no longer, and made up his mind to go back, if but to hear tidings whether she yet were living in the convent. He realized, of course, that under no circumstances could he ever again speak to her of his love. He had put himself on the side of her conscience against his own cause ; but he felt that he owed it to himself to dissipate uncertainty regarding her fate. This done, he could return, however sadly, and take up the duties of his life with better heart.

X.

One Sunday afternoon he got off at the little station. From one of the rustic loungers on the platform he learned that old Ezra and Martha had gone the year before to live with a son in a distant State, and that their scant acres had been absorbed" in the convent domain.

Slowly he took his way across the sombre fields. Once more he reached the brown foot-path and the edge of the pale, thin corn. Once more the summoning whistle of the quail came sweet and clear from the depths of a neighboring thicket. Silently in the reddening west were rising the white cathedrals of the sky. It was on yonder hill-top he had first seen her, standing as though transfigured in the evening light. Overwhelmed by the memories which the place evoked, he passed on towards the convent. The first sight of it in the distance smote him with a pain so sharp that a groan escaped his lips as from a reopened wound.

It was the hour of the vesper service. Entering the church he sat where he had sat before. How still it was, how faint the autumnal sunlight stealing in through the sainted windows, how motionless the dark company of nuns seated on one side of the nave, how rigid the white rows of novices on the other!

With sad fascination of search his eyes roved among the black-shrouded devotees. She was not there. In the organ-loft above, a voice, poor and thin, began to pour out its wavering little tide of song. She was not there, then. Was her soul already gone home to Heaven?

Noiselessly from behind the altar the sacristine had
come forth and begun to light the candles. With eyes
strained and the heart gone out of him he hung upon
the movements of her figure. A slight, youthful figure
it was—slighter, as though worn and wasted; and the
hands which so firmly bore the long taper looked too
white and fragile to have upheld aught heavier than the
stalk of a lily.

With infinite meekness and reverence she moved
hither and thither about the shrine, as though each
footfall were a step nearer the glorious Presence, each
breath a prayer. One by one there sprang into being,
beneath her touch of love, the silvery spires of sacred
flame. No angel of the night ever more softly lit the
stars of heaven. And it was thus that he saw her for
the last time—folded back to the bosom of that faith
from which it was left him to believe that he had all
but rescued her to love and happiness, and set, as a
chastening admonition, to tend the mortal fires on the
altar of eternal service.

Looking at her across the vast estranging gulf of
destiny, heart-broken, he asked himself in his poor
yearning way whether she longer had any thought of
him or longer loved him. For answer he had only the
assurance given in her words, which now rose as a
benediction in his memory:

"If He will deign to hear the ceaseless, fervent petition of one so erring, He will not leave you unhappy on
account of that love for me which in this world it will
never be allowed me to return."

One highest star of adoration she kindled last, and
then turned and advanced down the aisle. He was sitting close to it, and as she came towards him, with irre-

sistible impulse he bent forward to meet her, his lips
parted as though to speak, his eyes implored her for
recognition, his hands were instinctively moved to attract her notice. But she passed him with unuplifted
eyes. The hem of her dress swept across his foot. In
that intense moment, which compressed within itself
the joy of another meeting and the despair of an eternal
farewell—in that moment he may have tried to read
through her face and beyond it in her very soul the
story of what she must have suffered. To any one else,
on her face rested only that beauty, transcending all description, which is born of the sorrow of earth and the
peace of God.

Mournful as was this last sight of her, and touched
with remorse, he could yet bear it away in his heart
for long remembrance not untempered by consolation.
He saw her well ; he saw her faithful ; he saw her bearing the sorrows of her lot with angelic sweetness.
Through years to come the beauty of this scene might
abide with him, lifted above the realm of mortal changes
by the serenitude of her immovable devotion.

XI.

There was thus spared him knowledge of the great
change that had taken place regarding her within the
counsels of the Order; nor, perhaps, was he ever to
learn of the other changes, more eventful still, that were
now fast closing in upon her destiny.

When the Creator wishes to create a woman, the
beauty of whose nature is to prefigure the types of an
immortal world, he endows her more plenteously with

the faculty of innocent love. The contravention of this faculty has time after time resulted in the most memorable tragedies that have ever saddened the history of the race. He had given to the nature of Pauline Cambron two strong, unwearying wings: the pinion of faith and the pinion of love. It was his will that she should soar by the use of both. But they had denied her the use of one; and the vain and bewildered struggles which marked her life thenceforth were as those of a bird that should try to rise into the air with one of its wings bound tight against its bosom.

After the illness which followed upon the events of that terrible day, she took towards her own conduct the penitential attitude enjoined by her religion. There is little need to lay bare all that followed. She had passed out of her soft world of heroic dreams into the hard world of unheroic reality. She had chosen a name to express her sympathy with the sorrows of the world, and the sorrows of the world had broken in upon her. Out of the white dawn of the imagination she had stepped into the heat and burden of the day.

Long after penances and prayers were over, and by others she might have felt herself forgiven, she was as far as ever from that forgiveness which comes from within. It is not characteristic of a nature such as hers to win pardon so easily for such an offence as she considered hers. Indeed, as time passed on, the powers of her being seemed concentred more and more in one impassioned desire to expiate her sin, for, as time passed on, despite penances and prayers, she realized that she still loved him.

As she pondered this she said to herself that peace would never come unless she should go elsewhere and

begin life over in some place that was free from the
memories of her fall, there was so much to remind her
of him.   She could not go into the garden without recalling the day when they had walked through it side
by side.   She could not cross the threshold of the
church without being reminded that it was the scene
of her unfaithfulness and of her exposure.   The graveyard, the foot-path across the fields, the observatory—
all were full of disturbing images.   And therefore she
besought the Mother Superior to send her away to
some one of the missions of the Order, thinking that
thus she would win forgetfulness of him and singleness
of heart.

But while the plan of doing this was yet being considered by the Mother Superior, there happened one of
those events which seem to fit into the crises of our
lives as though determined by the very laws of fate.
The attention of the civilized world had not yet been
fixed upon the heroic labors of the Belgian priest, Father Damien, among the lepers of the island of Molokai.   But it has been stated that near the convent are
the monks of La Trappe.   Among these monks were
friends of the American priest, Brother Joseph, who for
years was one of Father Damien's assistants; and to
these friends this priest from time to time wrote letters,
in which he described at great length the life of the
leper settlement and the work of the small band of
men and women who had gone to labor in that remote
and awful vineyard.   The contents of these letters
were made known to the ecclesiastical superior of the
convent; and one evening he made them the subject
of a lecture to the assembled nuns and novices, dwelling
with peculiar eloquence upon the devotion of the three

Franciscan Sisters who had become outcasts from human society that they might nurse and teach leprous girls, until inevitable death should overtake them also.

Among that breathless audience of women there was one soul on whom his words fell with the force of a message from the Eternal. Here, then, at last, was offered her a path-way by following meekly to the end of which she might perhaps find blessedness. The real Man of Sorrows appeared to stand in it and beckon her on to the abodes of those abandoned creatures whose sufferings he had with peculiar pity so often stretched forth his .hand to heal. When she laid before the Mother Superior her petition to be allowed to go, it was at first refused, being regarded as a momentary impulse ; but months passed, and at intervals, always more earnestly, she renewed her request. It was pointed out to her that when one has gone among the lepers there is no return; the alternatives are either life-long banishment, or death from leprosy, usually at the end of a few years. But always her reply was :

" In the name of Christ, Mother, let me go !"

Meantime it had become clear to the Mother Superior that some change of scene must be made. The days of Sister Dolorosa's usefulness in the convent were too plainly over.

It had not been possible in that large household of women to conceal the fact of her unfaithfulness to her vows. As one black veil whispered to' another—as one white veil communed with its attentive neighbor—little by little events were gathered and pieced together, until, in different forms of error and rumor, the story became known to all. Some from behind window lattices had watched her in the garden with the young stranger

on the day of his visiting the convent. Others had
heard of his lying wounded at the farm-house. Still
others were sure that under pretext of visiting old
Martha she had often met him in the fields. And then
the scene on the steps of the church, when she had returned soiled and torn and fainting.

So that from the day on which she arose from her
illness and began to go about the convent, she was
singled out as a target for those small arrows which
the feminine eye directs with such faultless skill at one
of its own sex. With scarcely perceptible movements
they would draw aside when passing her, as though to
escape corrupting contact. Certain ones of the younger Sisters, who were jealous of her beauty, did not fail
to drop innuendoes for her to overhear. And upon
some of the novices, whose minds were still wavering
between the Church and the world, it was thought that
her example might have a dangerous influence.

It is always wrong to judge motives; but it is possible that the head of the Order may have thought it
best that this ruined life should take on the halo of
martyrdom, from which fresh lustre would be reflected
upon the annals of the Church. However this may be,
after about eighteen months of waiting, during which
correspondence was held with the Sandwich Islands, it
was determined that Sister Dolorosa should be allowed
to go thither and join the labors of the Franciscan
Sisters.

From the day when consent was given she passed
into that peace with which one ascends the scaffold or
awaits the stake. It was this look of peace that Gordon had seen on her face as she moved hither and
thither about the shrine.

Only a few weeks after he had thus seen her the
day came for her to go.   Of those who took part in the
scene of farewell she was the most unmoved.   A month
later she sailed from San Francisco for Honolulu ; and
in due time there came from Honolulu to the Mother
Superior the following letter.   It contains all that remains of the earthly history of Pauline Cambron :

XII.

"KALAWAO, MCLOKAI, HAWAIIAN ISLANDS,
"*January 1, 188—*.

"DEAR MOTHER,—I entreat you not to let the sight of
this strange handwriting, instead of one that must be
so familiar, fill you with too much alarm.   I hasten to
assure you that before my letter closes you will understand why Sister Dolorosa has not written herself.

"Since the hour when the vessel sailed from the American port, bearing to us that young life as a consecrated
helper in our work among these suffering outcasts of
the human race, I know that your thoughts and prayers
have followed her with unceasing anxiety ; so that first
I should give you tidings that the vessel reached Honolulu in safety.   I should tell you also that she had a
prosperous voyage, and that she is now happy—far happier than when she left you.   I know, likewise, that
your imagination has constantly hovered about this
island, and that you have pictured it to yourself as the
gloomiest of all spots in the universe of God ; so that
in the next place I should try to remove this impression
by giving you some description of the island itself,
which has now become her unchanging home.

"The island of Molokai, then, on which the leper settlement has been located by the Government, is long,
and shaped much like the leaf of the willow-tree. The
Sandwich Islands, as you well know, are a group of vol-
canoes out of which the fires have for the most part long
since died. Molokai, therefore, is really but a mountain of cooled lava, half of which perhaps is beneath the
level of the sea. The two leper villages are actually
situated in the cup of an ancient crater. The island
is very low along the southern coast, and slopes gradually to its greatest altitude on the northern ridge, from
which the descent to the sea is in places all but per-
pendicular. It is between the bases of these northern
cliffs and the sea that the villages are built. In the
rear of them is a long succession of towering precipices
and wild ravines, that are solemn and terrible to behold; and in front of them there is a coast line so
rough with pointed rocks that as the waves rush in
upon them spray is often thrown to the height of fifty
or a hundred feet. It is this that makes the landing at
times so dangerous; and at other times, when a storm
has burst, so fatal. So that shipwrecks are not unknown, dear Mother, and sometimes add to the sadness
of life in this place.

"But from this description you would get only a mistaken idea of the aspect of the island. It is sunny and
full of tropical loveliness. The lapse of centuries has
in places covered the lava with exquisite verdure. Soft
breezes blow here, about the dark cliffs hang purple
atmospheres, and above them drift pink and white
clouds. Sometimes the whole island is veiled in gold-
en mist. Beautiful streams fall down its green precipices into the sea, and the sea itself is of the most brill-

iant blue. In its depths are growths of pure white corals, which are the homes of fishes of gorgeous colors.

"If I should speak no longer of the island, but of the people, I could perhaps do something further still to dissipate the dread with which you and other strangers must regard us. The inhabitants are a simple, generous, happy race; and there are many spots in this world — many in Europe and Asia, perhaps some in your own land — where the scenes of suffering and death are more poignant and appalling. The lepers live for the most part in decent white cottages. Many are the happy faces that are seen among them; so that, strange as it may seem, healthy people would some times come here to live if the laws did not forbid. So much has Christianity done that one may now be buried in consecrated ground.

"If all this appears worldly and frivolous, dear Mother, forgive me! If I have chosen to withhold from you news of her, of whom alone I know you are thinking, it is because I have wished to give you as bright a picture as possible. Perhaps you will thus become the better prepared for what is to follow.

"So that before I go further, I shall pause again to describe to you one spot which is the loveliest on the island. About a mile and a half from the village of Kalawao there is a rocky point which is used as an irregular landing-place when the sea is wild. Just beyond this point there is an inward curve of the coast, making an inlet of the sea; and from the water's edge there slopes backward into the bosom of the island a deep ravine. Down this ravine there falls and winds a gleaming white cataract, and here the tropical vegetation grows most beautiful. The trees are wreathed

18

with moist creepers; the edges and crevices of the lava
blocks are fringed with ferns and moss.   Here the
wild ginger blooms and the crimson lehua.   Here grow
trees of orange and palm and punhala groves.   Here
one sees the rare honey-bird with its plumage of scarlet
velvet, the golden plover, and the beautiful white bos'un-
bird, wheeling about the black cliff heights.   The spot is
as beautiful as a scene in some fairy tale.   When storms
roll in from the sea the surf flows far back into this ravine, and sometimes—after the waters have subsided—
a piece of wreckage from the ocean is left behind.

" Forgive me once more, O dear Mother! if again I
seem to you so idle and unmeaning in my words.   But
I have found it almost impossible to go on; and, besides, I think you will thank me, after you have read
my letter through, for telling you first of this place.

" From the day of our first learning that there was a
young spirit among you who had elected, for Christ's
sake, to come here and labor with us, we had counted
the days till she should arrive.   The news had spread
throughout the leper settlement.   Father Damien had
made it known to the lepers in Kalawao, Father Wen-
dolen had likewise told it among the lepers in Kala-
paupa, and the Protestant ministers spoke of it to their
flocks.   Thus her name had already become familiar
to hundreds of them, and many a prayer had been offered up for her safety.

" Once a week there comes to Molokai from Honolulu
a little steamer called *Mokolii*.   When it reached here last
Saturday morning it brought the news that just before
it sailed from Honolulu the vessel bearing Sister Dolorosa had come into port.   She had been taken in charge
by the Sisters until the *Mokolii* should return and make

the next trip. I should add that the steamer leaves at about five o'clock in the afternoon, and that it usually reaches here at about dawn of the following morning in ordinary weather.

"And now, dear Mother, I beseech you to lay my letter aside! Do not read further now. Lay it aside, and do not take it up again until you have sought in prayer the consolation of our divine religion for the sorrows of our lives.

"I shall believe that you have done this, and that, as you now go on with the reading of my letter, you have gained the fortitude to hear what I have scarcely the power to write. Heaven knows that in my poor way I have sought to prepare you !

"As it was expected that the steamer would reach the island about dawn on Saturday morning, as usual, it had been arranged that many of us should be at the landing-place to give her welcome. But about midnight one of the terrific storms which visit this region suddenly descended, enveloping the heavens, that had been full of the light of the stars, in impenetrable darkness. We were sleepless with apprehension that the vessel would be driven upon the rocks—such was the direction of the storm—long before it could come opposite the villages : and a few hours before day Father Damien, accompanied by Father Conradi, Brother James, and Brother Joseph, went down to the coast. Through the remaining hours of the night they watched and waited, now at one point, and now at another, knowing that the vessel could never land in such a storm. As the dawn broke they followed up the coast until they came opposite that rocky point of which I have already spoken as being an irregular landing-place.

"Here they were met by two or three men who were
drenched with the sea, and just starting towards the villages, and from them they learned that, an hour or two
before, the steamer had been driven upon the hidden
rocks of the point. It had been feared that it would
soon be sunk or dashed to pieces, and as quickly as
possible a boat had been put off, in which were the
leper girls that were being brought from Honolulu.
There was little hope that it would ever reach the shore,
but it was the last chance of life. In this boat, dear
Mother, Sister Dolorosa also was placed. Immediately afterwards a second boat was put off, containing the
others that were on board.

"Of the fate of the first boat they had learned nothing.
Their own had been almost immediately capsized, and,
so far as they knew, they were the sole survivors. The
Hawaiians are the most expert of swimmers, being almost native to the sea ; and since the distance was short,
and only these survived, you will realize how little chance
there was for any other.

"During the early hours of the morning, which broke
dark and inexpressibly sad for us, a few bodies were
found washed ashore, among them those of two leper
girls of Honolulu. But our search for her long proved
unavailing. At length Father Damien suggested that
we follow up the ravine which I have described, and it
was thither that he and Brother Joseph and I accordingly went. Father Damien thought it well that I
should go with them.

"It was far inland, dear Mother, that at last we found
her. She lay out-stretched on a bare, black rock of lava,
which sloped upward from the sea. Her naked white
feet rested on the green moss that fringed its lower

edge, and her head was sheltered from the burning sun by branches of ferns. Almost over her eyes—the lids of which were stiff with the salt of the ocean—there hung a spray of white poppies. It was as though nature would be kind to her in death.

"At the sight of her face, so young, and having in it the purity and the peace of Heaven, we knelt down around her without a word, and for a while we could do nothing but weep. Surely nothing so spotless was ever washed ashore on this polluted island! If I sinned, I pray to be forgiven; but I found a strange joy in thinking that the corruption of this terrible disease had never been laid upon her. Heaven had accepted in advance her faithful spirit, and had spared her the long years of bodily suffering.

"At Father Damien's direction Brother Joseph returned to the village for a bier and for four lepers who should be strong enough to bear it. When they came we laid her on it, and bore her back to the village, where Mother Marianne took the body in charge and prepared it for burial.

"How shall I describe her funeral? The lepers were her pall-bearers. The news of the shipwreck had quickly spread throughout the settlement, and these simple, generous people yield themselves so readily to the emotion of the hour. When the time arrived, it seemed that all who could walk had come to follow her to the church-yard. It was a moving sight—the long, wavering train of that death-stricken throng, whose sufferings had so touched the pity of our Lord when he was on earth, and the desolation of whose fate she had come to lessen. There were the young and the old alike, Protestants and Catholics without distinction, children with their faces so strangely aged with ravages of the leprosy, those advanced in years with theirs so mutilated and marred. Others, upon whom the leprosy had made such advances that they were too weak to walk, sat in their cottage doors and lifted their husky voices in singing that wailing native hymn in which they bemoan their hopeless fate. Some of the women, after a fashion of their own, wore large wreaths of blue blossoms and green leaves about their withered faces.

"And it was thus that we lepers—I say we lepers because I am one of them, since I cannot expect long to escape the disease—it was thus that we lepers followed her to the graveyard in the rock by the blue sea, where Father Damien with his own hands had helped to dig her grave. And there, dear Mother, all that is mortal of her now rests. But we know that ere this she has heard the words : 'I was sick and ye visited me.'

"Mother Marianne would herself have written, but she was called away to the Leproserie.

"SISTER AGATHA."

POSTHUMOUS FAME; OR, A LEGEND OF THE BEAUTIFUL.

Posthumous Fame; or, a Legend of the Beautiful.

I.

THERE once lived in a great city, where the dead were all but innumerable, a young man by the name of Nicholas Vane, who possessed a singular genius for the making of tombstones. So beautiful they were, and so fitly designed to express the shadowy pain of mortal memory or the bright forecasting of eternal hope, that all persons were held fortunate who could secure them for the calm resting-places of their beloved sleepers. Indeed, the curious tale was whispered round that the bereft were not his only patrons, but that certain personages who were peculiarly ambitious of posthumous fame—seeing they had not long to live, and unwilling to intrust others with the grave responsibility of having them commemorated — had gone to his shop and secretly advised with him respecting such monuments as might preserve their memories from too swift oblivion.

However this may fall out, certain it is that his calling had its secrets ; and once he was known to observe that no man could ever understand the human heart until he had become a maker of tombstones. Whether the knowledge thus derived should make of one a laughing or a weeping philosopher, Nicholas himself remained a joyous type of youthful manhood—so joyous, in fact, that a friend of his who wrought in color, strolling one day into the workshop where Nicholas stood surrounded by the exquisite shapes of memorial marbles, had asked to paint the scene as a representation of Life chiselling to its beautiful purposes the rugged symbols of Death, and smiling as it wove the words of love and faith across the stony proofs of the universal tragedy.   Afterwards, it is true, a great change was wrought in the young artisan.

He had just come in one morning and paused to look around at the various finished and unfinished mortuary designs.

"Truly," he said to himself all at once, "if I were a wise man, I'd begin this day's business by chiselling my own head-stone.   For who knows but that before sunset my brother the grave-digger may be told to build me one of the houses that last till doomsday!   And what man could then make the monument to stop the door of *my* house with?   But why should I have a monument?   If I lie beneath it, I shall not know I lie there. If I lie not there, then it will not stand over me.   So, whether I lie there, or lie not there, what will it matter to me then?   Aye ; but what if, being dead only to this world and living in another, I should yet look on the monument erected to my memory and therefore be the happier?   I know not ; nor to what end we are vexed with this desire to be remembered after death.   The prospect of vanishing from a poor, toilsome life fills us with such consternation and pain!   It is therefore we strive to impress ourselves ineffaceably on the race, so that, after we have gone hence, or ceased to be, we may still have incorporeal habitation among all coming generations."

Here he was interrupted by a low knock at the door. Bidden to come in, there entered a man of delicate physiognomy, who threw a hurried glance around and inquired in an anxious tone :

"Sir, are you alone?"

"I am never alone," replied Nicholas in a ringing voice; "for I dwell hard by the gate-way of life and death, through which a multitude is always passing."

"Not so loud, I beseech you," said the visitor, stretching forth his thin, white hands with eager deprecation. "I would not, for the world, have any one discover that I have been here."

"Are you, then, a personage of such importance to the world?" said Nicholas, smiling, for the stranger's appearance argued no worldly consideration whatsoever. The suit of black, which his frail figure seemed to shrink away from with very sensitiveness, was glossy and pathetic with more than one covert patch. His shoes were dust-covered and worn. His long hair went round his head in a swirl, and he bore himself with an air of damaged, apologetic, self-appreciation.

"I am a poet," he murmured with a flush of pain, dropping his large mournful eyes beneath the scrutiny of one who might be an unsympathetic listener. "I am a poet, and I have come to speak with you privately of my—of the—of a monument. I am afraid I shall be forgotten. It is a terrible thought."

"Can you not trust your poems to keep you remembered?" asked Nicholas, with more kindliness.

"I could if they were as widely read as they should be." He appeared emboldened by his hearer's gentleness. "But, to confess the truth, I have not been accepted by my age. That, indeed, should give me no

pain, since I have not written for it, but for the great
future to which alone I look for my fame."

"Then why not look to it for your monument also?"

"Ah, sir!" he cried, "there are so many poets in the
world that I might be entirely overlooked by posterity,
did there not descend to it some sign that I was held
in honor by my own generation."

"Have you never noticed," he continued, with more
earnestness, "that when strangers visit a cemetery they
pay no attention to the thousands of little head-stones
that lie scattered close to the ground, but hunt out the
highest monuments, to learn in whose honor they were
erected? Have you never heard them exclaim: 'Yonder
is a great monument! A great man must be buried
there. Let us go and find out who he was and what he
did to be so celebrated.' Oh, sir, you and I know that
this is a poor way of reasoning, since the greatest monuments are not always set over the greatest men. Still
the custom has wrought its good effects, and splendid
memorials do serve to make known in years to come
those whom they commemorate, by inciting posterity to
search for their actions or revive their thoughts. I war-
rant you the mere bust of Homer—"

"You are not mentioning yourself in the same breath
with Homer, I hope," said Nicholas, with great good-
humor.

"My poems are as dear to me as Homer's were to
him," replied the poet, his eyes filling.

"What if you *are* forgotten? Is it not enough for
the poet to have lived for the sake of beauty?"

"No!" he cried, passionately. "What you say is a
miserable error. For the very proof of the poet's vocation is in creating the beautiful. But how know he has

created it? By his own mind? Alas, the poet's mind tells him only what is beautiful to *him*! It is by fame that he knows it—fame, the gratitude of men for the beauty he has revealed to them! What is so sweet, then, as the knowledge that fame has come to him already, or surely awaits him after he is dead?"

"We labor under some confusion of ideas, I fear," said Nicholas, "and, besides, are losing time. What kind of mon—"

"That I leave to you," interrupted the poet. "Only, I should like my monument to be beautiful. Ah, if you but knew how all through this poor life of mine I have loved the beautiful! Never, never have I drawn near it in any visible form without almost holding my breath as though I were looking deep, deep into God's opened eyes. But it was of the epitaph I wished to speak."

Hereupon, with a deeper flush, he drew from a large inside breast-pocket, that seemed to have been made for the purpose, a worn duodecimo volume, and fell to turning the much-fingered pages.

"This," he murmured fondly, without looking up, "is the complete collection of my poems."

"Indeed!" exclaimed Nicholas, with deep compassion.

"Yes, my complete collection. I have written a great deal more, and should have liked to publish all that I have written. But it was necessary to select, and I have included here only what it was intolerable to see wasted. There is nothing I value more than a group of elegiac poems, which every single member of my large family —who are fine critics — and all my friends, pronounce very beautiful. I think it would be a good idea to inscribe a selection from one on my monument, since

those who read the selection would wish to read the
entire poem, and those who read the entire poem would
wish to read the entire collection. I shall now favor
you with these elegies."

"I should be happy to hear them; but my time!"
said Nicholas, courteously. "The living are too im-
patient to wait on me; the dead too patient to be de-
frauded."

"Surely you would not refuse to hear one of them,"
exclaimed the poet, his eyes flashing.

"Read *one*, by all means." Nicholas seated himself
on a monumental lamb.

The poet passed one hand gently across his forehead,
as though to brush away the stroke of rudeness; then,
fixing upon Nicholas a look of infinite remoteness, he
read as follows:

> " He suffered but he murmured not;
>   To every storm he bared his breast;
> He asked but for the highest lot:
>   To be a bard above the rest."

"If you ask but for the common lot," interrupted
Nicholas, "you should rest content to be forgotten."

But before the poet could reply, a loud knock caused
him to flap the leaves of the " Complete Collection " together with one hand, while with the other he gathered
the tails of his long coat about him, as though preparing
to pass through some difficult aperture. The exaltation
of his mood, however, still showed itself in the look and
tone of proud condescension with which he said to
Nicholas:

"Permit me to retire at once by some private pass-way."

Nicholas led him to a door in the rear of the shop, and there, with a smile and a tear, stood for a moment watching the precipitate figure of the retreating bard, who suddenly paused when disappearing and tore open the breast of his coat to assure himself that his beloved elegies were resting safe across his heart.

The second visitor was of another sort. He hobbled on a cork leg, but inexorably disciplined the fleshly one into old-time firmness and precision. A faded military cloak draped his stalwart figure. Part of one bushy gray eyebrow had been chipped away by the same sword-cut that left its scar across his battle-beaten face.

"I have come to speak with you about my monument," he said in a gruff voice that seemed to issue from the mouth of a rusty cannon. "Those of my old comrades that did not fall at my side are dead. My wife died long ago, and my little children. I am old and forgotten. It is a time of peace. There's not a boy who will now listen to me while I tell of my campaigns. I live alone. Were I to die to-morrow my grave might not have so much as a head-stone. It might be taken for that of a coward. Make me a monument for a true soldier."

"Your grateful country will do that," said Nicholas.

"Ha?" exclaimed the veteran, whom the shock of battle had made deaf long ago.

"Your country," shouted Nicholas, close to his ear, "your country—will erect a monument—to your memory."

"My country!" The words were shot out with a reverberating, melancholy boom. "My country will do no such a thing.   How many millions of soldiers have fallen on her battle-fields !   Where are their monuments?   They would make her one vast cemetery."

" But is it not enough for you to have been a true soldier?   Why wish to be known and remembered for it?"

" I know I do not wish to be forgotten," he replied, simply.   "I know I take pleasure in the thought that long after I am forgotten there will be a tongue in my monument to cry out to every passing stranger, ' Here lies the body of a true soldier.'   It is a great thing to be brave !"

" Is, then, this monument to be erected in honor of bravery, or of yourself?"

" There is no difference," said the veteran, bluntly. " Bravery *is* myself."

" It is bravery," he continued, in husky tones, and with a mist gathering in his eyes that made him wink as though he were trying to see through the smoke of battle—" it is bravery that I see most clearly in the character of God.   What would become of us if he were a coward?   I serve him as my brave commander ; and though I am stationed far from him and may be faint and sorely wounded, I know that he is somewhere on the battle-field, and that I shall see him at last, approaching me as he moves up and down among the ranks."

" But you say that your country does not notice you —that you have no friends; do you, then, feel no resentment ?"

" None, none," he answered quickly, though his head dropped on his bosom.

" And you wish to be remembered by a world that is willing to forget you ?"

He lifted his head proudly. "There are many true men in the world," he said, "and it has much to think of. I owe it all I can give, all I can bequeath; and I can bequeath it nothing but the memory of a true man."

One day, not long after this, there came into the workshop of Nicholas a venerable man of the gravest, sweetest, and most scholarly aspect, who spoke not a word until he had led Nicholas to the front window and pointed a trembling finger at a distant church-spire.

"You see yon spire?" he said. "It almost pierces the clouds. In the church beneath I have preached to men and women for nearly fifty years. Many that I have christened at the font I have married at the altar; many of these I have sprinkled with dust. What have I not done for them in sorrow and want! How have I not toiled to set them in the way of purer pleasures and to anchor their tempest-tossed hopes! And yet how soon they will forget me! Already many say I am too old to preach. Too old! I preach better than I ever did in my life. Yet it may be my lot to wander down into the deep valley, an idle shepherd with an idle crook. I have just come from the writing of my next sermon, in which I exhort my people to strive that their names be not written on earthly monuments or human hearts, but in the Book of Life. It is my sublimest theme. If I am ever eloquent, if I am ever persuasive, if I ever for one moment draw aside to spiritual eyes the veil that discloses the calm, enrapturing vistas of eternity, it is when I measure my finite strength against this mighty task. But why? Because they are the sermons of my own aspiration. I preach them to my own soul. Face to face with that naked soul I pen those

19

sermons—pen them when all are asleep save the sleep-
less Eye that is upon me. Even in the light of that
Eye do I recoil from the thought of being forgotten.
How clearly I foresee it! Ashes to ashes, dust to dust!
Where then will be my doctrines, my prayers, my ser-
mons?"

"Is it not enough for you to have scattered your
handful of good broadcast, to ripen as endlessly as the
grass? What if they that gather know naught of him
that sowed?"

"It is not enough. I should like the memory of *me*
to live on and on in the world, inseparable from the
good I may have done. What am I but the good that
is in me? 'Tis this that links me to the infinite and
the perfect. Does not the Perfect One wish his goodness to be associated with his name? No! No! I
do not wish to be forgotten!"

"It is mere vanity."

"Not vanity," said the aged servitor, meekly. "Wait
until you are old, till the grave is at your helpless feet:
it is the love of life."

But some years later there befell Nicholas an event
that transcended all past experiences, and left its impress on his whole subsequent life.

II.

The hour had passed when any one was likely to
enter his shop. A few rays of pale sunlight, straggling
in through crevices of the door, rested like a dying halo
on the heads of the monumental figures grouped around.
Shadows, creeping upward from the ground, shrouded
all else in thin, penetrable half-gloom, through which

the stark gray emblems of mortality sent forth more solemn suggestions. A sudden sense of the earthly tragedy overwhelmed him. The chisel and the hammer dropped from his hands and, resting his head on the block he had been carving, he gave himself up to that mood of dim, distant reverie in which the soul seems to soar and float far above the shock and din of the world's disturbing nearness. On his all but oblivious ear, like the faint washings of some remote sea, beat the waves of the city's tide-driven life in the streets outside. The room itself seemed hushed to the awful stillness of the high aerial spaces. Then all at once this stillness was broken by a voice, low, clear, and tremuluous, saying close to his ear:

"Are you the maker of gravestones?"

"That is my sad calling," he cried, bitterly, starting up with instinctive forebodings.

He saw before him a veiled figure. To support herself, she rested one hand on the block he had been carving, while she pressed the other against her heart, as though to stifle pain.

"Whose monument is this?"

"A neglected poet's who died not long ago. Soon, perhaps, I shall be making one for an old soldier, and one for a holy man, whose soul, I hear, is about to be dismissed."

"Are not some monuments sadder to make than others?"

"Aye, truly."

"What is the saddest you ever made?"

"The saddest monument I ever made was one for a poor mother who had lost her only son. One day a woman came in who had no sooner entered than she sat down and gave way to a passionate outburst of grief."

"'My good woman,' I said, 'why do you weep so bitterly?'

"'Do not call me good,' she moaned, and hid her face.

"I then perceived her fallen character. When she recovered self-control she drew from her sinful bosom an old purse filled with coins of different values.

"'Why do you give me this?' I asked.

"'It is to pay for a monument for my son,' she said, and the storm of her grief swept over her again.

"I learned that for years she had toiled and starved to hoard up a sum with which to build a monument to his memory, for he had never failed of his duty to her after all others had cast her out. Certainly he had his reward, not in the monument, but in the repentance which came to her after his death. I have never seen such sorrow for evil as the memory of his love wrought in her. For herself she desired only that the spot where she should be buried might be unknown. This longing to be forgotten has led me to believe that none desire to remembered for the evil that is in them, but only for some truth, or beauty, or goodness by which they have linked their individual lives to the general life of the race. Even the lying epitaphs in cemeteries prove how we would fain have the dead arrayed on the side of right in the thoughts of their survivors. This wretched mother and human outcast, believing herself to have lost everything that makes it well to be remembered, craved only the mercy of forgetfulness."

"And yet I think she died a Christian soul."

"You knew her, then?"

" I was with her in her last hours. She told me her story. She told me also of you, and that you would accept nothing for the monument you were at such care to make. It is perhaps for this reason that I have felt some desire to see you, and that I am here now to speak with you of—"

A shudder passed over her.

" After all, that was not a sad, but a joyous monument to fashion," she added, abruptly.

" Aye, it was joyous. But to me the joyous and the sad are much allied in the things of this life."

" And yet there might be one monument wholly sad, might there not?"

"There might be, but I know not whose it would be."

" If she you love should die, would not hers be so?"

"Until I love, and she I love is dead, I cannot know," said Nicholas, smiling.

" What builds the most monuments?" she asked, quickly, as though to retreat from her levity.

" Pride builds many — splendid ones. Gratitude builds some, forgiveness some, and pity some. But faith builds more than these, though often poor, humble ones; and love!—love builds more than all things else together."

" And what, of all things that monuments are built in memory of, is most loved and soonest forgotten?" she asked, with intensity.

" Nay, I cannot tell that."

" Is it not a beautiful woman? This, you say, is the monument of a poet. After the poet grows old, men love him for the songs he sang; they love the old soldier for the battles he fought, and the preacher for his remembered prayers. But a woman! Who loves her

for the beauty she once possessed, or rather regards
her not with the more distaste? Is there in history
a figure so lonely and despised as that of the woman
who, once the most beautiful in the world, crept back
into her native land a withered hag? Or, if a woman
die while she is yet beautiful, how long is she remembered? Her beauty is like heat and light—powerful
only for those who feel and see it."

But Nicholas had scarcely heard her. His eyes had
become riveted upon her hand, which rested on the
marble, as white as though grown out of it under the
labors of his chisel.

"My lady," he said, with the deepest respect, "will
you permit me to look at your hand? I have carved
many a one in marble, and studied many a one in life;
but never have I seen anything so beautiful as yours."

He took it with an artist's impetuosity and bent over
it, laying its palm against one of his own and stroking
it softly with the other. The blood leaped through his
heart, and he suddenly lifted it to his lips.

"God only can make the hand beautiful," he said.

Displaced by her arm which he had upraised, the
light fabric that had concealed her figure parted on her
bosom and slipped to the ground. His eyes swept over
the perfect shape that stood revealed. The veil still
concealed her face. The strangely mingled emotions
that had been deepening within him all this time now
blended themselves in one irrepressible wish.

"Will you permit me to see your face?"

She drew quickly back. A subtle pain was in his
voice as he cried:

"Oh, my lady? I ask it as one who has pure eyes for
the beautiful."

"My face belongs to my past. It has been my sorrow; it is nothing now."

"Only permit me to see it!"

" Is there no other face you would rather see?"

Who can fathom the motive of a woman's questions?

" None, none!"

She drew aside her veil, and her eyes rested quietly on his like a revelation. So young she was as hardly yet to be a woman, and her beauty had in it that seraphic purity and mysterious pathos which is never seen in a woman's face until the touch of another world has chastened her spirit into the resignation of a saint. The heart of Nicholas was wrung by the sight of it with a sudden sense of inconsolable loss and longing.

"Oh, my lady!" he cried, sinking on one knee and touching his lips to her hand with greater gentleness. " Do you indeed think the beauty of a woman so soon forgotten? As long as I live, yours will be as fresh in my memory as it was the moment after I first saw it in its perfection and felt its power."

"Do not recall to me the sorrow of such thoughts." She touched her heart. " My heart is a tired hour-glass. Already the sands are wellnigh run through. Any hour it may stop, and then—out like a light! Shapeless ashes! I have loved life well, but not so well that I have not been able to prepare to leave it."

She spoke with the utmost simplicity and calmness, yet her eyes were turned with unspeakable sadness towards the shadowy recesses of the room, where from their pedestals the monumental figures looked down upon her as though they would have opened their marble lips and said, " Poor child! Poor child!"

" I have had my wish to see you and to see this place.

Before long some one will come here to have you carve
a monument to the most perishable of all things. Like
the poor mother who had no wish to be remembered—"

Nicholas was moved to the deepest.

"I have but little skill," he said. "The great God
did not bestow on me the genius of his favorite children of sculpture. But if so sad and sacred a charge
should ever become mine, with his help I will rear such
a monument to your memory that as long as it stands
none who see it will ever be able to forget you. Year
after year your memory shall grow as a legend of the
beautiful."

When she was gone he sat self-forgetful until the
darkness grew impenetrable. As he groped his way
out at last along the thick guide-posts of death, her
voice seemed to float towards him from every head-
stone, her name to be written in every epitaph.

The next day a shadow brooded over the place. Day
by day it deepened. He went out to seek intelligence
of her. In the quarter of the city where she lived he
discovered that her name had already become a nu-
cleus around which were beginning to cluster many
little legends of the beautiful. He had but to hear re-
citals of her deeds of kindness and mercy. For the
chance of seeing her again he began to haunt the neighborhood; then, having seen her, he would return to his
shop the victim of more unavailing desire. All things
combined to awake in him that passion of love whose
roots are nourished in the soul's finest soil of pity and
hopelessness. Once or twice, under some pretext, he
made bold to accost her; and once, under the stress of
his passion, he mutely lifted his eyes, confessing his
love; but hers were turned aside.

Meantime he began to dream of the monument he chose to consider she had committed to his making. It should be the triumph of his art ; but more, it would represent in stone the indissoluble union of his love with her memory. Through him alone would she enter upon her long after-life of saint-like reminiscence.

When the tidings of her death came, he soon sprang up from the prostration of his grief with a burning desire to consummate his beloved work.

"Year after year your memory shall grow as a legend of the beautiful."

These words now became the inspiration of his masterpiece. Day and night it took shape in the rolling chaos of his sorrow. What sculptor in the world ever espoused the execution of a work that lured more irresistibly from their hiding-places the shy and tender ministers of his genius? What one ever explored with greater boldness the utmost limits of artistic expression, or wrought in sterner defiance of the laws of our common forgetfulness?

III.

One afternoon, when people thronged the great cemetery of the city, a strolling group were held fascinated by the unique loveliness of a newly erected monument.

"Never," they exclaimed, "have we seen so exquisite a masterpiece. In whose honor is it erected?"

But when they drew nearer, they found carved on it simply a woman's name.

"Who was she?" they asked, puzzled and disappointed. " Is there no epitaph?"

" Aye," spoke up a young man lying on the grass

and eagerly watching the spectators.   "Aye, a very fitting epitaph."

"Where is it?"

"Carved on the heart of the monument!" he cried,
in a tone of triumph.

"On the heart of the monument?   Then we cannot
see it."

"It is not meant to be seen."

"How do *you* know of it?"

"I made the monument."

"Then tell us what it is."

"It cannot be told.   It is there only because it is
unknown."

"Out on you!   You play your pranks with the living and the dead."

"You will live to regret this day," said a thoughtful
by-stander.   "You have tampered with the memory of
the dead."

"Why, look you, good people," cried Nicholas, springing up and approaching his beautiful master-work. He
rested one hand lovingly against it and glanced around
him pale with repressed excitement, as though a long-
looked-for moment had at length arrived.   "I play no
pranks with the living or the dead.   Young as I am, I
have fashioned many monuments, as this cemetery will
testify.   But I make no more.   This is my last; and as
it is the last, so it is the greatest.   For I have fashioned
it in such love and sorrow for her who lies beneath it
as you can never know.   If it is beautiful, it is yet an
unworthy emblem of that brief and transporting beauty
which was hers; and I have planted it here beside her
grave, that as a delicate white flower it may exhale the
perfume of her memory for centuries to come.

"Tell me," he went on, his lips trembling, his voice faltering with the burden of oppressive hope—"tell me, you who behold it now, do you not wed her memory deathlessly to it? To its fair shape, its native and unchanging purity?"

"Aye," they interrupted, impatiently. "But the epitaph?"

"Ah!" he cried, with tenderer feeling, "beautiful as the monument is to the eye, it would be no fit emblem of her had it not something sacred hidden within. For she was not lovely to the sense alone, but had a perfect heart. So I have placed within the monument that which is its heart, and typifies hers. And, mark you!" he cried, in a voice of such awful warning that those standing nearest him instinctively shrank back, "the one is as inviolable as the other. No more could you rend the heart from the human bosom than this epitaph from the monument. My deep and lasting curse on him who attempts it! For I have so fitted the parts of the work together, that to disunite would be to break them in pieces; and the inscription is so fragile and delicately poised within, that so much as rudely to jar the monument would shiver it to atoms. It is put there to be inviolable. Seek to know it, you destroy it. This I but create after the plan of the Great Artist, who shows you only the fair outside of his masterpieces. What human eye ever looked into the mysterious heart of his beautiful!—that heart which holds the secret of inexhaustible freshness and eternal power? Could this epitaph have been carved on the outside, you would have read it and forgotten it with natural satiety. But uncomprehended, what a spell I mark it exercises! You will—nay, you *must*—remember it forever! You will speak of it to others. They will come. And thus in ever-widening circle will be borne afar the memory of her whose name is on it, the emblem of whose heart is hidden within. And what more fitting memorial could a man rear to a woman, the pure shell of whose beauty all can see, the secret of whose beautiful being no one ever comprehends?"

He walked rapidly away, then, some distance off, turned and looked back. More spectators had come up. Some were earnestly talking, pointing now to the monument, now towards him. Others stood in rapt contemplation of his master-work.

Tears rose to his eyes. A look of ineffable joy overspread his face.

"Oh, my love!" he murmured, "I have triumphed. Death has claimed your body, heaven your spirit; but the earth claims the saintly memory of each. This day about your name begins to grow the Legend of the Beautiful."

The sun had just set. The ethereal white shape of the monument stood outlined against a soft background of rose-colored sky. To his transfiguring imagination it seemed lifted far into the cloud-based heavens, and the evening star, resting above its apex, was a celestial lamp lowered to guide the eye to it through the darkness of the descending night.

IV.

Mysterious complexity of our mortal nature and estate that we should so desire to be remembered after death, though born to be forgotten! Our words and deeds, the influences of our silent personalities, do in-

deed pass from us into the long history of the race and
abide for the rest of time: so that an earthly immortality is the heritage, nay, the inalienable necessity, of
even the commonest lives; only it is an immortality
not of self, but of its good and evil. For Nature sows
us and reaps us, that she may gather a harvest, not of
us, but from us. It is God alone that gathers the harvest of us. And well for us that our destiny should be
that general forgetfulness we so strangely shrink from.
For no sooner are we gone hence than, even for such
brief times as our memories may endure, we are apt to
grow by processes of accumulative transformation into
what we never were. Thou kind, kind fate, therefore—
never enough named and celebrated — that biddest the
sun of memory rise on our finished but imperfect lives,
and then lengthenest or shortenest the little day of
posthumous reminiscence, according as thou seest there
is need of early twilight or of deeper shadows!

Years passed. City and cemetery were each grown
vaster. It was again an afternoon when the people
strolled among the graves and monuments. An old
man had courteously attached himself to a group that
stood around a crumbling memorial. He had reached
a great age; but his figure was erect, his face animated
by strong emotions, and his eyes burned beneath his
brows.

"Sirs," said he, interposing in the conversation, which
turned wholly on the monument, "you say nothing of
him in whose honor it was erected."

"We say nothing because we know nothing."

"Is he then wholly forgotten?"

"We are not aware that he is at all remembered."

"The inscription reads: 'He was a poet.' Know you none of his poems?"

"We have never so much as heard of his poems."

"My eyes are dim; is there nothing carved beneath his name?"

One of the by-standers went up and knelt down close to the base.

"There *was* something here, but it is effaced by time —Wait!" And tracing his finger slowly along, he read like a child :

    " He — asked — but — for — the — highest — lot.

"That is all," he cried, springing lightly up. "Oh, the dust on my knees!" he added with vexation.

"He may have sung very sweetly," pursued the old man.

"He may, indeed!" they answered, carelessly.

"But, sirs," continued he, with a sad smile, "perhaps you are the very generation that he looked to for the fame which his own denied him; perhaps he died believing that *you* would fully appreciate his poems."

"If so, it was a comfortable faith to die in," they said, laughing, in return. "He will never know that we did not. A few great poets have posthumous fame : we know *them* well enough." And they passed on.

"This," said the old man, as they paused elsewhere, "seems to be the monument of a true soldier : know you aught of the victories he helped to win?"

"He may not have helped to win any victories. He may have been a coward. How should *we* know? Epitaphs often lie. The dust is peopled with soldiers." And again they moved on.

"Does any one read his sermons now, know you?" asked the old man as they paused before a third monument.

"Read his sermons!" they exclaimed, laughing more heartily. "Are sermons so much read in the country you come from? See how long he has been dead! What should the world be thinking of, to be reading his musty sermons?"

"At least does it give you no pleasure to read 'He was a good man?'" inquired he, plaintively.

"Aye; but if he was good, was not his goodness its own reward?"

"He may have also wished long to be remembered for it."

"Naturally; but we have not heard that his wish was gratified."

"Is it not sad that the memory of so much beauty and truth and goodness in our common human life should perish? But, sirs,"—and here the old man spoke with sudden energy—"if there should be one who combined perfect beauty and truth and goodness in one form and character, do you not think such a rare being would escape the common fate and be long and widely remembered?"

"Doubtless."

"Sirs," said he, quickly stepping in front of them with flashing eyes, "is there in all this vast cemetery not a single monument that has kept green the memory of the being in whose honor it was erected?"

"Aye, aye," they answered, readily. "Have you not heard of it?"

"I am but come from distant countries. Many years ago I was here, and have journeyed hither with much desire to see the place once more. Would you kindly show me this monument?"

"Come!" they answered, eagerly, starting off. "It is the best known of all the thousands in the cemetery. None who see it can ever forget it."

"Yes, yes!" murmured the old man. "That is why I have—I foresaw— Is it not a beautiful monument? Does it not lie—in what direction does it lie?"

A feverish eagerness seized him. He walked now beside, now before, his companions. Once he wheeled on them.

"Sirs, did you not say it perpetuates the memory of her—of the one—who lies beneath it?"

"Both are famous. The story of this woman and her monument will never be forgotten. It is impossible to forget it."

"Year after year—" muttered he, brushing his hand across his eyes.

They soon came to a spot where the aged branches of memorial evergreens interwove a sunless canopy, and spread far around a drapery of gloom through which the wind passed with an unending sigh. Brushing aside the lowest boughs, they stepped in awe-stricken silence within the dank, chill cone of shade. Before them rose the shape of a gray monument, at sight of which the aged traveller, who had fallen behind, dropped his staff and held out his arms as though he would have embraced it. But, controlling himself, he stepped forward, and said, in tones of thrilling sweetness:

"Sirs, you have not told me what story is connected with this monument that it should be so famous. I conceive it must be some very touching one of her whose name I read—some beautiful legend—"

"Judge you of that!" interrupted one of the group, with a voice of stern sadness and not without a certain look of mysterious horror. "They say this monument was reared to a woman by the man who once loved her. She was very beautiful, and so he made her a very beautiful monument. But she had a heart so hideous in its falsity that he carved in stone an enduring curse on her evil memory, and hung it in the heart of the monument because it was too awful for any eye to see. But others tell the story differently. They say the woman not only had a heart false beyond description, but was in person the ugliest of her sex. So that while the hidden curse is a lasting execration of her nature, the beautiful exterior is a masterpiece of mockery which her nature, and not her ugliness, maddened his sensitive genius to perpetrate. There can be no doubt that this is the true story, as hundreds tell it now, and that the woman will be remembered so long as the monument stands—aye, and longer—not only for her loathsome— Help the old man !"

He had fallen backward to the ground. They tried in vain to set him on his feet. Stunned, speechless, he could only raise himself on one elbow and turn his eyes towards the monument with a look of preternatural horror, as though the lie had issued from its treacherous shape. At length he looked up to them, as they bent kindly over him, and spoke with much difficulty:

"Sirs, I am an old man—a very old man, and very feeble. Forgive this weakness. And I have come a long way, and must be faint. While you were speaking my strength failed me. You were telling me a story— were you not ?—the story—the legend of a most beautiful woman, when all at once my senses grew confused

20

and I failed to hear you rightly. Then my ears played
me such a trick! Oh, sirs! if you but knew what a
damnable trick my ears played me, you would pity me
greatly, very, very greatly. This story touches me. It
is much like one I seemed to have heard for many years,
and that I have been repeating over and over to myself
until I love it better than my life. If you would but go
over it again—carefully—very carefully."

"My God, sirs!" he exclaimed, springing up with the
energy of youth when he had heard the recital a second
time, "tell me *who* started this story! Tell me *how* and
where it began!"

"We cannot. We have heard many tell it, and not
all alike."

"And do they—do you—believe—it is—true?" he
asked, helplessly.

"We all *know* it is true; do not *you* believe it?"

"I can never forget it!" he said, in tones quickly
grown harsh and husky. "Let us go away from so pitiful a place."

It was near nightfall when he returned, unobserved,
and sat down beside the monument as one who had
ended a pilgrimage.

"They all tell me the same story," he murmured,
wearily. "Ah, it was the hidden epitaph that wrought
the error! But for it, the sun of her memory would
have had its brief, befitting day and tender setting.
Presumptuous folly, to suppose they would understand
my masterpiece, when they so often misconceive the
hidden heart of His beautiful works, and convert the
uncomprehended good and true into a curse of evil!"

The night fell. He was awaiting it. Nearer and
nearer rolled the dark, suffering heart of a storm;

nearer towards the calm, white breasts of the dead.
Over the billowy graves the many-footed winds suddenly fled away in a wild, tumultuous cohort.   Overhead,
great black bulks swung heavily at one another across
the tremulous stars.

Of all earthly spots, where does the awful discord of
the elements seem so futile and theatric as in a vast
cemetery?   Blow, then, winds, till you uproot the trees!
Pour, floods, pour, till the water trickles down into the
face of the pale sleeper below!   Rumble and flash, ye
clouds, till the earth trembles and seems to be aflame!
But not a lock of hair, so carefully put back over the
brows, is tossed or disordered.   The sleeper has not
stretched forth an arm and drawn the shroud closer
about his face, to keep out the wet.   Not an ear has
heard the riving thunderbolt, nor so much as an eyelid
trembled on the still eyes for all the lightning's fury.

But had there been another human presence on the
midnight scene, some lightning flash would have revealed the old man, a grand, a terrible figure, in sympathy
with its wild, sad violence.   He stood beside his masterpiece, towering to his utmost height in a posture of
all but superhuman majesty and strength.   His long
white hair and longer white beard streamed outward on
the roaring winds.   His arms, bared to the shoulder,
swung aloft a ponderous hammer.   His face, ashen-
gray as the marble before him, was set with an expression of stern despair.   Then, as the thunder crashed,
his hammer fell on the monument.   Bolt after bolt,
blow after blow.   Once more he might have been seen
kneeling beside the ruin, his eyes strained close to its
heart, awaiting another flash to tell him that the inviolable epitaph had shared in the destruction.

For days following many curious eyes came to peer into the opened heart of the shattered structure, but in vain.

Thus the masterpiece of Nicholas failed of its end, though it served another. For no one could have heard the story of it, before it was destroyed, without being made to realize how melancholy that a man should rear a monument of execration to the false heart of the woman he once had loved; and how terrible for mankind to celebrate the dead for the evil that was in them instead of the good.

THE END.

www.ingramcontent.com/pod-product-compliance
Lightning Source LLC
Chambersburg PA
CBHW020240290326
41929CB00045B/1112